NIETZSCHE'S GREAT POLITICS

NIETZSCHE'S GREAT POLITICS

HUGO DROCHON

PRINCETON UNIVERSITY PRESS

Princeton and Oxford

press.princeton.edu
Cover image: Friedrich Nietzsche, c. 1868
Cover design by Jess Massabrook

First paperback printing, 2018
Paper ISBN 978-0-691-18069-4

Cloth ISBN 978-0-691-16634-6
Library of Congress Control Number: 2015958004

British Library Cataloging-in-Publication Data is available

This book has been composed in
DIN 1452 Std & Sabon Next LT Pro

DEDICATED TO THE MEMORY OF
ISTVAN HONT

CONTENTS

ACKNOWLEDGMENTS   ix
EDITIONS AND TRANSLATIONS USED   xiii
ABBREVIATIONS   xv

INTRODUCTION   1

CHAPTER 1. THE GREEKS   24
   SOCRATES AND GREEK CULTURE   26
   PLATO'S LEGISLATIVE MISSION   36
   CONCLUSION   47

CHAPTER 2. THE STATE   49
   WAGNER AND SLAVERY   52
   "THE GREEK STATE"   55
   THE DECAY OF THE MODERN STATE   60
   BEYOND THE MODERN STATE   64
   CONCLUSION   67

CHAPTER 3. DEMOCRACY   71
   DEMOCRACY IN THE *KAISERREICH*   75
   DEMOCRACY AND ARISTOCRACY   78
   MISARCHISM, CHRISTIANITY, AND HERD MORALITY   80
   DEGENERATION AND THE GOOD EUROPEAN   82
   CASTE SOCIETY   88
   SLAVERY   91
   CONCLUSION   97

CHAPTER 4. PHILOSOPHY AND POLITICS   105
   THE WILL TO POWER   106
   THE ETERNAL RETURN   110
   THE OVERMAN   115
   CONCLUSION: POLITICAL PERFECTIONISM   126

CHAPTER 5. REVALUATION — 129
NIETZSCHE'S *NACHLASS* AND HIS LAST WORKS — 135
THE *PASSAGE À L'ACTE* — 144
CONCLUSION — 151

CHAPTER 6. GREAT POLITICS — 153
PETTY POLITICS — 156
GREAT POLITICS — 160
RELEARNING POLITICS — 165
THE WAR OF SPIRITS — 170
CONCLUSION — 176

CONCLUSION: NIETZSCHE NOW — 180

BIBLIOGRAPHY — 185
INDEX — 197

ACKNOWLEDGMENTS

Friedrich Nietzsche was not enamored with origins, but at least one fundamental stage in the genealogy of this book was my PhD "Nietzsche's Great
Politics and His Revaluation Project," which I completed at Cambridge in
2012. During that time, and indeed continuing to this day, Melissa Lane has
proven to be a model of academic supervision and direction, and has always
demanded the best of me, for which I am eternally grateful. The late Istvan
Hont also served as a true inspiration and intellectual father figure, and he
is acutely missed. Although my work did not fall into his immediate field of
inquiry, he made me confront the real issues at stake, and why they mat-
tered, in a way that will undoubtedly influence the rest of my research. This
book is dedicated to his memory.

Thanks to Duncan Kelly and Keith Ansell-Pearson for examining the dis-
sertation, and doing their best to put it on the right track. Thanks also to
Martin Ruehl for his advice both on and off the basketball court, and while
the latter can unfortunately no longer be, I look forward to more Nietzschean adventures in the future.

Since 2013, I have had the great fortune to be part of a Leverhulme-
funded project on Conspiracy and Democracy, based at the Centre for
Research in the Arts, Social Sciences, and Humanities in Cambridge. My
research colleagues there—Tanya Filer, Rolf Fredheim, Rachel Hoffman,
Nayanika Mathur, Andrew McKenzie-McHarg, and Alfred Moore—under
the benevolent watchful eyes of Richard Evans, John Naughton, and David
Runciman, have made for an exceptionally stimulating and fertile environment. I would especially like to thank David Runciman, who made
not solely my position but also this book possible, for offering a true exemplar of academic acuity, career support, and life values that I will endeavor, although invariably fail, to emulate. Many thanks also to Andrew
McKenzie-McHarg for having taken the time to read large parts of this
book, and always offering incisive and helpful comments, suggestions, and

spot-on stylistic tips; in this you are certainly more Nietzschean than I will ever be.

At Princeton University Press, I would like to thank Al Bertrand for having confidence in this project from the start, and his assistants Quinn Fusting and Jaime Estrada. Thanks also to Kathleen Cioffi for production assistance, and Cindy Milstein for her patient and professional copyediting in this difficult time for her. Tracy Strong and another anonymous reviewer provided warmly encouraging and helpful remarks. They saved me from many mistakes, and those that remain are purely my own. I am indebted to Adrian Moore and Patricia Williams for permission to view Bernard Williams's unpublished piece "Can There Be a Nietzschean Politics" from his private papers, and the late Geoffrey Hawthorn for facilitating this. This text is not available to the public, was not intended by Williams for publication, and therefore cannot be treated as an accurate record of his views. There is no reliable evidence that it is the text of his talk in Cambridge.

I have had both the immense pleasure and great honor to discuss my work with a number of different people over the last while, across the United Kingdom, France, Germany, Italy, and the United States. There are simply too many to be able to mention here, and picking out a few is naturally an arbitrary enterprise. But those I fail to mention should recognize themselves here and know my thanks in any case: Christa Davis Acampora, Thomas Brobjer, Yannis Constantinidès, Don Dombowsky, Manuel Dries, Raymond Geuss, George Kateb, Duncan Large, Enrico Mueller, Jan-Werner Mueller, Alexander Nehamas, David Owen, Aaron Ridley, Heike Schotten, Herman Siemens, Andreas Urs Sommer, Yannick Souladié, and Werner Stegmaier. Thanks also to my friends and colleagues at Cambridge: Duncan Bell, Jocelyn Betts, Christopher Bickerton, Annabel Brett, Christopher Brooke, Joseph Canning, John Dunn, Anna Hont, Joel Isaac, Samuel James, Christopher Meckstroth, Glen Rangwala, John Robertson, Or Rosenboim, Magnus Ryan, Paul Sagar, Richard Serjeantson, Micheal Sonenscher, Gareth Stedman Jones, Tim Stuart-Buttle, Helen Thompson, Sylvana Tomaselli, Damian Valdez, and Waseem Yaqoob.

For the last three years I have lived at 118 Thoday Street with Thomas Hopkins and Alexis Papazoglou. They have been life companions in every sense of the word, and I would like to thank them both here, while wishing them the best in their future lives and careers. Thomas Hopkins in particular has been an intellectual companion since our PhD years, and I have little doubt that that companionship will last a lifetime.

None of this, of course, would have been possible without my family. I'm grateful to my parents, Annie and Tommy Halferty, for their unfailing emotional and financial support; and my sister, Maud, her husband, Chris, and my nephews and niece, Scott, Thomas, and Lara, all a constant source of joy. Thanks also to my aunt Anne-Marie Wagnon for her education.

I finished writing this book in Sicily, and while it is not exactly *aus Messina*, Pauline Blistène has certainly made my life an idyll.

Chapter 2 was first accepted for publication as "Nietzsche: Theorist of the State?" in *History of Political Thought* (forthcoming). A shorter version of chapter 3, without sections 5 and 6, will appear as "'An Old Carriage with New Horses': Nietzsche's Critique of Democracy" in *History of European Ideas* (forthcoming).

EDITIONS AND TRANSLATIONS USED

The reference critical edition of Friedrich Nietzsche's work is Giorgio Colli, Mazzino Montinari, et al., *Werke: Kritische Gesamtausgabe* (KGW) in forty volumes, along with its abridged fifteen-volume paperback edition, *Sämtliche Werke: Kritische Studienausgabe* (KSA). For translations of the main published works, I have relied on the Cambridge University Press editions (see the bibliography). For the unpublished notes, I have primarily relied on Frank Cameron and Don Dombowsky's anthology *Political Writings of Friedrich Nietzsche*, and also consulted Walter Kaufmann's edition of *The Will to Power* and, to a lesser extent, Richard Gray's translation of *Unpublished Writings from the Period of Unfashionable Observations*. Other translations of the late *Nachlass* are my own. Nietzsche's letters are organized into eight volumes by Colli and Montinari in *Sämtliche Briefe: Kritische Studienausgabe* (KSB). When possible, I have used Christopher Middleton's translations in *Selected Letters of Friedrich Nietzsche*. Other translations are my own. I cited letters by addressee and date.

ABBREVIATIONS

AC: *The Antichrist*
AOM: *Assorted Opinions and Maxims* (HH II)
BGE: *Beyond Good and Evil*
BT: *The Birth of Tragedy*
CW: *The Case of Wagner*
D: *Daybreak*
DD: *Dithyrambs of Dionysus*
DS: *David Strauss, the Confessor and the Writer* (UM I)
EH: *Ecce Homo*
FEI: *On the Future of Our Educational Institutions*
GM: *On the Genealogy of Morality*
GS: *The Gay Science*
GSt: *The Greek State*
HC: *Homer's Contest*
HH: *Human, All Too Human* (I)
HL: *On the Uses and Disadvantages of History for Life* (UM II)
KSA: *Sämtliche Werke: Kritische Studienausgabe*
KSB: *Sämtliche Briefe: Kritische Studienausgabe*
NCW: *Nietzsche contra Wagner*
PL: *Lectures on Plato*
PPP: *Pre-Platonic Philosophers*
PTAG: *Philosophy in the Tragic Age of the Greeks*
SE: *Schopenhauer as Educator* (UM III)
TI: *Twilight of the Idols*
UM: *Untimely Meditations*
WB: *Richard Wagner in Bayreuth* (UM IV)
WS: *The Wandered and His Shadow* (HH II)
Z: *Thus Spoke Zarathustra*

NIETZSCHE'S GREAT POLITICS

INTRODUCTION

Friedrich Nietzsche's impact on the world of culture, philosophy, and the arts is uncontested, but his contribution to political thought remains mired in controversy. The source of that controversy resides in his political misappropriation by the Nazis during World War II, and we are still counting the cost of that appropriation for contemporary scholarship today. So the price that Walter Kaufmann—in his seminal *Nietzsche: Philosopher, Psychologist, Antichrist*, first published in 1950, now in its fourth edition—paid to rescue Nietzsche from the philosophical abyss he had fallen into after the war was to deny him any interest in politics.[1] Instead, Kaufmann reconstructed Nietzsche as a German humanist whose sole preoccupation was the revival of an "un-" or indeed "antipolitical" high culture. We are unquestionably indebted to Kaufmann for restoring Nietzsche to his rightful place in the philosophical canon, but this image of an unpolitical Nietzsche has cast a long shadow over Nietzsche interpretation in the second half of the twentieth century, and still haunts later work by, for instance, Bernard Williams, Alexander Nehamas, and Brian Leiter, among others. More recently, Nietzsche has been enlisted into attempts to refound American democracy on a radicalized, postmodern, and *agonistic* basis.[2] Representative of this strand are political theorists such as Bonnie Honig, Wendy Brown, Dana Villa, William Connolly, and Mark Warren, alongside more specifically Nietzsche scholars such as Lawrence Hatab, Alan Schrift, and David Owen. This involves mining Nietzsche for various intellectual resources—often drawn from what is conceived to be his "postmodern" philosophy, separated out from his disappointingly, on this account, "premodern" conception of politics—to be reshaped in the process of formulating a new account of demo-

---

[1] Walter Kaufmann, *Nietzsche: Philosopher, Psychologist, Antichrist* (Princeton, NJ: Princeton University Press, 1974). A new fourth edition with a foreward by Alexander Nehamas came out in 2013.

[2] Christa Davis Acampora, *Contesting Nietzsche* (Chicago: University of Chicago Press, 2013).

cratic politics. But we are no closer to understanding what politics meant *for him*.

The aim of this book is to offer an account of Nietzsche's politics that restores him to his time—namely, late nineteenth-century Germany and Europe. It will argue that Nietzsche, in contrast to Kaufmann and others, does make a (highly interesting) contribution to political thought, but his contribution must be understood within its own context and not against the backdrop of the Nazi regime. Moreover, that contribution will turn out to be much more hierarchical than the current democratic readings allow for, which raises the question of how much contact the later postmodern construal of Nietzsche retains with its nineteenth-century original, and therefore of what use is it to call on Nietzsche, outside his undeniable intellectual prestige, for one's cause.

The figure who dominated Nietzsche's political context was Otto von Bismarck, and in fact Nietzsche's productive life maps itself almost perfectly onto Bismarck's era: he served as a medical orderly in the Franco-Prussian War (1870–71), Bismarck's final war in view of German unity; published his first book, *The Birth of Tragedy*, in 1872; and descended into madness in 1889, a year before Bismarck was forced to resign. Perhaps the defining feature of Bismarck's reign was *grosse Politik*: the "power politics" of German unification and maintenance of this newfound greatness within the European balance of power.[3] International politics, on this account, was meant to have primacy over domestic concerns, meaning that other policies such as the notorious Kulturkampf—the "cultural struggle" against German Catholics—were meant to serve as handmaidens to "grand politics." Against those who claim that Nietzsche had no interest in politics, Nietzsche consistently and thoughtfully engaged with the notion from at least *Human, All Too Human* (1878) onward. At first he was critical of grand politics, linking it to slave-morality-infused concepts such as mass democracy, fragmentation, mediocrity, religion, dynastic politics, and philistinism. But with *Beyond Good and Evil* (1886) he transformed what he labeled "petty politics" into his own theory of what "great politics" should truly be: the master-morality politics of unifying Europe through a cultural elite "good European" caste—which has as its ideal the intermarriage of Prussian officers and Jewish financiers—to serve as a geopolitical counterweight to Russia and the British Empire. Indeed, Nietzsche's final notebook is titled "Great Politics," and there he develops in the most systematic manner his vision of what such politics ought to amount to. That notebook, along with much of the late *Nachlass* (Nietzsche's unpublished notes), has yet to be translated into English and represents an untapped source that this book draws on.

---

[3] See Tracy Strong, "'Wars the Like of Which One Has Never Seen': Reading Nietzsche and Politics," in *Friedrich Nietzsche*, ed. Tracy Strong (Farnham, UK: Ashgate, 2009), xi–xxxiii.

Williams was one of the most prominent moral philosophers of the late twentieth and early twenty-first centuries, and much of his work developed in dialogue with Nietzsche. In *Shame and Necessity* (1993), his celebrated work on the Greeks, Williams explains that "Nietzschean ideas will recur in this inquiry, and, above all, he sets its problem, by joining in a radical way the questions of how we understand the Greeks and of how we understand ourselves."[4] Later in *Truth and Truthfulness* (2002), whose subtitle is *An Essay in Genealogy*, he repeated the claim that "the problems that concern this book were discovered, effectively, by Nietzsche."[5]

Williams also took a keen interest in Nietzsche's political writings, but ultimately concluded in *Shame and Necessity* that Nietzsche "did not offer a politics." Yet in the process of doing so, he identified a number of desiderata that Nietzsche would have to meet for him to be considered to have done so. Pinpointing the answers to these questions is a helpful way of making more precise what Nietzsche's contribution to political theory might be. Williams writes:

> Although Nietzsche moved beyond the conception of the world as aesthetic phenomenon that is prominent in his major, early, work devoted to the Greeks, *The Birth of Tragedy*, he did not move to any view that offered a coherent politics. He himself provides no way of relating his ethical and psychological insights to an intelligible account of modern society—a failing only thinly concealed by the impression he gives of having thoughts about modern politics that are determinate but terrible. But we need a politics, in the sense of a coherent set of opinions about the ways in which power should be exercised in modern societies, with what limitations and to what ends.[6]

So there are four elements that comprise a "coherent" politics according to Williams: "ethical and psychological insights," "an intelligible account of modern society," the ability to relate these insights to this account of society, and "a coherent set of opinions about the ways in which power should be exercised in modern societies, with what limitations and to what ends." For Nietzsche to have a politics, he therefore would need to relate his (undeniable, in Williams's eyes) ethical and psychological insights—for instance, his analysis of master and slave morality, and his theory of the "death of God"—to an intelligible account of modern politics—namely, that of the state, democracy, and international politics.[7] Moreover, he must posit a vi-

[4] Bernard Williams, *Shame and Necessity* (Berkeley: University of California Press, 2008), 10.

[5] Bernard Williams, *Truth and Truthfulness: An Essay in Genealogy* (Princeton, NJ: Princeton University Press, 2002), 12.

[6] Williams, *Shame and Necessity*, 10–11.

[7] See "Nietzsche Minimalist Moral Psychology," "Introduction to *The Gay Science*," and "Unbearable Suffering," all in Bernard Williams, *The Sense of the Past: Essays in the History of*

sion of how power should be exercised in his ideal society, with what limitations and to what ends. To this account we should add something like a political strategy: given his understanding of modern politics and his advocating of a future ideal, how does Nietzsche propose we move from one to the other? What is his political program?

It is the task of this book to answer these questions. It will argue that Nietzsche offers a highly intelligible account of modern society, specifically in his critique of the modern *Kulturstaat*—the new German "culture-state"—modern democracy, and as we just saw above, international politics. He is able to relate his numerous ethical and psychological insights to this critique, such as in associating his theory of the death of God with the democratic decay of the modern state, and judging his contemporary power politics from the perspectives of master and slave morality. In terms of how power should be distributed in society, he posits a vision of the future comprising two separate spheres—a high cultural one, and a lower democratic one—with their own respective fields of responsibilities, but which importantly retain a degree of exchange between them. Finally, in his later work and notes, he starts to articulate a political strategy of how to achieve this ideal society, notably through his call for the founding of a "party of life" whose goal will be to carry out his great politics.

In an unpublished paper titled "There Are Many Kinds of Eyes," Williams fleshed out some of his claims concerning his rejection of a Nietzschean politics.[8] He opens by reiterating the claim that "Nietzsche did not have much conception of politics," although he adds that

> he had some political opinions, of an aristocratic character; he had a well-known dislike of socialism, liberalism, equality, democracy and so on. But as Mark Warren has well argued, he had not the faintest idea of the nature of a modern state. His general political conceptions, such as they were, were largely drawn from the ancient world and were not so much reactionary as archaic. Indeed, he had a poor sense not just of the modern state but of a modern society: it might even be said, of any society at all.[9]

Philosophy, ed. Myles Burnyeat (Princeton, NJ: Princeton University Press, 2006), 299–310, 331–24, 331–37, respectively.

[8] Bernard Williams, "There Are Many Kinds of Eyes," in *The Sense of the Past: Essays in the History of Philosophy*, ed. Myles Burnyeat (Princeton, NJ: Princeton University Press, 2006), 325–30. We have no exact dating for the paper, but its themes resonate well with what Williams was saying about Nietzsche in *Shame and Necessity*.

[9] Ibid., 326–27. The reference is to Mark Warren, *Nietzsche and Political Thought* (Cambridge, MA: MIT Press, 1991), 209, which argues that Nietzsche combines, unsuccessfully, a "postmodern philosophy with a premodern politics."

So Nietzsche had no sense of the modern state, or in fact modern society or perhaps even simply society at all, and only offered an archaic view of politics. In the same text, Williams continues by rehearsing a common view about the purportedly "solitary" nature of Nietzsche's project:

> His models of overcoming and transforming *our* values, which is his most enduring concern, tend to be personal, individualistic, occasionally heroic. Often the undertaking is regarded as an expression simply of a personal endeavor, like that of an artist; sometimes it takes on a historical transformative note, as though the individual's feat of transvaluation will itself change society. . . . [H]e leaves us for the most part with an image of some solitary figure bringing new values into existence, an image which, brought into relation to a transformation of society, is bound to have a certain pathos about it.[10]

But perhaps Williams's most substantive engagement with the content of Nietzsche's political writings came during a panel discussion on "Nietzsche's Critique of Liberalism" at the University of Chicago in 1995. There he delivered a paper titled "Can There Be a Nietzschean Politics?" which was pitched as a response to an earlier paper given by Martha Nussbaum, called "Is Nietzsche a Political Thinker?"[11]

Williams, as we have seen above, continued his engagement with Nietzsche throughout his life, but that this paper was delivered six years after he gave the Sather Lectures at Berkeley in 1989—which formed the basis for *Shame and Necessity*—suggests that the position he expressed there on Nietzsche's politics was not to be the final one he adopted for the rest of his life. Even though in the paper the content of Nietzsche's writings on politics left Williams, as we will now explore, feeling rather discouraged, at the same time he believed to have found a way for Nietzsche's thought to animate our own reflection on politics, which I will return to in the conclusion to this book.

In the paper, anticipating much of the subsequent debate about Nietzsche's relation to democracy, Williams interests himself in Nietzsche's so-called middle period, conventionally understood as the period stretching from *Human, All Too Human* (1878) to *Thus Spoke Zarathustra* (1883). This

---

[10] Ibid., 327.

[11] This paper was published a couple of years later as Martha Nussbaum, "Is Nietzsche a Political Thinker?" *International Journal of Philosophical Studies* 5, no. 1 (1997): 1–13. For a critique of this article, see chapter 2. Williams declined permission to publish his contribution on the grounds that it was a "work in progress" and written as a response to Nussbaum rather than a freestanding piece. I am indebted to Adrian Moore and Patricia Williams for permission to view this paper from Williams's private papers, and the late Geoffrey Hawthorn for facilitating this.

period is thought to represent the phase between Nietzsche's early enthusiasm for Richard Wagner from *The Birth of Tragedy* to the *Untimely Meditations* (1873–76), and his later work starting with *Zarathustra* where Nietzsche develops his own "philosophy" of the "will to power," "eternal return," and "overman."

During this period, Williams sees Nietzsche as more calm, moderate, and almost scientific in tone, as indeed he is often presented in the secondary literature, and—most important—more favorable to "democratic, egalitarian and liberal tendencies."[12] In contrast, Williams describes Nietzsche's later period as "visionarily prophetic," with not only a tone of "rigorous resistance to equality and liberalism" but also one "favoring radical and heroic change."[13] For Williams, Nietzsche's politics of "aristocratic radicalism," as Nietzsche's first translator and promoter, the Dane Georg Brandes, had labeled it, was primarily of the cultural and spiritual kind, and did not amount to a serious political program. Echoing what he had written previously in "There Are Many Kinds of Eyes," Nietzsche's political proposals, Williams observes, were "nostalgic and poorly informed images of past societies or, again, simply the dream of an isolated intellectual to bring modernity under his hammer."[14] This was followed by a renewed rejection of Nietzsche's grasp of the modern state, and on the basis of Nietzsche's concept of the "pathos of distance" and critique of equality—that equality can only hold between people of roughly equal power—Williams closes his paper with a reflection on the relation between power and right. He concludes that there is a potentially unresolvable tension between the two—in the process dismissing some of the democratic agonistic readings of Nietzsche inspired by Hannah Arendt—but that this tension is a feature of modern politics, which Nietzsche's thinking allows us to see, and does not arise from a tension within Nietzsche's thinking itself.

If *Shame and Necessity* provides us with a structural framework within which to address more precisely, through its different desiderata, the question of whether Nietzsche offers a "coherent" politics, Williams's own engagement with the content of Nietzsche's political writings in the paper "Can There Be a Nietzsche Politics?" affords us a springboard from which to raise a number of the themes I wish to discuss in this book, and as such can serve, in a certain manner, as its *fil conducteur*.

Much like Williams in *Shame and Necessity*, we must start with the Greeks. My first chapter begins with Nietzsche's interpretation of the ancients, focusing in on what Nietzsche terms—moving away from the more

---

[12] Bernard Williams, "Can There Be a Nietzschean Politics? (unpublished manuscript), 2–3.
[13] Ibid., 4.
[14] Ibid., 6–7.

conventional "pre-Socratics"—the "Pre-Platonic Philosophers," alongside Plato and Socrates. Plato is the pivotal figure here because he is the first "hybrid" philosopher. Previously all philosophers, in Nietzsche's eyes, were "pure" in the sense that their philosophy sprung naturally from their own personality. Yet Plato is a mixture of different types of philosophies and personalities: Socrates and Heraclitus are prominent, but not only. Another key difference is that the pre-Platonics all aimed for the "salvation of the whole"—that is, their philosophies, Socrates's included, aimed at the spiritual purification of their polis, whereas Plato only looked for the salvation of his small sect. He is the first to "fight against his time" and has the desire to "found a new state." The reason the earlier philosophers were pure had to do with the fact that their philosophy arose from a fundamentally healthy culture. Socrates marks the transition away from this healthy culture because he was the first to realize that the Greek's instincts had turned decadent. Nevertheless, according to Nietzsche, he remains pure in his dialectical method and desire to save Athens. After Socrates's death Plato sees the only salvation for philosophy in the future coming of philosopher-kings.

Straddling two different eras—that of the healthy Greeks and their decay into moralism, an era that we are still, according to Nietzsche, in today—Plato is therefore a focal point in Nietzsche's early history of philosophy. He was also the first to think a way out of it. His "legislative mission," as Nietzsche describes Plato's project, thus serves as a model for Nietzsche's own. That mission is comprised of two facets: to legislate for a new state, and train the men who would found it with him. It will be the mission of Nietzsche's "new philosophers" to legislate for a new type of society, and in his late call for the founding of a party of life, which will play a crucial role in the elaboration of his political strategy, Nietzsche thinks up an institution within which those men who will found this new state with him can be trained. But Nietzsche clearly saw that while a healthy philosophy could only spring from a healthy culture, it was not the role of philosophy to try to restore that type of culture. Nietzsche, still at this moment under the influence of Wagner, instead thought music would play that part. Later Nietzsche would suggest his own methods for cultural regeneration, and these would turn out to be much more political.

Nietzsche's published texts, particularly *The Birth of Tragedy* and *Twilight of the Idols* (1888), will feature strongly in this chapter, but the main content of it will be drawn from unpublished sources of that time, notably "Philosophy in the Tragic Age of the Greeks" along with his lectures on the "Pre-Platonic Philosophers" and Plato; the latter two in fact provide much of the substance for the former. I will draw out the intimate relationship these published and unpublished texts entertain with one another, although this brings me to the question of Nietzsche's (quite-substantial) *Nachlass*—his unpublished notes—and what to do with them. Bernd Magnus has separated Nietzsche interpreters into two blocs: "lumpers" and "splitters,"[15] Lumpers are those who take Nietzsche's writings en bloc, making no distinction between his published and unpublished work, whereas the splitters prioritize the published work. In general in this work I tend to side with the splitters in the sense that I find that the majority of Nietzsche's thoughts expressed in the notebooks make their way, in some form or another, into the published texts. As such, the notes are helpful in illuminating or clarifying a certain idea or text, perhaps also helping to tract their evolution, but the published material remains central. This is the case for the majority of Nietzsche's work, especially throughout his active publishing period that makes up most of his adult life. But I suspend this judgment at two moments, which represent the extremities of Nietzsche's corpus: the beginning and the end.

At the beginning of his career Nietzsche had planned to publish a number of works that were to accompany and complement his first book, *The Birth of Tragedy*. These include "Philosophy in the Tragic Age of the Greeks" and his lecture series on "The Future of Our Educational Institutions"—which he considered to form a triptych with *The Birth*—and the "Five Prefaces to Five Unwritten Books."[16] Most of these were in near-complete form, but were subsequently abandoned by Nietzsche because of the falling out with the academic community that resulted from *The Birth*. For reasons of their often near-finalized state, and the role they were meant to play with *The Birth*, I include these unpublished writings in my study. At the other end of the spectrum we come to the controversy concerning Nietzsche's planned "major work," "The Will to Power," which I will examine in more detail in chapter 5. Suffice it to say for now that the final notes are indispensable to at the very least get a grasp of what Nietzsche was ultimately planning before he was taken away by madness, and may indeed be central to our understanding of Nietzsche's project for a great politics.

One aspect I wish to emphasize in this chapter is the strong continuity that obtains between Nietzsche's early and later views of Socrates and Plato. This raises the issue of how one is to read Nietzsche. Should we see Nietzsche's thought as one "in becoming," as has frequently been suggested by the more "continental" readings of Nietzsche, in which he gradually deepens and expands his reflection on his chosen topics over the course of his writings?[17] Or should we distinguish sharply between three different peri-

---

[15] Bernd Magnus, "Nietzsche's Philosophy in 1888: The Will to Power and the Übermensch," *Journal of the History of Philosophy* 24, no. 1 (1986): 79–98.

[16] See Tracy Strong, "Nietzsche and the Political: Tyranny, Tragedy, Cultural Revolution, and Democracy," *Journal of Nietzsche Studies* 35–36 (Spring–Fall 2008): 48–66.

[17] Mazzino Montinari, "Nietzsche's Unpublished Writings from 1885 to 1888; or, Textual

ods in Nietzsche's life, which Nietzsche himself appears to allude to in *Ecce Homo*: an earlier phase, marked by the influence of Wagner, comprising *The Birth of Tragedy* and the *Untimely Meditations*; followed by a more "critical" phase where Nietzsche seeks emancipation from Wagner and starts to develop his own philosophy (*Human, All Too Human* to *Thus Spoke Zarathustra*, as discussed above); to a final, mature stage, beginning with *Zarathustra* (although in chapter 5, I will argue that this must be understood as a "singular" work, to which all posterior work will refer back to) that sees Nietzsche in full control of his thoughts?

I want to suggest that these two approaches need not be antithetical, and in fact may be complementary. In terms of politics, there are strong continuities between what Nietzsche writes on the state, democracy, and international politics over the course of his early, middle, and later periods, and often we can see a later period explicitly referring back to an earlier one, as I will explore over the course of this book. Nietzsche's thoughts on these topics are certainly not static—they evolve, deepen, and expand over time—but the kernel of his views on those matters remain remarkable consistent. Yet one of the main claims I want to make in this book is that it is through his revaluating of grosse Politik from the perspective of master politics that Nietzsche starts to develop something recognizable as a politics, and thus that there is a difference between Nietzsche's earlier and later views of politics, which stem from the discovery of his philosophical concepts. Instead of seeing a tension between these two views, however, I find both strands of interpretation mutually enlightening. The continuity in Nietzsche's thought is to be found in his rejection of the grand politics of his day, which is remarkably consistent over the course of his writings from *Human, All Too Human* to his last notebook. But when Nietzsche brings his notions of master and slave morality to bear on international politics, he is able to recast that same kernel in a new light: the grand politics he criticizes is relabeled petty politics, while the new policy he puts forward—which can been seen as an inversion of this petty politics—he titles (true) great politics.

One of the implications of the in-becoming reading of Nietzsche is that his later work will be richer and deeper than his earlier work, not simply due to the effect of accumulation, but also because of the deepening of his *philosophical* reflection, which, as we just saw, has an impact on his *political* thinking. This gives credit to the view that Nietzsche's fuller contribution to political thought is best found in his later work, notably in how it is articulated through the notion of great politics, which becomes much more prominent over time, rather than focusing on the supposed proto-democratic thinking of his middle period.

Criticism and the Will to Power," in *Reading Nietzsche*, ed. Mazzino Montinari, trans. Greg Whitlock (Champaign: University of Illinois Press, 2003), 80–102.

In my second chapter, I turn to tackling Williams's claim that Nietzsche had a poor grasp of the state. I will argue that against someone like Brian Leiter, Nietzsche does offer a theory of the state and its justification. By placing Nietzsche's early, unpublished text "The Greek State" alongside what he says about the birth of the state in *The Genealogy of Morality* (1887)—and there are good reasons to read both texts side by side—we can see that for Nietzsche, the birth of the state can be located in the conquering horde that are the infamous "blond beasts of prey," who seize on an unformed population and establish a hierarchical society. But this original act of violence is justified, according to Nietzsche, because it allows for the development of genius and culture through a division of labor. It leads to, as he puts it in *The Birth*, the justification of the world and existence as an aesthetic phenomenon.

Nietzsche did not confine his analysis to the ancient state, and he turns his gaze to the modern nation-state, particularly in its Kulturstaat variety, which he was highly critical of. Here we start to get a better sense of the intelligible account of modern society that Williams denies Nietzsche has. If with the Greeks the state existed as a means to genius, the modern culture-state instrumentalizes culture for its own end, notably by arrogating to itself the best talents and forcing them to work for the sole promotion of the state, instead of following their own true path to culture. Yet Nietzsche sees some hope for the future, in the sense that as the ancient state did not last, nor would the modern one, which he believes will "decay" because of the demands modern democracy will make on it, and which it will not be able to meet. This has to do with Nietzsche's famous declaration of the death of God in *The Gay Science* (1882)—already we can see Nietzsche relating his philosophical insights to his account of modern society—that once religion can no longer provide the support to the state it once did, and that the state comes to be seen simply as an "instrument of the popular will, then the modern state will become obsolete and be replaced by "better suited institutions." "Private companies" (*Privatgesellschaften*) will take over the business of the state, including those activities that are the "most resistant remainder of what was formerly the work of the government"—that is, "protecting the private person from the private person."

We should not, however, understand the decay of the *modern* state as the death of the state tout court. Instead, we should understand it as the superseding of the modern state, much like that of the ancient state by the modern, by a new type of entity. This entity will take on a more regulatory and minimalist function, allowing private companies to take over the role they formerly played, including that of protecting the private person from the private person, but still maintaining overall jurisdiction; the key here is the difference between the state and government. There will be space, within this new configuration, for culture, and Nietzsche speculates about the role new cultural "institutions" can play as counterparts to the private companies.

We can pause at this juncture to note that the cultural mission Nietzsche ascribes to these new institutions are strongly communal ones, thus challenging the view Williams rehearses about the solitary nature of Nietzsche's revaluative project.[18] Indeed, the figures that Nietzsche calls on, from the "republic of geniuses" to the "free spirits," good Europeans, new philosophers, and the party of life, are all conceived of in the plural. And while the *Übermensch* is mostly styled in the singular, particularly in *Zarathustra*, this has more to do with the exceptionalism of their appearance; in *The Antichrist* (1888), Nietzsche is clear that there have been a number of these "lucky hits" in the past. Regardless of how many overmen may appear in the future, the ground from which they may appear—the soil of Nietzsche's revaluative project—is undeniably collective.

Williams is quite aware of Nietzsche's speculation about the state's decay, asking in his paper whether "the belief in the power of the state can survive the decline of the belief in religion. In this context Nietzsche indeed foresees the excesses of privatization, predicting that even the prison service may be handed over to private companies when people's belief in the state finally declines."[19] Williams associates this view with Nietzsche's middle period, and while it is certainly the case that the claim about the state's decay is first made in *Human, All Too Human*, that passage from *Human* is again explicitly quoted in *Twilight of the Idols*, from Nietzsche's later period, underlining the strong continuities of this theme over the course of his writings. The repetition of this claim also makes it, to my mind, Nietzsche's final prognosis of the modern state's future. Nor should we understand Nietzsche as being reticent about the future "excesses" of privatization; he is rather looking forward to "new stories in the history of mankind," which he is hoping will be "good ones," where culture can be restored to its true path outside the clutches of the modern state.

A key figure in this chapter, and for Nietzsche's engagement with the Greeks more generally, is Wagner. Nietzsche's theory of the state arose in the first place from a disagreement with Wagner over the role slavery played in ancient Greece, and therefore whether it was needed to re-create high culture in Germany. It must be understood that for the early German Romantics, the ancient Greeks were their single reference point, in what makes for a strange historical arc that leads, on their account, from ancient times directly to nineteenth-century Germany, while eliding everything else in between.

---

[18] Tracy Strong had already challenged this view in his *Friedrich Nietzsche and the Politics of Transfiguration* (Champaign: University of Illinois Press, 2000).

[19] Williams, "Can There Be a Nietzschean Politics?" 3.

Their politics was crucial too; Nietzsche calls the Greeks the "political men *as such*." What this allows us to see is that exactly as Wagner's "total revolution" necessarily involved both art and politics—Wagner believed that the liberation of the modern factory slave was essential to the successful completion of his cultural revolution—so it was for Nietzsche as well. On the question of slavery, however, Nietzsche begged to disagree. In a chapter on the state and slavery originally intended for *The Birth*, he argued that "slavery belongs to the essence of a culture." This did not sit well with Wagner's more left-leaning tendencies, and it appears that the offending chapter was removed at his insistence. What that disagreement obscured was the fact that for Nietzsche, and certainly from the onset of his writing career, politics and art were inseparable. That Nietzsche was not advocating the same politics as Wagner in the re-creation of Greek high culture should not blind us to the reality that the overall structure of this total revolution remained the same. Indeed, Nietzsche's enduring commitment to those views is testified to by the fact that he offered a word-for-word copy of the chapter, now titled "The Greek State," to Cosima Wagner for Christmas 1872 (i.e., after *The Birth* had been published earlier in the year) as part of his "Five Prefaces to Five Unwritten Books"—a poisoned gift if there ever was one. Moreover, *The Genealogy* echoes the opinions expressed in that essay, and in so doing offers a public endorsement of his earlier, unpublished views.

If for Nietzsche politics and art are inseparable, I do not mean to suggest that they are the same. This is a view that has become popular of late, which characterizes Nietzsche's politics as "cultural politics," understood in the sense that it is through cultural means that a political transformation can be effected.[20] It is often how Nietzsche's project for a "revaluation of all values" is presented, as being solely of the cultural or spiritual kind, much in the same way Williams does. But building on the structural similarity between Wagner's total revolution and Nietzsche's own project that I develop in the first part of the book—namely, that the project for a cultural renewal contains both a necessary, if independent, political facet—in the second part I will argue more attentively that Nietzsche's revaluation of all values also has an indispensable political aspect to it, notably articulated through the notion of great politics. If we desire to understand what such a cultural politics could amount to, we must understand what the political element of that politics is meant to entail. What is puzzling about this view is that although it recognizes that Nietzsche does write about politics, it refuses to look at these writings on their own terms, instead casting them as cultural demands. To my mind, this makes understanding Nietzsche's political writ-

---

[20] See Jennifer Ratner-Rosenhagen, *American Nietzsche: A History of an Icon and His Ideas* (Chicago: University of Chicago Press, 2012).

ings on their own grounds even more urgent, so that we may correctly theorize their relationship to the cultural aspect of his work.

While for Nietzsche one cannot have high culture without it being rooted in a hierarchical society, this does not mean that the spheres of art and politics overlap perfectly. Although one cannot exist without the other—or to be more precise, the sphere of higher art cannot exist without a politics of rank—they both, in Nietzsche's work, retain a degree of autonomy from one another. If in his early life Nietzsche's cultural sphere takes a Wagnerian form, it will take a distinctively more Nietzschean shape over time. For the sphere of politics it is the same: while Nietzsche maintains throughout his life that a caste society is essential to underpin a high culture, the exact relationship that the two castes entertain with one another—the higher and the lower—evolve over the course of his writings. Tracking his historical interests, initially Nietzsche posits a society in which the higher is placed firmly above the lower, much like it was with his interpretation of the Greeks, yet later he advocates a somewhat more horizontal relationship between the two in a vision of a future societal organization, which nevertheless retains a key transferral of resources from the lower to the higher.[21] It will be the object of chapter 3 to fully explore that relationship.

I should clarify at this point that I do not mean to suggest in this book that Nietzsche is first and foremost a political thinker. His prime concern is culture, and I have no wish to deny that. What I want to refuse is that one can have a reflection about Nietzsche's views on culture that is completely divorced from his views on politics. I do not wish to exclude the possibility of an analytic distinction, but on the one hand, I want to deny that for Nietzsche there can and should be a separation between the two, and on the other, I want to affirm that if we are interested in Nietzsche's view of culture we must interest ourselves in the conditions that made that culture, for Nietzsche, possible—and what did not.

There has been a strong push in the recent literature, particularly in discussions surrounding Nietzsche's notion of the pathos of distance, that attempt to portray Nietzsche as having himself come to see how the two might be separated, but in chapter 3 I will give reasons for wanting to resist such a move, at least in terms of how Nietzsche saw it. Some have tried to argue that we need not see politics and art as closely intertwined as Nietzsche did, and those contentions have to be assessed on their own merits—something I will not attempt to do here. Yet if we take Nietzsche's views about culture seriously, then we must try hard to understand in the first instance what Nietzsche himself said about it. Whatever that might be must

---

[21] On this point, see also John Richardson, *Nietzsche's System* (Oxford: Oxford University Press, 2002).

surely be of interest to those who are concerned about the relationship culture entertains with politics today.

Chapter 3 also takes aim at Williams's view, which anticipated much of the contemporary debate on the matter, that Nietzsche's so-called middle period is more sympathetic to democracy. This, I will argue, is mistaken. While it is certainly the case that Nietzsche in this period approaches democracy from its own point of view, positing that what it must aim for is more independence, he nonetheless concludes that democracy will ultimately serve as a means toward forming a new type of aristocracy. In the section Williams relies on in *The Wanderer and His Shadow*, which has as its title "The Age of Cyclopean Building" (WS 275)—hardly the most democratic of imageries—Nietzsche clearly states that the democratization of Europe is a link in the chain to what he calls those "tremendous prophylactic measure." Moreover, he explains that the independence-inducing "stone barriers" and "trellises" that are built by the gray and sullen democratic workers to keep out the barbarians will in fact ultimately be used by a future "higher artist of horticulture," who will erect a new higher culture on the basis democracy provides. This vision of a forthcoming aristocracy using democratic tools with which to build a new culture is strikingly similar to the one found in *Beyond Good and Evil*, belonging to Nietzsche's later period, where he notes that what he is trying to say is that "the democratization of Europe is at the same time an involuntary exercise in the breeding of *tyrants*—understanding that word in every sense, including the most spiritual." Thus while Nietzsche made certain statements in his middle period that have supplied inspiration for a number of postmodern reconceptualizations of democratic politics, his own view is that democracy will lead to a new type of aristocracy. Nor can this middle period be considered to be especially singular, as in his later work he reaffirmed his vision of democracy serving as building blocks toward a new nobility.

Analyzing Nietzsche's theory of democracy will continue to provide substance to the view that Nietzsche does, pace Williams, offer an intelligible account of modern society. He is, for one, quite capable of discerning behind the facade of democratic politics taking place in the new *Reichstag* the fact that it is still Bismarck who is holding the reins of power and implementing his realpolitik, in the process dispelling the notion that democratic politics is meant to be more pacific. Nietzsche also hits on a number of critiques of modern democracy—the problem of minorities and secession; the difficulty of finding a unanimous democratic basis to institute an electoral system—that have become classics in the field. In this sense the secondary literature is right in depicting Nietzsche as one of the sharpest critics of modern democracy, but at the same time he cannot be restricted to being only that, as his theory of the future superseding of democracy also provides a positive vision of what politics might become. Furthermore, and building on chapter 2 where we will see how the notion of the death of God informed his theory of the democratic decay of the modern state, many of Nietzsche's most famous pronouncements about democracy—that it represents the political arm of Christianity; that it is best described as a form of "misarchism," the mind-set of being against everything that dominates and wants to dominate; that it represents not solely a form of spiritual but also physiological degeneration, an example of the darker European races regaining the upper hand against the original blond beasts of prey—take their lead from his concept of slave morality, thereby underlining how Nietzsche continues to relate his ethical and psychological insights to his account of modern politics.

In the process of exploring these ideas, we will come into contact with some of Nietzsche's more unsavory statements. I do not, as has sometimes been the case in recent scholarship, simply want to brush these under the carpet, but at the same time there are two points I want to emphasize. The first is that while Nietzsche undeniably toys with eugenic ideas, in particular in his later reflections on "breeding," he is hardly the only one in his day to do so; such ideas were in that period quite ubiquitous, and frequently part and parcel of accepted scientific discourse, as we will see.[22] Nor, it must be said, does that immediately make him the preserve of the Far Right; that thinking has a longer legacy in European left-wing thought than we would often like to admit.[23] Indeed, it is not surprising that someone who is so interested in education, culture, and health should have more than a passing interest in the topic. While I by no means want to absolve him of his responsibilities, I do find that this type of language sometimes sees Nietzsche a prisoner of his own time. Second, it should also be clear that against certain writers like Joseph-Arthur, comte de Gobineau for whom race was the key concern, for Nietzsche it was morality, which does not map itself perfectly onto questions of race. Williams is quick to the mark here spotting that at least one and perhaps two (depending on whether by "Arabs" Nietzsche had in mind the Berbers, typically thought to have been more fairheaded) of the figures Nietzsche lists as his infamous blond beasts of prey—the Arabs and the Japanese—could not have been blond.[24] In any case, we can hardly understand Nietzsche's call for a mixing of Prussian military officers with Jews in view of creating the good Europeans as a ringing endorsement of a vulgar Aryanism, whose main theses Nietzsche, as a trained philologist, would have been patently aware of.

[22] On breeding, see John Richardson, *Nietzsche's New Darwinism* (Oxford: Oxford University Press, 2008).

[23] See Dan Stone, *Breeding Superman: Nietzsche, Race, and Eugenics in Edwardian and Interwar Britain* (Liverpool: Liverpool University Press, 2002).

[24] Williams, "Can There Be a Nietzschean Politics," 7.

It would be remiss of a book on Nietzsche not to discuss his principle philosophical concepts—the notions of the will to power, eternal return, and Übermensch—and this will be the task of chapter 4. So if chapters 1 and 5 are principally concerned with the structure of Nietzsche's political project, and chapter 2, 3, and 6 with the content of that project, chapter 4 stands a little aside in dealing primarily with Nietzsche's philosophy. But it will not aim to offer a comprehensive interpretation of these ideas, which would require three more separate studies. Rather, it aims to propose a political reading of the terms in question. Starting with the will to power, it will link that notion strongly to what Nietzsche says about the Greek agon, particularly in the early essay "Homer's Contest," which appeared alongside "The Greek State" in Nietzsche's "Five Prefaces to Five Unwritten Books." There Nietzsche discusses the two opposing yet twin patron deities of the agon—the good and the bad Eris—and how the "wicked" eldest leads to strife and destruction, whereas the younger promotes a positive contest that is not only beneficial to the competitors in question but also captured, through the different institutions of the agon, for the benefit of the city-state as a whole. It is through this institutional setup that we can glean a sense of how Nietzsche's future party of life is to be internally structured, and what form the "war of spirits" it will be brought to fight against its enemies, the "Christian Reich" and the "party of Christianity," will take. On the topic of the party of life, the political role that Nietzsche's "doctrine" of the eternal return plays is in separating ascending from descending life, and thus serving as a selective device for separating those who are to join the party from those who are not.

One prominent strand that has appeared in recent American interpretations of Nietzsche has been to tie him to debates about ethical perfectionism, and one entry point into that discussion has been Nietzsche's highly debated concept of the Übermensch. The line here—one I wish to challenge—is that we should understand that figure in Nietzsche's writing as some form of perfected humanity. But the true question is, to my mind, what *type* of humanity is to be perfected? If it is to be modern man, then in Nietzsche's eyes, as Zarathustra comes to quickly realize in his opening speech in the marketplace, the perfection of that type leads not to the Übermensch but instead exactly to his opposite—the "last man." In fact, if we are to translate the *Über* in Übermensch as "over," then what Nietzsche appears to be saying is that the overman represents precisely the overcoming of modern man into something new, in the same way the ancient philosophers represented the overcoming of the ancient poets—a thought I will explore in this chapter. This Emersonian perfectionist reading therefore seems quite at odds with Nietzsche's project, particularly the democratic element of universal self-creation that goes along with it, when we know Nietzsche's views about the hierarchical nature of high culture. But if that *ethical* perfectionist reading of Nietzsche does not hold, John Rawls's account of Nietzsche's *political* perfectionism put forward in *A Theory of Justice*—that society should be organized with the sole goal of creating new geniuses—might be closer to the mark. Indeed, while Rawls's reconstruction may be a fair reflection of Nietzsche's early views of political organization, his later years, as I have suggested above, see a more subtle account of what the interaction between the different spheres of that caste society might look like, thereby lowering Nietzsche on the scale of political perfectionism—from extreme to more moderate—that Rawls offers us.

Near the end of his productive life Nietzsche, as Tracy Strong has rightly highlighted, starts to become impatient with simply remaining a "spectator" to the politics of his time.[25] He desires to enter the political arena; he wants to act. Why this sudden desire? If we hark back to the relationship that Nietzsche's project entertained with Wagner's total revolution, we can see the logic behind this move. Having expounded from *Zarathustra* onward his philosophy of the will to power, eternal return, and overman—the new theoretical underpinning to his project, after abandoning Wagner's *"artist's* metaphysics"—Nietzsche naturally returns to the other, inseparable aspect of the revolution: politics. And if what Nietzsche learned from the Greeks was that a healthy philosophy only sprung from a healthy culture, then there is every reason to start with politics, as first the instincts—Nietzsche's politics has a strong educational aspect to it—and then the structure on which that culture can come about needs to be restored. To begin with philosophy itself would be to simply perpetuate the moralism it is already rooted in. Williams himself may have intuited such a move in *Shame and Necessity*. In discussing the possible "structural substitutions" one would need to better relate the Greek world to our own, Williams alights on the fact that "Napoleon remarked to [Johann Wolfgang] Goethe that what fate was in the ancient world, politics was in the modern, and in the same spirit Benjamin Constant said that the significance of the supernatural in ancient tragedy could be transferred to the modern theatre only in politics terms."[26] Politics having replaced tragedy in the modern world, Nietzsche, having himself internalized such a transformation, should in his recovery of the Greeks instinctively turn to it.

A good sense of Nietzsche's final intentions can only be acquired through a close philological study of Nietzsche's final plans, especially his plans for a famous *Hauptwerk*, which had for a long time the title "The Will to Power." This will be the focus of chapter 5. And while I completely subscribe to

[25] See Tracy Strong, "Nietzsche's Political Aesthetics," in *Nietzsche's New Seas: Explorations in Philosophy, Aesthetics, and Politics*, ed. Michael Gillespie and Tracy Strong, trans. Thomas Heilke (Chicago: University of Chicago Press, 1988), 153–76.

[26] Williams, *Shame and Necessity*, 164.

Mazzino Montinari's—the eminent editor of Nietzsche's work—analysis of the fraudulent nature of the editions compiled by Nietzsche's sister after his death, I am less convinced by his conclusion that when Nietzsche transformed his "Will to Power" project into one of a "Revaluation of All Values" that signaled the end of everything he wanted to achieve. Nietzsche certainly may have achieved everything he wanted to achieve philosophically and intellectually at the end of his sane life, but before the onset of madness he was turning to the other aspect of his mission: politics. This is why Nietzsche's late texts and notes on great politics are so crucial: they are a fundamental part of his "Revaluation of All Values," and in fact served as the planned title for his book 4 of the magnum opus—*The Antichrist* was meant to be book 1—and offer a vision of how that project was meant to be accomplished. Moreover, they explain why the project was never completed in full literary form, as the end point of it was in a different register—one of political action.

My sixth and final chapter will flesh out the vision of Nietzsche's great politics that I opened with—one that advocates the unification of continental Europe through a good European ruling class, and whose aim is to foster a new European culture that is specially called on to guarantee world culture. The notion of great politics, as I have been arguing, represents the best way to my mind of meeting Williams's challenge as laid down in *Shame and Necessity*: of whether Nietzsche offers a "coherent politics." Nietzsche instantly, both in his second *Untimely Meditation* and *Human, All Too Human*, seizes on the novelty of the power politics of his day, and quickly links that type of politics to the arrival of the masses on the political stage. He also is able to see how in this new configuration domestic politics is to serve as the handmaiden of international politics, as I will examine in more detail in this chapter in relation to colonization and the Kulturkampf. As such, and building on his analysis of the modern state and modern democracy, Nietzsche yet again demonstrates his ability to offer an "intelligible account of modern society." In relating master and slave morality to this account—revaluing the slave-like grand politics of his time into petty politics and supplying a new vision of great politics on the basis of master morality—Nietzsche thereby fulfills the first three desiderata that Williams had set out: to 3) relate his 1) "ethical and psychological insights" to an 2) intelligible account of modern politics. Furthermore, as we saw in chapter 3, Nietzsche is able to 4) posit a vision of a future society divided into two spheres, each with its own responsibilities and goals, which the vision of great politics is able to add to. Finally, in starting to fill out the content of what such a great politics should look like, particularly in his call for the founding of a party of life that is to fight a war of spirits against the Christian Reich, Nietzsche begins to formulate a political strategy for successfully moving from his contemporary society to his ideal future.

That Nietzsche's conception of great politics serves as the best inlet into theorizing his politics is one of the core claims of this book. To get a good grasp of what that politics amounts to, three methodological moves are made that demark it from other studies in the field. First, that to correctly understand what Nietzsche's vision of great politics entails it must be placed back within its own context of late nineteenth-century international politics. Second, that Nietzsche's late notes need to be taken into consideration to fully flesh out that vision. These notes have yet to be entirely translated into English, particularly Nietzsche's last notebook titled "Great Politics," and remain to a certain degree unexplored. They therefore comprise the innovative source material this book draws from for its study. Lastly, that there are strong continuities across Nietzsche's writings on politics throughout his active life, which both goes against the grain of much contemporary scholarship that focuses on Nietzsche's middle period and reinforces the view that Nietzsche's later period, because of the depth of its reflection, is of more interest to those who aim to understand what politics meant for him.

The key context for Nietzsche's vision of great politics is the so-called great game being played by Britain and Russia over control of India and Afghanistan. Whoever controlled that area, so it was thought at the time, controlled the world. Many of the international events of the period—whether that be the Russo-Turkish War of 1877–78, Congress of Berlin (1878), or general "scramble for Africa" and its denouement in the Berlin Conference of 1884–85—shed light on Nietzsche's statements about great politics in both *Human, All Too Human* and *Beyond Good and Evil*, and are central to our understanding of them. Perhaps most pivotal is the Panjdeh Incident (1885), which took place one year before the publication of *Beyond Good and Evil*, where Russian troops seized an area of Afghanistan, almost triggering a full-scale conflict with Britain (diplomacy saved the day). It is in reaction to these events that Nietzsche demands that Russia become more aggressive so that Europe can unify and become more aggressive in return, which signals his revaluation of the grand politics he had so far decried into a truly Nietzschean great politics.

There are a number of different conceptions of politics at work here whose relationships need to be elucidated. Nietzsche, as is well known, had little time for the internal politics of democracies, elections, and party competition—what he describes as the "miserable, ephemeral gossip of politics" in his preface to *The Antichrist*—which he was used to seeing as being beneath him. In this sense Nietzsche is the antipolitical thinker he is so frequently made out to be. But he also, however, wanted to reopen what for him was the true question of political legislation, now that Christianity no longer held sway over a portion of the population, which was what type of humanity we want to become. This transcendence of everyday politics is matched in the international sphere: Nietzsche rejects as petty politics the grand posturing and jostling for territory that the Great Powers engage in, instead positing the unification of Europe as the basis for a new European culture. Thus, if Nietzsche's engagement with the international politics of his day helps us make better sense of his different pronouncements on great politics, it also allows him to develop the geopolitical facet—the unification of Europe as a counterweight to Russia and England—of this vision.

Williams was quite aware that Nietzsche had little time for what he labeled petty politics, and that his own politics would seek to transcend such a practice. He writes in his paper that "the notion of being 'antipolitical' has a special significance in terms of the rejection of the politics of parties and in general of the modern state, the politics, one might say, of politicians, and it is hardly in dispute that Nietzsche had small patience for that." But this leads Williams to conclude that Nietzsche gave up on politics altogether: "There was no way in which ideas of aristocratic radicalism or whatever could be inserted into the politics of Bismarckian Germany, nor did he think that there was any route, whether revolutionary or not, to replace Bismarckian Germany with a field of political action in which the ideas of aristocratic radicalism could be expressed."[27] The main claim of this book is that it is precisely through the notion of great politics that Nietzsche was able to link his aristocratic radicalism to the politics of Bismarckian Germany. In revaluating the petty antipolitics of modern states, parties, and politicians into a great politics of European unification through a pan-racial and pan-national elite, Nietzsche, pace Williams, was able to find a field of political action in which his aristocratic radicalism could be expressed. This is, to my mind, the element Williams was missing for him to answer in the affirmative the question that formed the title of his paper: whether there could be a such a thing as a Nietzschean politics.

The vision of his ideal future society that Nietzsche leaves us with, of one divided into two spheres, with the first dedicated to art, and the other to democratic politics, allows us to address one of the final questions Williams raises in his paper in reference to the notion of the pathos of distance. Given that "Nietzsche's master is distinguished from [Georg Wilhelm Friedrich] Hegel's precisely in the respect that he does not require recognition," Williams asks, then "this leaves us less than clear why the masters need the slaves at all."[28] It is indeed the case that Nietzsche's masters do not need the Hegelian recognition of their slaves, but their existence is required for two reasons. First, it is from the surplus of their work that the masters are liberated from having to work for their own subsistence, and therefore can fully engage in their pursuit of high art; second, it is in looking down and outward on the "slaves" that their souls are pushed toward the even higher de-

[27] Williams, 'Can There Be a Nietzschean Politics?" 2, 10.
[28] Ibid., 12.

mands and expectations they place on themselves as an internal form of demarcation. And while with Nietzsche there can never be an equality of power between individuals but only an order of rank, a degree of equality of power can obtain between the two future spheres Nietzsche imagines because of their respective size and power, and hence a degree of equality. This potential reconciliation between aristocratic and democratic modes of life was a theme Williams was particularly interested in, yet one he was unable to resolve, believing it to be an inherent tension in modern politics.[29] Nietzsche offers us at least one way of thinking about it.

Mine is not the first study to use great politics as an inlet into Nietzsche's political thought, although the prominence of those who do not see it primarily as a cultural phenomenon, much like Williams, has dwindled over the years. Even Bruce Detwiler, for a long time the standard-bearer of the "political" Nietzsche, while admitting that if one is serious about understanding Nietzsche's politics then one must focus on the notion of great politics, fails to heed his own advice and concentrates instead, again much like Williams, on the putatively proto-democratic views of his middle period.[30] One must return to the lead up to World War II to rediscover great politics as the focal point in interpreting Nietzsche's politics. The reasons for that are patently clear, and reside in the political context, but that does not make the debate any less intriguing; quite the contrary. In fact, one of the problems with Kaufmann's interpretation of Nietzsche is that it paints all that came before him with the same brushstroke. While there is no doubt that the National Socialist reading of Nietzsche was the politically dominant one on both sides of the war divide—Bertrand Russell labeled the war "Nietzsche's war"—the same could not be said of the intellectual milieu. It was Alfred Baeumler who was responsible for the characterization of Nietzsche as a "Hitler prophecy," as Thomas Mann put it, and he wielded much force from his position as head of pedagogy in Berlin for the Nazi regime. It is also in part his fault that the controversy surrounding "The Will to Power" grew over the period, as Baeumler based his quite-dubious interpretation on that text.[31] But his was hardly the only voice.

For one, during the first part of the twentieth century Nietzsche was an inspiration across the political spectrum, and one of the main points of discussion was how to successfully combine him with Karl Marx.[32] Indeed,

---

[29] Ibid., 13.

[30] Bruce Detwiler, *Nietzsche and the Politics of Aristocratic Radicalism* (Chicago: University of Chicago Press, 1990).

[31] On Baumler, see also Michael Halberstam, *Totalitarianism and the Modern Conception of Politics* (New Haven, CT: Yale University Press, 2000).

[32] See Steven Aschheim, *The Nietzsche Legacy in Germany, 1890–1990* (Berkeley: University of California Press, 1994). Compare Max Weber's later comment that one could measure a scholar's integrity by their intellectual posture toward Marx and Nietzsche.

we can note that the unpolitical phase of Nietzsche interpretation has been quite a minority one over the course of over a century of Nietzsche interpretation—twenty-five years to be precise, from the publication of Kaufmann's *Nietzsche* in 1950 to Strong's *Friedrich Nietzsche and the Politics of Transfiguration* exactly twenty-five years later in 1975.[33] Before that, one of the first book-length studies of Nietzsche was Ernst Bertram's *Nietzsche: Attempt at a Mythology* (1918), written under the auspices of the George circle.[34] Martin Heidegger's relation to Nietzsche is famously complicated, and he claimed that it is through his war-years lectures on Nietzsche that he turned and fought against Nazism. Whatever is to be said about that assertion, it is certainly the case that Heidegger disagreed with Baeumler's interpretation of the concepts of the will to power and eternal return. Nonetheless, in the final analysis Heidegger had a tendency to renationalize Nietzsche's European vision of great politics into an agon or struggle between different cultures, which seems to have brought him to justifying the Nazi invasion of the Mediterranean, construing grand politics as the de facto victory of force.[35]

Still through all this Karl Jaspers's book on Nietzsche (1936), recognized as one of the first truly scholarly studies of him, was written explicitly against the Nazi interpretation: "In the years 1934 and 1935, I also intended to marshal against the National Socialists the world of thought of the man whom they had proclaimed as their own philosopher."[36] There Jaspers devoted his longest chapter to discussing grosse Politik, which he saw as the most promising entry point into theorizing Nietzsche's politics. In spite of its *parti pris* for Jaspers's own *Existenzphilosophie*, that text remains a great source of inspiration, and many of the themes it develops will also be treated here, although not from the same perspective.

Of course Williams's interest in Nietzsche's political thought stemmed from his interest in what a Nietzschean politics would look like *today*. He opens his paper with the line: "The question I am asking in my title is whether there are Nietzschean ideas that can be of some distinctive use in thinking about issues of politics for us today."[37] But he was well aware that to start answering that question, one must first ask what Nietzsche's politics meant for him: "To ask this is obviously not the same as to ask whether

[33] Strong, *Friedrich Nietzsche and the Politics of Transfiguration*.

[34] Ernst Bertram, *Nietzsche: Attempt at a Mythology* (Champaign: University of Illinois Press, 2009). See also Melissa Lane and Martin Ruehl, eds., *A Poet's Reich: Politics and Culture in the George Circle* (London: Camden House, 2011).

[35] Martin Heidegger, *Nietzsche*, vols. 1–4 (San Francisco: HarperCollins, 1991).

[36] See the preface to the second and third editions in Karl Jaspers, *Nietzsche: An Introduction to the Understanding of His Philosophical Activity* (Baltimore: Johns Hopkins University Press, 1997), xiii.

[37] Williams, "Can There Be a Nietzschean Politics?" 1.

Nietzsche himself held political opinions, and what they were." Answering that second question is the main aim of this book, and one I hope it will be judged on. It is only on the basis of that response, as Williams recognized, that we can start to get a sense of the answer to the first question.

Nietzsche's political opinions, or at least Williams's interpretation of them, left him feeling rather discouraged, for reasons I have explored above. Yet we need not be disheartened, and I will contend over the course of this book that they were in fact much more encouraging than Williams allowed them to be. In fact, many of the themes Nietzsche deals with—the geopolitics of Afghanistan, Russian threat, superseding of the European nation-state by a supranational entity, privatization of public services, globalization of politics, and persistence of hierarchies in modern society—resonate strongly in the world we inhabit today, thus making a full recovery of them especially urgent.

In answer to Williams's question, I will argue that there *is* a Nietzschean politics, but that it is first and foremost a politics for the nineteenth century. Yet in the process of doing so, I hope to bring to light numerous insights, prognostics, theories, and themes that can be of some use to us in thinking about politics today.

CHAPTER 1
THE GREEKS

Looking back over his life in 1888—"What I Owe to the Ancients" serves as the starting point for Nietzsche's "autobiography" *Ecce Homo*—Nietzsche declares that *The Birth of Tragedy*, first published in 1872, was his "first revaluation of all values' (TI Ancients 5). It is from this "soil"—that is, his study of the Greeks—that his "will," his *abilities* grow." During this time Nietzsche had noted a series of reflections on *The Birth* in preparation for his "Revaluation of All Values," demonstrating that the book and its themes were on his mind, and a number of letters of December 1888 echo this sentiment.[1] To his confidant Heinrich Köselitz, whom he had dubbed "Peter Gast," Nietzsche claims on December 22 that "since the last four weeks I understand my works," singling out *The Birth* as "something indescribable, *profound*, tender, happy" (KSB 8). But he does not only claim to fully understand his books for the first time; he adds that he now "values" them, concluding that he is "absolutely convinced that everything has been successful, since the beginning—that everything tends toward unity." "I have done everything very well, without realizing it," he opines, feeling "for the first time up to the task."

The purpose of this chapter is to take seriously Nietzsche's claim that *The Birth* was his first revaluation, less in terms of acquiring a better understanding of *The Birth* itself, than in view of gaining an insight into what the project for a revaluation of all values entails.[2] I am less interested in following

---

[1] See KSA 13, 14 [14–46], 16 [40], 17 [3]. Nietzsche titles the notes "Art in *The Birth of Tragedy*," some of which were to be incorporated into Nietzsche's review of *The Birth* in *Ecce Homo*.

[2] For a discussion of translating *Umwerthung* into English, see Duncan Large, "A Note on the Term 'Umwerthung,'" *Journal of Nietzsche Studies* 39 (2010): 5–11. I concur with Large's view that "revaluation" might be a better rendering of the term because it emphasizes valuing anew rather than across, as with "transvaluation." Moreover, I find the financial tonality of revaluation apt, as Nietzsche explains in a letter written on May 23, 1888, to Georg Brandes: "'Revaluation all values.' Do you understand this phrase? The alchemist is in fact the most

Heidegger in wanting to read into Nietzsche's early writings the embryonic forms of his main philosophical theories—the will to power, eternal return, and even perhaps overman, although I am sympathetic to certain aspects of that claim, as I will return to in chapter 4—but rather I wish to posit a *structural* similarity—in terms of the respective parts and overall purpose, instead of the actual content, which importantly will change—between *The Birth* and the "Revaluation."[3] What I mean to suggest is that Nietzsche's goal with his revaluation project will remain the same as that of *The Birth*: restoring a healthy culture as the ancient Greeks had from which true philosophy can grow. And while he will maintain that to do so a hierarchical society is indispensable, he will come to reject certain aspects he thought necessary for such a transformation to take place. This latter will arise mainly from his split with Wagner: Nietzsche will come to reject Wagner's anti-Semitism, pan-German nationalism, and return to the "true essence of Christianity," the latter of which he claimed not to have been particularly taken with in the first place (BT P 5).

The relationship that *The Birth of Tragedy* entertains with Wagner's total revolution will be the subject of the following chapter, especially how a disagreement over the role slavery played in the production of the Greek drama—the purest art form in history that Wagner's own *Gesamtkunstwerk*, his "total work of art," aimed to revive—obscured the political character of Nietzsche's first work. The focus of this chapter, instead, will be on the soil from which Nietzsche claims his "abilities grow": the Greeks. From his study of the Greeks, Nietzsche will garner a number of insights. First, as we have just seen, and again as will be examined more closely in the next chapter, a slave class is indispensable for culture. Nietzsche will remain faithful to this inference for the rest of his intellectual career, and we will have reason to return to it on numerous occasions throughout the book. Second, only from a healthy culture can genuine philosophers appear. One does not reestablish a healthy culture through decadent philosophy; rather, one must first restore the healthy instincts that are a prerequisite to a healthy culture. Finally, from his interpretation of Plato's legislative mission, Nietzsche will glean a political strategy comprised of two elements: legislating for a new state, and training the men who will found it with him.

---

praiseworthy man there is: I mean he who transforms scoria, detritus, into something precious, even into gold. Only he enriches: the others contend themselves with trading. My task is rather curious this time round: I asked myself what has been until now the most hated, feared, despised by humanity: and it is precisely that which I have made my 'gold' " (KSB 8).

[3] Heidegger suggests that Nietzsche's "doctrine of the eternal return" and the revaluation theme are both presaged in his youthful writings "Fate and History" and "Free Will and Fate." See Martin Heidegger, *Nietzsche* (San Francisco: HarperCollins, 1991), 2:135.

SOCRATES AND GREEK CULTURE

Nietzsche concurred with Wagner that only the ancient Greeks had attained the highest form of culture. For Wagner they had achieved "drama," the highest form of art that combined all its expressions (dance, tone, and poetry), which his own "total artwork" aimed to reproduce. *The Birth of Tragedy* echoes the view that the Greeks had produced the highest art form, which Nietzsche would call tragedy, and the book concludes with a stirring defense of Wagner's project—something it has often been criticized for.[4] But for Nietzsche the Greeks were also the first to produce something else—something they have so far remained unrivaled at producing: philosophers.

Nietzsche developed this thought in "Philosophy in the Tragic Age of the Greeks," drafted in an incomplete form in 1873, itself drawn from a lecture series that Nietzsche had worked on and given in Basel throughout the 1870s, of which he wrote out a full manuscript version in 1872.[5] Ironically, "Philosophy in the Tragic Age of the Greeks" remained incomplete due to Wagner, who insisted Nietzsche turn his attention to writing a polemical tract, which was to become the first *Untimely Meditation*, against David Strauss. Nietzsche, however, thought his study indispensable, conceiving it as a "hook" to *The Birth of Tragedy*.[6] Nietzsche had started to work on the theme at the same time as he was writing *The Birth*, as the passing remarks on Heraclitus, among others, hint at.[7] In fact, through the notions of the "aesthetic man" and "child at play," Heraclitus, the hero of Nietzsche's study and the philosopher to whom he was to remain—by his own avowal—the closest to, already appears as the antithesis of the "Socratism in ethics" that caused the downfall of tragedy and consequently the Greeks.[8] If the Greeks are therefore the soil from which Nietzsche's desires and abilities grow, his studies of the "Pre-Platonic Philosophers," as the lecture series are known, comprised his first harvest.

[4] See Ulrich von Wilamowitz-Moellendorf, *"Zukunftsphilologie,"* in *Der Streit um Nietzsches "Geburt der Tragödie,"* ed. Karlfried Gründer (Hildesheim: Georg Olms Verlag, 1989), 27–55; trans. and ed. Babette Babich, *"Future* Philology!*" New Nietzsche Studies* 4 (2000): 1–32. Walter Kaufmann in his seminal *Nietzsche: Philosopher, Psychologist, Antichrist* (Princeton, NJ: Princeton University Press, 1974) argued that the true ending of BT should be considered to be BT 16, as beyond that it is simply a uncritical elegy to Wagner.

[5] See Greg Whitlock's introduction to his *The Pre-Platonic Philosophers: Friedrich Nietzsche* (Champaign: University of Illinois Press, 2001), xxii–xxx.

[6] In a draft dedication to Cosima Wagner, Nietzsche explains that in PTAG, he "pursues the thoughts he had first developed in BT."

[7] For Heraclitus, see BT 11, 19, 24; for Anaxagoras, see BT 12; for Pythagoras, see BT 11. Not to mention, of course, Socrates.

[8] See EH BT 3.

His second was in his preparation for the "Revaluation of All Values." In a letter to Carl von Gersdorff of April 5, 1873, anticipating his visit to Bayreuth where he would read sections of "Philosophy in the Tragic Age" to the Wagners, indicating that it is "still very far from a standard form of a book," Nietzsche explains that he has already made three attempts to synthesize the pre-Platonic philosophers. The first was his 1865 study of Democritus through Friedrich Lange's *History of Materialism*.[9] The second was his lectures on the pre-Platonics, and his third was "Philosophy in the Tragic Age." He writes: "I have become increasingly harder toward myself and must still allow much time to pass in order to consider another treatment (the *fourth* on this same theme)."[10] This fourth systematic treatment would only come when Nietzsche (re)turns to his revaluation project, having in the meantime developed his own philosophical position, finding its fullest expression in "The Problem of Socrates" and "What I Owe to the Ancients" in *Twilight of the Idols*. Indeed, it appears that Nietzsche reread his studies during that time—even annotating "Philosophy in the Tragic Age"—and consequently there are remarkable continuities, as we will see, between these earlier and later treatments.[11]

The thesis of "Philosophy in the Tragic Age" is that the Greeks have "*justified* philosophy once and for all simply because they have philosophized" (PTAG 1). They justify philosophy because for them it sprung from a healthy culture, characterized—anticipating the first *Untimely Meditation*—as the "unity of style." Only from such a genuine culture can philosophy manifest itself as "helpful, redeeming, or prophylactic." As Nietzsche puts it, there is an "iron law" that binds a philosopher to a genuine culture. As such, the Greeks began philosophizing at the "right time," which is to say in the "midst of good fortune, at the peak of mature manhood, as a pursuit springing from the ardent joyousness of courageous and victorious maturity." When they engaged in philosophy, they did so as "civilized human beings," with "highly civilized aims." Their activity—though they were "quite unconscious of it," as Nietzsche observes—tended toward the "healing and purification of the whole" (PTAG 2).[12]

[9] For Nietzsche on Democritus, see Paul Swift, *Becoming Nietzsche: Early Reflections on Democritus, Schopenhauer, and Kant* (Lanham, MD: Lexington, 2005); Jessica Berry, "Nietzsche and Democritus: The Origins of Ethical Eudaimonism," in *Nietzsche and Antiquity: His Reaction and Response to the Classical Tradition*, ed. Paul Bishop (Rochester, NY: Camden House, 2004), 98–113. On Nietzsche and Lange, see George Stack, *Lange and Nietzsche* (Berlin: De Gruyter, 1983).

[10] Quoted in Whitlock, *The Pre-Platonic Philosophers*, xxvi.

[11] As such, Strong is quite right in drawing, as he does throughout his work, a strong link between BT and the revaluation.

[12] See also Catherine Zuckert, "Nietzsche's Rereading of Plato," *Political Theory* 13, no. 2 (1985): 220.

While a healthy culture can exist without philosophy, or with a moderate exercise of it—the Romans lived, according to Nietzsche, their "best period" without it (PTAG 1)—when philosophy takes root in an unhealthy society it spells disaster for both itself and the society in question. "Where could we find an instance of cultural pathology that philosophy restored to health?" Nietzsche asks. If a culture is sick, then philosophy will make it even sicker. When a culture is disintegrating, philosophy is unable to reintegrate the individual back into the group. This is vital because a people is characterized not so much by its great men but instead by the way in which it "recognizes and honors" them. When the philosopher takes root in a healthy culture, he "shines like a stellar object of the first magnitude." In contrast, in a degenerate one, he appears as a "chance wanderer," "lonely in a totally hostile environment that he either creeps past or attacks with clenched fists"; or again, as a "comet, incalculable and therefore terror inspiring."[13] The Greeks thus "justify" philosophy, according to Nietzsche, because only among them the philosopher is neither a chance wanderer nor a comet. In fact, they produced the "archetypes of philosophical thought," to which posterity, in Nietzsche's view, has not made an essential contribution to since. These archetypes constitute the republic of geniuses that stretches from Thales to Socrates. They are what Nietzsche variously calls either "monolithic" or "one-sided," settling on the term "pure types" of philosophers, as while they may influence one another—calling and bridging out to one another through the "desolate intervals of time"—they are all the "first-born sons of philosophy" because they all generated from within themselves their own personal, fundamental idea (e.g., for Thales everything is water, and for Heraclitus everything is fire) (PTAG 1–2).

With Plato, however, starts something new. If the republic of geniuses consists of pure philosopher types of the "one idea," Plato is the first great mixed type, both in his philosophy—his doctrine of Ideas combines Socratic, Pythagorean, and Heraclitean elements, and therefore should not be considered, according to Nietzsche, an entirely original conception—and personality, which mingles the features of a "regally proud Heraclitus with the melancholy, secretive and legislative Pythagoras and the reflective dialectician Socrates" (PTAG 2).[14] All philosophers after Plato are such mixed types. Furthermore, instead of working for the "healing and purification of the whole," the mixed types are founders of sects, in opposition to the previous unity of style.[15] If their philosophy also sought salvation, it is only for

[13] This is, needless to say, a rather good description of how Nietzsche saw himself.

[14] In his lecture series on Plato, to which I will turn in the next section, Nietzsche sums up Plato's philosophy as such: "1. the Heraclitean movement of all things; 2. the stable 'Ideas' of Socrates; 3. the Pythagorean transmigration of the souls as intermediary between the two, the science of reminiscence" (PL I 2 [VII]).

[15] See also GS 149: "Pythagoras and Plato . . . aimed at founding new religions. . . . [T]hey just reached the point of founding sects."

THE GREEKS | 29

the individual or a small group of people—the sect. Rather than protect their native land, philosophers, with Plato, become exiles, "conspiring against their fatherland."

This is in effect one of the fundamental differences between Socrates and Plato, and it is a political difference: while Socrates is still a "good citizen" who tries to help his fellow countrymen, Plato desires, as I will explore further in the following section, to overthrow his contemporary polis to found a new state.[16] We now also understand the meaning of the title of the lecture series "The Pre-Platonic Philosophers": the separation occurs between the pure types from Thales to Socrates and the mixed types starting with Plato. The existence of an "Athenian school," comprised of Socrates, Plato, and Aristotle—and hence before them the more conventionally called pre-Socratics—is hereby challenged by Nietzsche: Plato is a mixed type consisting of non-Athenian elements such as Heraclitus and the Pythagoreans. But more fundamentally: Why this disjuncture? To answer that question we must turn to Nietzsche's understanding of Socrates and Plato, who stand on either side of the turning point, and thereby investigate his account of the decadence of the Greeks.

Nietzsche's relationship to Socrates has been the subject of an extensive and discordant debate, ranging from Socrates being depicted as Nietzsche's ultimate "villain" in the history of philosophy with Nietzsche himself as the final hero, to being presented by him as a "demigod," equal in stature to Apollo and Dionysus.[17] In what follows I will side with those who see Nietzsche's view of Socrates as inherently ambivalent, understood as Nietzsche being of two minds about Socrates: while he is the last genius of the republic of philosophers, Socrates is also the first decadent philosopher whose moralism corrupted all those after him.[18] So if Nietzsche takes on the Socratic role of being the "critic," "gadfly," or "bad conscience" of his time (PPP Socrates; HH 433; BGE 212; CW P), he rejects the moral method that Socrates employs. This position vis-à-vis Socrates is perhaps best summed up by an early note that Nietzsche pens, in which he remarks that "Socrates, to confess it frankly, is so close to me that I almost always fight with him" (KSA 8 6 [3]).[19] Nietzsche feels close to Socrates in being the gadfly of his time, yet fights against the legacy of his moralism. Moreover, as throughout

[16] See PL II 11: "Socrates was a good citizen, Plato a bad one, as [Barthold Georg] Niebuhr dared to say. This means that Plato fought to the death the political conditions in place and was an extremely radical revolutionary."

[17] See, respectively, Crane Brinton, *Nietzsche* (Cambridge, MA: Harvard University Press, 1948); Werner Dannhauser, *Nietzsche's View of Socrates* (Ithaca, NY: Cornell University Press, 1976); Walter Kaufmann, "Nietzsche's Attitude toward Socrates," in *Nietzsche: Philosopher, Psychologist, Antichrist*, 392.

[18] See Alexander Nehamas, *Nietzsche: Life as Literature* (Cambridge, MA: Harvard University Press, 2002), 30.

[19] See also Kaufmann, *Nietzsche*, 398.

the book, I want to underline certain basic continuities between Nietzsche's early and later thinking—in this case, his thinking on Socrates. Concentrating on Nietzsche's two most sustained early and late treatments of Socrates, both in *The Birth* and the early lectures on him in the "Pre-Platonic Philosophers," along with the later "The Problem of Socrates" in *Twilight of the Idols*—thus matching the time periods of the "first" (*The Birth of Tragedy*) and second "Revaluation of All Values"—I argue that Nietzsche's portrayal of Socrates in the "Problem" is a more systematic and worked-out account of the views already present in embryonic form in his early writings. As the lectures were never published during his lifetime, Nietzsche interspersed his thoughts on Socrates throughout his work, and I will do my best to link them with both the early studies and the "Problem" to again highlight their continuity.

In his lectures on Socrates, Nietzsche presents him within the paradigm of a pure type of the one idea. Socrates has a *"single* interest": the question of "what-so'er is good or evil in a house" (PPP Socrates).[20] Socrates is the first ethicist, and through this he becomes the first philosopher of life (*Lebensphilosoph*), because instead of life serving thought and knowledge, now knowledge is to serve life. Knowledge is the path to virtue, and knowledge is to be attained through dialectics, a radical new means.[21] Socratic philosophy is thus entirely practical as its only concern is with its ethical implications. Consequently, Socrates has no time for art and belongs to the "despisers of tragedy." Here we reconnect with the Socrates of *The Birth of Tragedy*, the dialectician who is only interested in the Logos, and whose supreme moral law "virtue is knowledge; sin is only committed out of ignorance; the virtuous man is a happy man" led to the death of Greek tragedy (BT 14). But is this image of Socrates as the pure life-philosopher of the lectures compatible with the destroyer of Greek tragedy in *The Birth*?

The first clue we find in "Philosophy in the Tragic Age of the Greeks," where if Nietzsche had claimed that the Greeks knew when to start philosophizing "at the right time," conversely they did not know when to stop at the right time, prolonging it into their "sterile old age" (PTAG 1). The Greeks persisted in philosophizing in a period of "affliction," thereby drawing it from a state of personal "moroseness." This would considerably diminish the Greeks' merit for "barbaric posterity," where philosophy would become but the "pious sophistries and sacrosanct hairsplittings of Christian dogmatics." Socrates, being the last in line in the republic of geniuses, is the target here. Though he is a pure philosopher of the one idea whose ethical reform aims for the "general salvation of the whole"—even appearing as a

---

[20] See also WS 6: "Socrates . . . loved to indicate the true compass and content of all reflection[:] . . . 'that which I encountered of good and ill in my own house.'"

[21] See also BT 12: "the Socratic principle 'Knowledge is virtue.'"

"breath of fresh air" for those of the earlier generation (PPP Socrates)—he is still philosophizing in a period of general affliction, in his own "sterile old age." Indeed, one of the strongest claims of *The Birth* was that the "phenomenon" of Socrates represented one of the characteristic signs of a "degenerate" culture (BT 17).[22] As Nietzsche would underscore in both the "Self-Criticism" and review of the work in *Ecce Homo*, expressing it in his newfound later term, Socrates is a decadent.[23]

Already we can see the solidarity between *The Birth* and "Philosophy in the Tragic Age" in interpreting the appearance of Socrates as an expression of a disintegrating culture. Nietzsche pursues this idea in his lectures on Socrates through emphasizing Socrates's "ugliness."[24] In stark contrast to the noble lineages of his predecessors, Socrates is plebeian. Not simply is he plebeian by birth, but more devastatingly, his character is plebeian: he is ugly, "suffers from the greatest passions," is prone to "violent outbursts," and even his manner of expression has the "aftertaste" of the "ugly and plebeian" (PPP Socrates). As a pure type of philosopher, whose philosophical system springs from Socrates's inner personality, the singularity of his appearance impacts directly on his philosophy. His dialectic method where human ethics is sought through knowledge breaks radically with both the whole of Greek education and his philosophical predecessors: "the entirety of older philosophy still belongs to the time of unbroken ethical instincts; Heraclitus, Anaxagoras, Democritus, Empedocles—each breathes Hellenic morality, yet each according to a different form of Hellenic ethics." This ancient Hellenic morality was essentially aristocratic, while Socrates's philosophy is "popular" and "for everyone" because it holds that virtue can be taught. As we saw in "Philosophy in the Tragic Age," a healthy philosophy can only spring from a healthy culture. That Socrates had to fight the instincts of the Greeks meant that their culture and his own instincts were decaying. Nietzsche had also discussed this notion of degenerating instincts in *The Birth*, where he describes how the "greatest statesmen, orators, poets, and artists" practiced their professions "only from instinct" (BT 13).[25] The "instinct-dissolving influence" of Socrates's dialectics and dissuasive role of

[22] See also HH 261: "With the Greeks everything goes quickly forward, but it likewise goes quickly downward; the movement of the whole machine is so accelerated that a single stone thrown into its wheels makes it fly to pieces. Socrates, for example, was such a stone."

[23] See BT Self-Criticism 1: "Might not this very Socratism be a sign of decline, of exhaustion, of sickness, of the anarchic dissolution of the instincts?" See also EH BT 1: "Socrates recognized for the first time as the instrument of Greek disintegration, as a typical decadent."

[24] For the link between Socrates's ugliness and decadence, see Yannick Souladié, "La Laideur de Socrates," *Nietzsche-Studien* 35 (2006): 29–46.

[25] See also BGE 191: "Didn't [Socrates] spend his whole life laughing at the shortcomings of his clumsy, noble Athenians, who, like all noble people, were men of instinct and could never really account for why they acted the way they did?"

his daemonium, in contrast to the fact that "in all productive people, it is precisely instinct that is the creative-affirmative force," negates the ancient Greek character that was founded on an unbroken Hellenic morality. Again to mark Socrates off from his forerunners, *The Birth* depicts him as the "single point around which so-called history turns and twists" (BT 15).

The Birth of Tragedy, "Philosophy in the Tragic Age of the Greeks," and the lectures on Socrates in the "Pre-Platonic Philosophers" all accord in their own way with the view that Socrates, his time, and his philosophy were decadent. Another point of contact between *The Birth* and lectures is the topic of the "dying Socrates." Indeed, this theme serves as a *fil conducteur* for much of Nietzsche's reflection on Socrates throughout the course of his work. Both *The Birth* and lectures posit that Socrates wanted death. He wanted death to demonstrate the dignity of his "divine mission" and domination of the human fear of death through knowledge and reasoning. With his death he overcame his own degenerate instincts, and in doing so, Socrates became both the last "exemplar" of the sage and the "new ideal" of the Hellenic youth, especially Plato. At his sentencing, he "speaks before posterity" (BT 13, 15; PPP Socrates). As Greg Whitlock—the editor of Nietzsche's "Pre-Platonic Philosophers" lectures—puts it, this "sacrifice" leads to the "Socratic cult of martyrdom."[26]

Returning to this theme of the dying Socrates in *The Gay Science*, Nietzsche sees in Socrates's "last word"—"O Crito, I owe Asclepius a Rooster"— as the betrayal of who he really was: Socrates was a pessimist who suffered from life as if it were a disease, and through his death wanted to take revenge on it (GS 340). While this thought may appear as new in Nietzsche's work, it is continuous with his vision of Socrates the decadent as developed previously. In fact, in *The Birth* Nietzsche had already discussed Nietzsche's last word, where at last Socrates "makes music," even dedicating a proemium to Apollo (BT 14). As is well known, it is the image of the "music-making Socrates" that Nietzsche would present in *The Birth* as the reconciliation of science and music, indicating that the Socrates who did not make music was certainly decadent (BT 15, 17).

Owing Asclepius the savior a rooster is again the scene with which Nietzsche opens and closes his discussion of "The Problem of Socrates" in *Twilight of the Idols*, one of his last texts. The "Problem" systematizes and clarifies—Nietzsche speaks of his "increasing lucidity"—the views that Nietzsche had developed of Socrates in his early writings. Referring explicitly back to *The Birth*—remember neither "Philosophy in the Tragic Age" nor the lectures were published—Nietzsche summarizes his earlier views of Socrates. He has one "equation," the hallmark of the genius of the one idea, which is "reason = virtue = happiness." He is ugly and of plebeian character—"almost

---

[26] See Whitlock, *The Pre-Platonic Philosophers*, 261–63.

a refutation for the Greeks"—therefore also a decadent. The more ancient noble "taste," Hellenic morality, is defeated through dialectics, which is a revenge Nietzsche exacts against life as portrayed by the "dying Socrates": an expression of his plebeian ressentiment. Recognizing that decadence had become a "universal affliction" in the sterile age he was living in, Socrates offers his cure—rationality—through his own sacrifice as the savior for the Greek crisis—a crisis so profound that the cure was adopted only as a "last resort," as a means of "self-preservation."[27] In this way, Socrates fulfills his role of philosophizing for the general salvation of the whole, though in the end, on his deathbed, he recognizes that the only real cure for the decadence—of which he is a symptom—is death (TI Problem).[28]

On the fascination that Socrates as savior exercised during his time, Nietzsche writes,

> Philosophers and moralists are lying to themselves when they think that they are going to extricate themselves from decadence by waging war on it. Extrication is not in their power; what they choose as a remedy, as an escape, is itself only another expression of decadence—they *change* the way it is expressed, but do not get rid of the thing itself. Socrates was a misunderstanding; *the whole morality of improvement, including that of Christianity, was a misunderstanding* (TI Problem 11).

We can see the germs of this final thought—in terms of decadence's advent with Christianity—in "Philosophy in the Tragic Age" when Nietzsche explains that the Greek's barbaric posterity reduced philosophy to "pious sophistries and the sacrosanct hairsplittings of Christian dogmatics."[29] Also

---

[27] There has been some suggestion that the self-preservative aspects of Socrates's philosophy are something that Nietzsche values positively. On this point, see, for instance, Christa Davis Acampora, "Nietzsche contra Homer, Socrates, and Paul," *Journal of Nietzsche Studies* 24 (Fall 2002): 25–53. This seems mistaken. Nietzsche, after all, concludes GS 340 with the statement that "even the Greeks," by which he means Socrates and his progeny, need to be overcome. In a late note, he explains that there is in fact nothing to be done about the existence of decadence. Instead, what needs to be done is to prevent decadence from infecting the still-healthy parts of the body (KSA 13 15 [31]), which is in line with what Nietzsche had stated in the third essay of *The Genealogy*: "That the sick should *not* make the healthy sick . . . ought to be the chief concern on earth" (GM III 14).

[28] The theme of Socrates as the "true eroticist" along with the links this entertains with the agon is also continued in both *The Birth* and "Problem" (BT 13: "Socrates, the true eroticist"; TI Problem 8: "Socrates was a great *erotic* too"). I will return to a discussion of the agon in the following chapters.

[29] See also the interesting parallel that Whitlock makes between Socrates's "cult of martyrdom" and decadent Christianity: "Although Nietzsche scarcely mentions Christianity in these lectures, making a connection between Socrates and Jesus Christ as a cult figure popularizing Platonism shows that he had already concluded that the Christian God-man, like Socrates, represents a decadent type hostile to life." (Whitlock, *The Pre-Platonic Philosophers*, 261–63).

in *The Birth*, Nietzsche had qualified as a "delusion" Socrates's belief that "by following the guiding thread of causality, thought reaches into the deepest abysses of being and is capable not only of knowing but also even of *correcting* being" (BT 15), implying that dialectics would not solve the problem the Greeks were facing. While the attack on the notion of the "morality of improvement" might appear new—Nietzsche identifies the start of his "war against morality" with the publication of *Daybreak* (EH Daybreak 1)—this should be seen as in line with Nietzsche's early rejection of Socrates's "moral method," notably in *The Birth*.

In the end, I think what gives this passage and the "Problem" in general its force is the fact that Nietzsche brings together his dispersed early thoughts on Socrates into a coherent unity. This unity, I have argued, existed intellectually in the early writings but was waiting to be systematized. As I have tried to bring out above, there is consequently an underlying continuity between his early and later thinking. What Nietzsche does is develop—for instance, by deepening the link between Socrates's posterity and Christianity—and clarify his early thoughts over the course of his work. Indeed, Nietzsche concludes the section with the line that "to *have* to fight the instincts—that is the formula for decadence: as long as life is *ascending*, happiness is equal to instinct" (TI Problem 11). As he had stated as early as "Philosophy in the Tragic Age," a healthy philosophy only springs from a healthy culture—there is an iron law that binds a true philosopher to a genuine culture, which is defined by the unity of its style—and therefore "extrication" through philosophy is not in the power of those who are already decadent; they merely "change" its expression.

Like most of the themes Nietzsche treats, his account of Socrates is a subtle one, consisting of both positive and negative elements. These mixed views of Socrates, and thus Nietzsche's ambivalent relationship to him, coexist in Nietzsche's thought from the outset, once we combine *The Birth* with the early, unpublished studies. Socrates is lauded as the final pure philosopher of the republic of geniuses, even a *Lebensphilosoph*, putting knowledge in the service of life. Perhaps Socrates's greatest achievement was identifying the Greeks'—and his own—slide into decadence, and his attempt at ethical reform. I think this is the Socrates that Nietzsche felt the closest to, serving as the critic, gadfly, or bad conscience of his time, and also attempting ethical reform.[30] The misunderstanding that Socrates caused, however, arose from the fact that the treatment he proposed exacerbated rather than cured the symptoms he was the first to recognize because it was drawn from his own decadent self. Here Nietzsche parts ways with Socrates: while

[30] For *Thus Spoke Zarathustra* as an attempt at ethical reform, see Peter Berkowitz, *Nietzsche: The Ethics of an Immoralist* (Cambridge, MA: Harvard University Press, 1995).

Nietzsche will accept that he is also a decadent, he will claim that he is the "opposite as well," and that his philosophy springs from an essentially healthy core (EH Wise 2).

From an early age, Nietzsche concluded that for there to be a healthy philosophy, it needed to be in harmony with the healthy instincts from which an authentic culture can grow. For an authentic philosophy to exist, *first* a healthy culture needed to be created: a healthy culture comes from healthy instincts. Only from this, *second*, can a genuine philosopher appear—the iron law that chains a true philosopher to a healthy culture—to dedicate his time to the general salvation and purification of the whole. Already in "Philosophy in the Tragic Age" Nietzsche had made it clear that philosophy would not help in regaining healthy instincts. Quite to the contrary, as the "Problem" concurs, it would make matters even worse. So in "Philosophy in the Tragic Age," Nietzsche suggests that healing and purification could be found either through Goethe's physics or Wagner's music (PTAG 1). We know that Nietzsche would come to reject Wagner's music as also being decadent (CW P), but in light of Nietzsche's later revaluation project it is worth noting that his early view was that a healthy culture would be restored not by philosophy but instead by something else.

There are other elements that Nietzsche will glean from his study of the Greeks for the purposes of his revaluation project, especially as it is put forth in *The Antichrist*, the original first book of the literary project, and they are worth relating briefly here. For example, Nietzsche accounts for the continuing occasional appearance of philosophers after the Greeks, those chance wanderers, as lucky hits (AC 3). But due to the decay of the Greeks, Nietzsche concludes that the philosopher should be something consciously "willed," and that society should be organized in such a way as to produce culture and the philosopher. In a *Nachlass* note of 1887 that serves as a plan for the "Revaluation of All Values," Nietzsche writes, "To establish an infrastructure on which becomes at last possible a *stronger* species. . . . State and society as infrastructure: global economic viewpoint, education as *breeding*" (KSA 12 9 [1]). Finally, Nietzsche will of course identify as good instincts the "increased feeling of power," using his subsequently found term, the will to power. Happiness is in the "feeling that power is *growing*," that resistance has been "overcome"; whereas conversely, degenerate instincts spring from the feeling of weakness, the desire for "peace at any price" instead of war, the desire for Christian virtue instead of Renaissance *virtù*, that which is "moraline-free" (AC 2).

If Nietzsche appears to follow Wagner's view that the philosophers are the true decadents of the Greeks, he does so with one important qualification, which he specifies in his review of *The Birth* in *Ecce Homo*: this does not apply to the "eminent" Greek philosophers, those from "two centuries *before* Socrates" (EH BT 3)—that is, the philosophers of the republic of geniuses from Thales to the Pythagoreans.[31] Nevertheless, with Socrates starts the great "misunderstanding" of decadent moralism that the whole of posterity would inherit, beginning with Plato, to whom I now turn. While Nietzsche felt strong affinities to Socrates's role as gadfly, in many ways Plato is even closer to him. Plato is the first true comet that all philosophers after him—and Nietzsche in particular—are doomed to be; he is the founder of a sect with whom he will fight against his time. Moreover, if Nietzsche felt a strong parallel between his own project and Socrates's ethical reform, Plato provides him with a vision on how to develop a political strategy to restore the authentic culture to which he aspires.

PLATO'S LEGISLATIVE MISSION

Nietzsche engages constantly with Plato throughout his writings. In an early note of 1871, he writes: "my philosophy *inverted Platonism*" (KSA 7 7 [156]), and this is echoed by Nietzsche's claim in the preface to *Beyond Good and Evil* (1886) that his "task" is to fight Plato's "dogmatist's error" of the "invention of pure spirit and the good in itself" (BGE P).[32] So Nietzsche sees his philosophical task as refuting Plato's philosophy. Plato's philosophy, as we have seen, is a mixed one, drawn from different influences, as is his personality. This also means that Plato combines both healthy and decadent elements, with the latter notably inherited from Socrates. Did the "evil Socrates" corrupt the "most beautiful outgrowth of antiquity," Nietzsche asks? "There is something in Plato's moral philosophy that does not really belong to him, but is there in spite of him, as it were: namely, the Socratism that he was really too noble for," Nietzsche concludes (BGE 190).[33]

To acquire a fuller understanding of Plato, certain misunderstandings concerning Nietzsche's relationship to him need to be elucidated, such as Nietzsche's comment in "What I Owe to the Ancients" in *Twilight of the Idols* that he finds Plato "boring" (TI Ancients 2). It must be stressed here that it is the *"artist* Plato" that Nietzsche finds boring, not the man, nor, in-

---

[31] See TI Ancients 3: "Philosophers really are the decadents of the Greek world, the countermovement to the ancient, noble taste."

[32] As with the PPP, Nietzsche's lectures on Plato were never published in his lifetime, so I will continue to highlight the continuities of Nietzsche's thought concerning him throughout his writing as I did for Socrates in the preceding section.

[33] On Plato's decadence, see also Plato's inability to understand tragedy because of his old age (D 157) and "fatigue" in general (D 542), which is not without recalling the sterile old age of the Greeks that Nietzsche criticized in PTAG 1. This is best summed up, again, in TI Problem 2: "Socrates and Plato as symptoms of decay, as agents of Greek disintegration," and EH BT 2: *"degenerate* instincts . . . Plato's philosophy."

THE GREEKS | 37

deed, his philosophy. He finds the artist Plato boring because he "mixes up all the forms of style," which makes him a *"first-rate* decadent of style." His dialogues are "this horribly smug, childlike type of dialectic" that would not strike anyone who has ever "read any good French writers" as "charming." In his early lectures on Plato in Basel (1871–76), to which I now turn, Nietzsche had already discussed the artist Plato (PL I 1, II 15) and had also labeled his dialectics as boring (PL I 1). In the preface to the lectures, he explains that Plato is a "tremendously able prose writer, mastering all registers" (PL P). He is thought to have composed dithyrambic poems in his youth, for which he showed "universal artistic gifts" (PL I 2 [3]), yet he burned them because of Socrates, who abhorred art and poetry.[34] In fact, it is attempting to reproduce Socratic dialectics in written form that leads to Plato's decadence as an artist. As Nietzsche had identified as early as *The Birth of Tragedy*, the Platonic dialogues were created by "mixing all available styles and forms together," breaking the strict older law about the unity of linguistic form that characterizes an authentic culture (BT 14). So if Plato mastered all forms, it is the mixing of them—mixing being the trait of the hybrid philosopher—that leads to his artistic decadence.

Nor is Nietzsche's disagreement with Plato fundamentally a *political* one. In the short essay "The Greek State" that I will consider more extensively in the next chapter, Nietzsche attributes to Plato's *"perfect state"*—the *Republic*—the first *"secret study of the connection between state and genius,"* wherein the actual aim of the ancient Greek state is discovered to be the production of Olympian men (GSt, 173). That a hierarchical society as described in the *Republic* is needed for philosophers to emerge is something that Nietzsche—through identifying the "cruel-sounding truth" that slavery is a necessary base from which Olympian men can take root and grow—is entirely in agreement with. Nietzsche's disagreement with Plato is consequently a *philosophical* one, as anticipated above. It is the decadent moralism that Plato inherited from Socrates, and Western philosophy inherited in turn from Plato as Platonism, that Nietzsche desires to reverse.[35]

---

[34] See also BT 14: "The youthful tragic poet Plato first burned his poetry in order to become a student of Socrates."

[35] There is some disagreement in the secondary literature over the nature of Nietzsche's engagement with Plato's philosophy. While Thomas Brobjer ("Nietzsche's Wrestling with Plato and Platonism," in *Nietzsche and Antiquity: His Reaction and Response to the Classical Tradition*, ed. Paul Bishop ed. [Rochester, NY: Camden House, 2004], 241–59) might be right in highlighting how Nietzsche did not have an *internal* engagement with Plato's philosophy, simply rejecting it out of hand, this does not have to imply, to my mind, that Nietzsche could not have engaged with Plato's philosophy in his rejection of it, perhaps from a more *external* viewpoint, in terms of rejecting a Platonic "being" in favor of Heraclitus's "becoming," as John Richardson has brought to the fore. See his "Plato's Attack on Becoming" and "Nietzsche's Theory of Becoming," in *Nietzsche's System* (Oxford: Oxford University Press, 2002), 89–108. See also George Stack, "Contra Platonism," in *Lange and Nietzsche*, 51: "[Nietzsche] is

But beyond the philosophical disagreement between Plato and Nietzsche lies a much more fundamental affinity that has to do with their respective projects, or at least Nietzsche's interpretation of what he took to be Plato's legislative mission. Recognizing the disintegration of ancient Greek culture, both want to restore philosophy to its rightful place.[36] They desire to make the (modern) world "safe for philosophy" again. Plato, famously, believed that to save philosophy, philosophers had to become kings, or kings had to become philosophers (PL I 2 [II]). Nietzsche, on the other hand, thought that a genuine culture needed to be restored, and from this healthy philosophers could once again appear. So while both fight against their time and lay a heavy emphasis on education, it is the starting point that, once again, they disagree on: Plato wants to begin with philosophy, while Nietzsche wants to start with culture (underpinned by a certain politics). We can also note that Plato's *Republic* can be conceived of wanting to save society as a whole, but that is a *new* type of society that is not yet in existence—he has no desire to save his contemporary polis, which he fights against—and the means to achieve that is through a select few. Nietzsche too directs his revaluative project through a small band, but in the future society he posits the artistic work of the few will also be to the benefit of the whole.

There is a disagreement between the two as to what type of philosopher should be king. Nietzsche writes that Plato excludes the "inspired artist entirely from his state"—an artist whom Nietzsche wants to foster—placing instead only the genius of "wisdom and knowledge" at the head of his perfect state, although he admits that this might be a result of the "rigid consequence of the Socratic judgment on art, which Plato, struggling against himself, adopted as his own" (GSt, 173). What unites them, however, is their shared diagnosis of the decadence of Greek culture—with Nietzsche of course believing that we still inhabit this decadence today—and their projects meet not only in wanting to restore this culture, though their understanding of what this amounts to diverges, but also in their politics.

For forcing Socrates to drink the hemlock, Nietzsche presents Plato's "determinate political goal" in his lectures on him as the desire to refound the Greek polis (PL I 2 [V]). To do so he develops a philosophical "system," and at the age of forty-one or forty-two, all that he was missing were the "men, whom he would make into philosophers, so that they can found with him

---

not so much concerned with the grounds for Plato's metaphysics, the arguments he offers in defense of his views, as he is with the reasons why this metaphysics was brought into being and its effects on man and his perception of his place in the universe."

[36] In the lectures Nietzsche explains that Plato fought against two enemies: the ancient Athenians who obstinately held on to their ancestral (decaying) customs, and the Sophists who (nihilistically) attacked all customs, thereby painting the picture of the disintegration of ancient Athens (see PL II 23).

someday the new state." There are in fact striking parallels between Nietzsche's interpretation of Plato's development and Nietzsche's own. Pursuing this thought, it is interesting to apply Nietzsche's understanding of Plato in his lectures to himself, in the same manner Nietzsche suggests in *Ecce Homo* that what he writes about on Wagner and Arthur Schopenhauer was really about him, *anticipando* (EH BT 4). If Socrates is a "semiotic for Plato," then Plato is a semiotic for Nietzsche (EH UM 3).[37]

The portrait that Nietzsche paints of Plato is of a young man first plunged into the darkest despair, but who becomes optimistic through learning Socratic dialectics (PL II 2–5). From there on Nietzsche explains that like all geniuses, Plato carried within him already between the ages of twenty to thirty all the seeds of his own greatness in embryonic form (PL I 1), and had achieved his complete philosophical system by the age of forty-one or forty-two—a philosophy reserved for the "few" (PL 2 [V–VII]).[38] The result was an unreserved belief in himself and the desire to be a model for others to follow, like his teacher Socrates before him. One can construe Nietzsche's development along surprisingly similar lines: Nietzsche adhered to Schopenhaurian pessimism in his youth before transforming that outlook into a "pessimism of strength" through his study, ironically, of the ancient Greeks (BT P 1).[39] As suggested in the introduction, aspects of Nietzsche's "philosophy" of the will to power and eternal return can be conceived of as being already present in embryonic form in *The Birth* and his writings of around that time, when he was in his late twenties. Between 1885 and 1886, when he was forty-one or forty-two, Nietzsche had not only just finished publishing *Thus Spoke Zarathustra*, the first work to expose all his philosophical notions, but he also presented in his letters what he was planning at the time as his magnum opus, "The Will to Power"—which already carried his project of revaluation as its subtitle—as his "philosophy."[40] In *Ecce Homo*, Nietzsche assuredly claims that he is a "destiny," and explains why he is so wise, clever, and writes such good books. Indeed, the desire to write such an "autobiography" cannot be disassociated from wanting to give oneself as an

---

[37] See also BGE 190: "Plato did everything he could to interpret something refined and noble into his teacher's [Socrates's] claim: above all, himself . . . varying it to the point of infinity and impossibility, into all his own masks and multitudes. . . . Plato at the front, Plato at the back, Chimaera in the middle." As I have argued above, Nietzsche's interpretation of Plato is also chimerical in the sense that he follows his legislative mission but rejects his moralism.

[38] See also AOM 271: "Plato's philosophy recalls the mid-thirties, when a cold and hot current are accustomed to buffet against one another."

[39] On Schopenhauer's influence on Nietzsche, in particular his filtering of Plato and Platonism, see Christopher Janaway, *Beyond Selflessness: Reading Nietzsche's Genealogy* (Oxford: Clarendon Press, 2009). See also George Simmel, *Nietzsche and Schopenhauer*, trans. Helmut Loiskandl, Deena Weinstein, and Michael Weinstein (Champaign: University of Illinois Press, 1991).

[40] See letters to Franz Overbeck, July 2, 1885, and his mother and sister, September 2, 1886.

exemplar.[41] Finally *The Antichrist*, the book of the revaluation of all values, is dedicated to the "very few" (AC P).[42]

These congruencies may appear to be more coincidental than profound, and there are of course several differences between the two. One notable disagreement concerns the use of mathematics in the education of the future philosopher: Plato notoriously finds it fundamental, while Nietzsche sides with Goethe in dismissing its importance.[43] Another is Nietzsche's labeling of Plato as a "moralist" (PL II 23)—a tendency he inherits from Socrates—while Nietzsche will present himself in *Ecce Homo* as the "first immoralist," the negator of Platonism-inspired Christian morality (EH Destiny 2–4). But I believe there are a number of aspects that Nietzsche garners from his interpretation of Plato's project that can help us better conceive Nietzsche's own.

The overarching aspect is the notion of the philosopher as legislator, from which will follow a political strategy. This is perhaps best summed up by the portrait of Plato as an "accomplished" philosopher that Nietzsche presented in his lectures on him: the philosopher must be a "legislator and founder of state," and to do so he employs *three* means: "founding the Academy, writing, and an untiring fight against his time" (PL II 11).[44] The different elements that Plato employs are well captured in Nietzsche's opening statement about Plato in his lectures, which I will presently turn to: Plato is a "political agitator, who wants to change the world in its entirety and is, *amongst other things*, and to that end, a writer. Founding the Academy for him is something much more important: he writes to strengthen in combat his companions of the Academy (PL P)." Nietzsche concurs with the view of the philosopher as legislator, and the three means he attributes to Plato

[41] On Nietzsche wanting to give himself as an exemplar, see Nehamas, *Nietzsche*.

[42] We can add a parallel between Nietzsche's interpretation of Plato's work methods and his own. Discussing the *Laws*, he explains that "we must understand Plato's manner of classifying his works like Goethe's. In a somewhat-arbitrary manner, a work is constituted. The *Republic* like the *Laws* are reconstitutions from writings of different periods of his life" (PL I 3 [Laws]). Nietzsche's work method, especially in his later years, also involved drafting a number of notes that he would then revise and organize into chapters to form a publishable book, although he might want to defend himself against the claim that such a selection might be "arbitrary."

[43] See PL II 15, where Nietzsche also discusses the artist Plato: "It has often been objected to Goethe his lack of knowledge of mathematics. To this Plato opposed the importance of mathematics: they are indispensable for understanding the theory of Ideas." Nietzsche, however, sides with Goethe: "Experience shows that the great artistic geniuses were not gifted in mathematics." Moreover, in his look at reforming the education system in the *Future of Our Educational Institutions*, which with its dialogue form has strong Platonic overtones, Nietzsche proposes that three subjects be taught: classics, philosophy, and German, with mathematics notably being absent.

[44] See also HH 261: "Plato was the incarnate desire to become the supreme lawgiver and founder of states."

provides him with a political strategy, a purpose to his writings, and a model of political activism. I do not mean to suggest that Nietzsche had developed all these notions fully from the beginning but rather that Plato's thinking provides a structure he would draw inspiration from and deepen over the course of his own thinking. Indeed, in developing a plan of action for the "men" he would win for his cause, as we will see in chapter 6, Nietzsche would come to build on Plato's own achievements.

Plato's legislative mission forms the "central point of the Platonic will" (PL I 2 [VII]). What is Plato's legislative mission? There are two main axes, from which other elements follow: first, the desire to legislate a new state, and second, to train the men to carry through the reform (PL I 2 [V]). There is both an ethical and political aspect to legislating a new state—ethical in the physical and moral training that Plato will impose on his men for them to be able to reform the state; political in actually giving laws to the ideal new state.[45]

Drawing inspiration from his interpretation of Plato, Nietzsche himself posits that true philosophers are legislators.[46] This is most explicitly stated in *Beyond Good and Evil* 211, where the passage in question represents perhaps the climax of the work, as witnessed in its highlighting.[47] There Nietzsche proclaims that true philosophers are *"commanders and legislators*; they say, 'That is how it *should* be!' [T]hey are the ones who first determine the 'where to?' and 'what for?' of people" (BGE 211). These legislators are "genuine philosophers," as opposed to the philosophical laborers in the "noble mode" such as Immanuel Kant and Hegel, who only "establish some large class of given values ... and press them into formulas, whether in the realm of *logic* or *politics* (morality) or *art*."[48] In simply reifying common sense, philosophical laborers are only perpetuating "herd morality" (BGE 202), whereas the task of true philosophers is to *"create values"* (BGE 211).[49]

[45] On "legislating manners" and how this leads to the "political instincts in the body," see also D 496.

[46] For more on the affinities between Nietzsche's and Plato's legislative projects, see Yannis Constantinidès, "Les législateurs de l'avenir: L'affinité des projets politiques de Plato et de Nietzsche," *Nietzsche-Cahiers de L'Herne* 73 (2005): 128–43. See also Henning Ottmann, *Philosophie und Politik bei Nietzsche* (Berlin: De Gruyter, 1999), 147–50.

[47] For aphorism 211 as a "peak" of BGE, and this topic more generally, see Laurence Lampert, "Nietzsche and Plato," in *Nietzsche and Antiquity: His Reaction and Response to the Classical Tradition*, ed. Paul Bishop (Rochester, NY: Camden House, 2004), 205: "The long aphorisms of that chapter are a gathering argument, which peaks with aphorism 211."

[48] For more on the philosopher as legislator, see Melissa Lane, "Founding as Legislating: The Figure of the Lawgiver in Plato's Republic." In *Dialogues on Plato's* Politeia *(Republic): Selected Papers from the Ninth Symposium Platonicum*, ed. Luc Brisson and Noboru Notomi (Berlin: Akademia Verlag, 2012), 104–14.

[49] Tellingly, the section on herd morality starts with Socrates: "People in Europe clearly *know* what Socrates claimed not to know. . . . [P]eople these days 'know' what is good and

By using the term "genuine philosophers," Nietzsche is implicitly referring back to the ancient philosophers of the tragic age that I explored in the preceding section. They also legislated values in coming up with their one idea, but the fundamental difference here is that their philosophy was in harmony with the society they inhabited. The values they posited were for the salvation of the whole. Due to the decline of Greek culture, however, philosophy becomes, with Socratic dialectics, essentially decadent philosophy. Modern philosophers who draw inspiration from their contemporary world, like Kant and Hegel, are thereby positing decadent herd morality. As Plato was the first in line of Greek culture's degeneration, he remains the paradigm of the true philosopher for Nietzsche because he legislated new values to change the society in which he lived. This again underlines the importance of the notion of the pre-Platonics: Plato is the first to legislate new values that go *against* his time. Unfortunately, as already examined above, the fact that his new values were drawn from moral dialectics meant that his new values were still decadent: a healthy culture had first to be restored—through nature or music—for a healthy philosophy to be able to appear again, and not, as Plato seemed to wish it, the other way around.

Zarathustra's task will be precisely to start writing new tables of laws, as is confirmed by the fundamental place that the section "On Old and New Tables" holds in *Zarathustra* (Z III Tables). Zarathustra will give two laws to the new nobility that he calls into being: to "love your *children's land*" and "*become hard*" (Z III 12, 29).[50] While these new tablets seem to focus more on the ethical aspect of legislation, in the emphasis on marriage, education, and the role of commander that the new nobility must take on to themselves, and that I will look at more fully over the course of the book, we nevertheless can already see the legislative project starting to spill over into the social and political realm. Moreover, we can see an even stronger move on Nietzsche's behalf into the political realm in his proclamation of a "law against Christianity" in conclusion to *The Antichrist*, with its ominous seventh proposition that "the rest follows from this." This is in line with Nietzsche's definition of the philosophical lawgiver in *Beyond Good and Evil*: "The philosopher as *we* understand him, we free spirits, . . . will make use of reli-

---

evil" (BGE 202). The following section is where Nietzsche first sketches the new philosophers (BGE 203).

[50] Both of these must be viewed within the perspective of the coming of the overmen, which will take place sometime in the future. These will be brought about through procreation and education (loving one's children's land), and one must be strong (hard) to remain on this path without being disturbed by Christian morality. On these, see, respectively, Verity Smith and Tracy Strong, "Trapped in a Family Portrait? Gender and Family in Nietzsche's Refiguring of Authority," in *Dialogue, Politics, and Gendre*, ed. Jude Browne (Cambridge: Cambridge University Press, 2013), 146–72; Tracy Strong, "The World as It Finds Us," in *Politics without Vision: Thinking without a Banister in the Twentieth Century* (Chicago: University of Chicago Press, 2012), 394.

gion for his breeding and education work, just as he will make use of the prevailing political and economic situation" (BGE 61), implying both an ethical and political aspect to the work.

From this legislative mission follow the three *means* that Nietzsche ascribes to Plato—a political strategy, a purpose to his writings, and a model of political activism—from which he himself will draw inspiration. The *first* means is a political strategy: if Plato had achieved his philosophy and had a determinate political goal by the age of forty-two, all that he was missing were the men whom he would make philosophers and with whom he would found this new state. Thus he establishes the Academy, the "sect" with which he will fight against his time (PL P, I 2 [VII]). Inspired by Wagner's thought, and especially his founding of "Wagner Societies" to raise funds for the Bayreuth *Festspielhaus*, Nietzsche saw from the beginning of his reflection the necessity of pursuing his aims not individually but rather through a group. Already in *The Birth* he anticipated how a "rising generation" would decide to "live resolutely" and re-create a tragic society (BT 18). That this passage is central for Nietzsche is demonstrated by the fact that he quotes it in his "Self-Criticism" of *The Birth* as a rebuttal to those who want to accuse him of Romanticism, charging that he had no positive project to offer but instead reverted to "metaphysical comfort" (BT P 7). The figures that Nietzsche calls on—the free spirits and new philosophers—are always conceived as a plurality. In his review of *The Birth* in *Ecce Homo*, most important, Nietzsche gives an explicitly political gloss to this "new generation" by introducing for the first time in his published writings the notion of the party of life (EH BT 4). It is for this party that Nietzsche will write, at the end of his intellectual life, a "politics," understood as a political strategy or program to achieve Nietzsche's desired society. This is thus already against the view that Nietzsche's thought is destined only for the "solitary wanderer."

The creation of the so-called sect of the Academy to train the men with whom he would found the new state leads us back to the reason Plato chose to write, which is the *second* means ("purpose to his writings"). The totality of the dialogues, Nietzsche explains, has as its goal the "teaching and education" of the men of the Academy in preparation for their legislative mission of reforming the state (PL I 1). Plato writes to "strengthen in combat his companions of the Academy" (PL P), and in establishing the Academy, he "sows for the future" (PL I 2 [VII]). He writes only for the training of his future philosopher-kings; before that writing had no sense for him, which explains why he only starts to write at the late age of forty-one.[51] But teaching and education took place first and foremost in the discussions in the

---

[51] "The *Phaedrus* is his first written work, and was not drafted until his forty-first year" (PL I 2 [VII]).

gardens of the Academy. Nietzsche explains, "Plato the writer is only an image of Plato the teacher, a simple reminiscence of the speeches in the gardens of the Academy" (PL P). This is why writing must imitate the oral form of teaching because it is simply a means of remembering the discussions of the Academy (PL I 1). Plato's written dialogues can therefore be understood as a reserve form of intellectual ammunition, where arguments would be consulted and brought to bear by the future philosopher-kings to refute opposing assertions in their intellectual struggle to reform the state.

In his description of Socrates's "Problem" of *Twilight of the Idols*, discussed in the previous section, Nietzsche had identified dialectics as a "new type of agon" that appealed to the agonistic drives of the Greeks (TI Problem 8). The new "wrestling matches" were intellectual contests to which Socrates was the first "fencing master." Plato's philosophy continues in this line: "Philosophy à la Plato is more accurately defined as an erotic contest, as the further development and internalization of the ancient gymnastics and its *presuppositions*" (TI Skirmishes 23). Like the Jesuits, Socrates and Plato use competition through dialectics as a method of education. The artist Plato also, according to Nietzsche in the lectures, engages in a continual artistic contest with the other writers of his time, though this becomes gradually dominated by the moralistic tendency that he inherits from Socrates.[52]

Nietzsche also understands his own writings to have an educative function, explaining that *Beyond Good and Evil*, for example, is to serve as a "*school of the gentilhomme*" (EH BGE 1). Moreover, in his writings he sows for the future. Declaring himself to be a destiny (EH Destiny), and that he will be born "posthumously" (AC P), the mission of the free Spirits, "philosophers of the future," and party of life he calls on is to carry through his future revaluation of all values. From his literary criticisms of Strauss in his first *Untimely Meditation* to his "Skirmishes" with a number of writers (Ernest Renan, Charles Augustin Saint-Beuve, George Eliot, and George Sand) in the *Twilight of the Idols*, Nietzsche, the avid reader of the *Revue des Deux Mondes*—the dominant literary review of the time—constantly engages in an artistic contest with his contemporary writers, too.[53] He demonstrates over the course of his works his "mastery of all registers"—between aphorisms (HH, D, GS, BGE, TI), dialogues (FEI, Z), essays (BT, UM, GM), autobiographies (EH, NCW), poetry (DD), and also composing music ("Hymn

[52] See PL II 15: "We must not forget in the *Phaedusa* and the *Symposium* the competition with the other writers of his time." See also PL I 1: "The *Republic* is much more important work than the *Gorgias* or the *Symposium*, but of much lesser aesthetic value. . . . [H]is artistic abilities are more and more repressed because of his Socratic knowledge, for example the *Laws*," of which Nietzsche would later write, "Very vague composition, contradictions, and a repetitive and boring dialogue" (PL I III [Laws]).

[53] See letter to Meta von Salis, December 29, 1888, KSB 8; letter to Ruggero Bonghi, end of December 1888, KSB 8.

to Life")—though retains the "good taste" not to decadently mix them all together into the one art form. There is little doubt that Nietzsche's writings themselves were meant as a challenge to their readers, knocking over the idols of the day (TI P 2). Finally, in exhorting mankind to "overcome" itself through teaching the figure of the overman (Z P 3), Nietzsche also demands of his readers and companions that they engage in a perpetual agon with themselves, so that they may continually overcome themselves.

The essential difference between Plato and Nietzsche in this regard is that the latter lives in a "literary age" (PL P, I 1).[54] Instead of education being conducted orally in the Academy as it was for the ancients, with writing simply being a method of remembering the speeches held there, the modern literary age reverses this relationship and makes writing the fundamental form of education. This is due to the "unchaining" of the philosopher in the post-Greek world from an authentic culture where they lived and acted out their philosophy publicly, as I have explored above. The end result is that the writings of today's philosopher appear as comets to their contemporary society, much as Nietzsche's writings must have appeared during his lifetime, where he struggled to develop a readership. Nietzsche of course tried to win students over to his cause—without much success either, it would appear—both from the University of Basel and the Pädegogium, which trained aspiring philologists at the secondary level, and the general public more broadly, notably through his public seminars series "On the Future of Our Educational Institutions."

But writing books had since become the main means of education and recruitment. Nietzsche writes to Erwin Rohde on December 15, 1870, that their "books serve as hooks to win over newcomers to the artistic brotherhood." This idea of books as hooks to win over newcomers reappears in Nietzsche's later writings. In his review of *Beyond Good and Evil* in *Ecce Homo*, he writes that "all my writings from this point on have been fish hooks," though still lamenting the lack of fish (EH BGE 1). He explains: "This involved slowly looking around for anyone related to me, for anyone who, out of strength, would give me a hand with *destruction*." The central difference here is that while the early Nietzsche was trying to recruit for Wagner's artistic brotherhood, come *Ecce Homo* Nietzsche is trying to recruit for his own "great war"—the revaluation of values.

If Plato is only secondarily a writer, he remains first and foremost, according to Nietzsche, a political agitator (PL P)—his *third* means at achieving reform ("a model of political activism").[55] He is, as a true Greek, "entirely a

---

[54] See also WS 87: "The age of speaking well is past, because the age of the city cultures is past. . . . [T]hat is why everyone who is a good European now has to learn *to write well*."

[55] In *Why Plato Wrote*, Danielle Allen ([Oxford: Wiley-Blackwell, 2010], 4) argues that Plato wrote to "effect political change." According to her, Plato is not only the "world's first systematic philosopher" but also the "western world's first think-tank activist and its first message

public man and only incidentally a literary man." When Nietzsche will turn to his revaluation of all values, this agitator aspect will be close to his mind, conceiving the publication of *The Antichrist*, as I will develop over the course of chapters 5 and 6, as an "agitation edition" that will cause an international uprising against the church and European powers it sanctions, especially the German Reich.[56] Combining both the style of the ancients and fact that Nietzsche lives in a literary age, the publication of *The Antichrist* will take the form of a "literary act."

Nietzsche, in sum, is opposed to Plato's style and philosophy, but in agreement, in a certain manner, with his politics. A similar type of judgment can also be passed on Nietzsche's view of the church: an agreement on certain aspects of its politics, but a rejection of its "philosophy." The links that Nietzsche draws between Plato and the church are well known. In the preface to *Beyond Good and Evil*, he states that "Christianity is Platonism for the 'people'" (BGE P). In "What I Owe to the Ancients" in *Twilight of the Idols*, Nietzsche returns to the theme, writing that for him Plato is so much at odds with the Hellenic instinct that he is "proleptically Christian—he already has 'good' as the highest concept" (TI Ancients 2). He adds: "And how much Plato there still is in the concept of 'church,' in the structure, system, and praxis of the church!" Much like with Plato's *Republic*, Nietzsche does have sympathy for certain aspects of the church as an institution—namely, its hierarchical structure. He also appreciates the fact that it has made certain things sacred—the Bible—in such a way that the great unwashed must wear gloves to touch it, and that it has retained—specifically the Jesuits have retained—in its method of education the notion of contest from the Greeks.[57] Indeed, one can easily see the link that Nietzsche suggests between Plato's sect of the Academy and the praxis of the church: the training of men to be priests, either to continue the work of the church or even in certain cases—think of Duc de Richelieu—reforming the state, and the Bible as the educational tool, as a reserve of arguments against non-

---

man." "He wrote . . . to change Athenian culture and thereby transform Athenian politics." Nietzsche agrees that Plato wanted to change Athenian culture and politics, but as an ancient Greek, did this above all as a public man, notably through his lectures at the Academy. Writing was only a secondary tool, to remember the discussions there. Yet in modernity, which is what Allen is fundamentally interested it, writing takes over that role.

[56] This return to the legislative nature of Nietzsche's study of the ancient Greeks is well captured in Rüdiger Safranski's *Nietzsche: A Philosophical Biography*, trans. Shelley Frisch (London: Granta, 2003).

[57] In general Nietzsche, as the good son of a Protestant pastor, believes that the Christian ascetic practice of cleanliness is something positive (see Z II Rabble: "I appreciate all that is clean"; GM III). See also HH 55, where Nietzsche lauds the "cunning and infamous arts of the Jesuits," admits that there is "only a difference in insight that divides them from him," and asks whether "given quite the same tactics and organization" we would be "equally good instruments or equally admirable in self-conquest, indefatigability, or devotedness."

believers. Nevertheless, much as Nietzsche is opposed to Plato's dogmatic philosophy of the good in itself, he fights against the philosophy of the church: Christianity. The subtitle of *The Antichrist* is *A Curse on Christianity.*

CONCLUSION

Taking as his starting point Nietzsche's conception of the philosopher as a legislator, Laurence Lampert has argued that "Nietzsche's Plato wrote esoterically and invented Platonism as an instrument of philosophical rule." In doing so, he affords himself the "right to lie."[58] This seems in line with what has been developed in this section: Plato as legislator coming up with a "philosophical system," stored in the dialogues, to serve as intellectual ammunition for the men he will train to reform the state.[59] We can add that Nietzsche undoubtedly saw in Plato a certain esotericism: he maintains that only a "small number" can fully understand the theory of Ideas, which he communicates "esoterically" to the few, and not to the "uninitiated" (PL I 2 [VII]). Nietzsche also discusses Plato's "noble lie." In fact, the theme is a recurring one throughout his work.[60] It is worth noting, however (contrary to some opinions that I we will return to) that Nietzsche does not see the noble lie in a bad light as such.[61] As he had stipulated already in the lectures on Plato and would repeat most explicitly in *The Antichrist*, the most important aspect of the lie is the "purpose" it is supposed to serve.[62]

What this engagement with Plato allows us to see is that Nietzsche is not only engaging in philosophy when writing his books but also that there may be broader structural roles that his publications play, notably in being hooks for attracting his readers to his cause, or again in attempting to agitate his time. We therefore should not limit ourselves to solely studying Nietzsche's published writings, as doing so might lead us to miss the over-

[58] Lampert, "Nietzsche and Plato," 217, 206.

[59] Lampert (ibid., 218) suggests that the question that should drive research concerning Nietzsche and Plato is whether "Nietzsche's understanding of Plato [can] help lead to a truer understanding of what both Plato and Nietzsche aimed at." In this section I have applied Nietzsche's understanding of Plato back onto himself as a way of answering Lampert's question with regard to Nietzsche.

[60] See variously HL 10: "Plato's *necessary lie*"; GM III 19: "the actual lie, the genuine, resolute 'honest' lie (listen to Plato about its values)"; TI Improves 5: "Plato [has never] doubted [his] *right* to lie"; AC 55: "the 'holy lie' . . . is not absent from Plato either."

[61] See Thomas Brobjer, "The Absence of Political Ideals in Nietzsche's Writings: The Case of the Laws of Manu and the Associated Caste Society," *Nietzsche-Studien* 27 (1998): 300–318.

[62] See PL II 25: "the noble lie, approved by the philosopher, which is to say the lie driven by a good intention"; AC 56: "In the end, it comes down to the *purpose* the lie is supposed to serve."

arching *purpose* that Nietzsche had in both composing and publishing his works. We should be attentive to Nietzsche's notes and letters where he gives indications of what he is trying to achieve, for fear that in focusing too exclusively on what he published we lose sight of his overall goal. Furthermore, we should not consider Nietzsche's books to be the ultimate horizon for the task he sets himself; his final "act" of the "Revaluation of All Values" is not only literary but also expresses itself outside philosophical prose: through poetry, music, and politics, as we will see in the second part of the book. Finally, his analysis of the pre-Platonic philosophers made him realize that only from a healthy culture can genuine philosophy grow, and his interpretation of Plato allowed him to think about how to formulate a political strategy. This he will develop later in his life through setting out the principles of his own great politics, which will constitute the indispensable political arm of his new total revolution, his revaluation of all values.

CHAPTER 2
THE STATE

It has often been said that if Nietzsche expresses various views about the state, these do not amount to anything systematic enough to be considered a political theory. Leiter, a prominent commentator on Nietzsche, has written that the "interpretative question" concerning Nietzsche's political philosophy is whether "scattered remarks and parenthetical outbursts add up to *systematic* views on questions of philosophical significance." His own view is that Nietzsche "has no political philosophy, in the conventional sense of a theory of the state and its legitimacy." If he "occasionally expresses views about political matters[,] . . . read in context, they do not add up to a theoretical account of any of the questions of political philosophy." Leiter explains that "the canon of political philosophers is composed of thinkers (like [Thomas] Hobbes, [John] Locke, and [Jean-Jacques] Rousseau) who have philosophical views about political questions—the state, liberty, law, justice, etc.—not thinkers whose views about *other* topics merely have 'implications' for politics." Instead Nietzsche, for Leiter, is an *"esoteric moralist,"* someone who "has views about human flourishing, views he wants to communicate at least to a select few," but for whom the "larger world, including its form of political and economic organization, is simply not his concern."[1]

By denying Nietzsche a reflection on politics, Leiter places himself in a long line of interpreters stretching back to the end of World War II. The first and perhaps still most prominent was Kaufmann. His seminal *Nietzsche: Philosopher, Psychologist, Antichrist*, first published in 1950 and now in its fourth edition, rescued Nietzsche from the philosophical abyss that he had fallen into after his misuse by the Nazis, which at the time, as mentioned earlier, had prompted Bertrand Russell to call the war "Nietzsche's war."[2] Kaufmann reconstructed Nietzsche as a German humanist whose sole pre-

---

[1] Brian Leiter, *Nietzsche on Morality* (London: Routledge, 2003), 292–97.

[2] Walter Kaufmann, *Nietzsche: Philosopher, Psychologist, Antichrist* (Princeton, NJ: Princeton University Press, 1974).

occupation was with an antipolitical culture. But the price he paid for rescuing Nietzsche from the "philosophical bestiary," as Alasdair MacIntyre described the place to which Nietzsche's Übermensch had been consigned, was to deny him any interest in politics.[3]

Kaufmann's line of argumentation still serves as a cue for many readings of Nietzsche, providing a starting point for authors such as Williams and Nehamas, and remains a powerful strand of interpretation today.[4] A number of different authors, including Keith Ansell-Pearson, Daniel Conway, Detwiler, and Dombowsky, have more recently questioned such a view, but the position remains firmly entrenched in the secondary literature.[5] The aim of this chapter is to contribute to this debate by approaching Nietzsche through one of the central themes of the history of political thought—namely, that of the state. By adopting this perspective, I wish to continue to challenge the view that Nietzsche held no interest in politics at all, and in doing so enrich the discussion about how his relation to political thought might best be understood.

An essential part of this approach is to pay particular attention to the context within which Nietzsche's theory of the state emerged—that is, a disagreement with Wagner over the role of slavery in the ancient city-state. This will be the focus of the first part of the chapter, which will also be concerned with the contrast Nietzsche draws of his own account of the origins of the state and that of the social contract tradition, the latter of which he dismisses as a "fantasy" in *On the Genealogy of Morality* (GM II 17). Yet in a youthful unpublished essay, "The Greek State," Nietzsche is quite clear that the state of nature is a Hobbesian *"bellum omnium contra omnes"* (GSt, 170). The task of the first part of the chapter will be to unpack the relationship between these two seemingly competing claims.[6]

In the second part, I will turn my attention to Nietzsche's theory of the decay of the state—a common theme in the history of political thought

[3] Alasdair MacIntyre, *After Virtue: A Study in Moral Theory* (London: Duckworth, 2013), 25.
[4] Bernard Williams, *Shame and Necessity* (Berkeley: University of California Press, 2008); Alexander Nehamas, *Nietzsche: Life as Literature* (Cambridge, MA: Harvard University Press, 2002).
[5] Keith Ansell-Pearson, *An Introduction to Nietzsche as Political Theory* (Cambridge: Cambridge University Press, 1994); Daniel Conway, *Nietzsche and the Political* (London: Routledge, 1997); Bruce Detwiler, *Nietzsche and the Politics of Aristocratic Radicalism* (Chicago: University of Chicago Press, 1990); Don Dombowsky, *Nietzsche's Machiavellian Politics* (Basingstoke, UK: Palgrave Macmillan, 2004).
[6] In this chapter, I will concentrate on Nietzsche's critique of the Hobbesian social contract rather than on Hobbes himself, as Nietzsche appears more to be attacking a certain position associated with Hobbes's political thought than engaging textually with him. For Nietzsche's knowledge of Hobbes, see Thomas Brobjer, *Nietzsche's Philosophical Context: An Intellectual Biography* (Champaign: University of Illinois Press, 2008).

and, indeed, the nineteenth century. What must be made clear here is that when Nietzsche talks about the state in his work, he is in fact referring to three related yet at the same time distinct instances, which follow chronologically. First is the ancient city-state, which Nietzsche lauds for providing the original platform for the development of high culture that could not have taken place beforehand. This state subsequently suffers a transformation into the modern nationalist Kulturstaat, which Nietzsche virulently condemns for its instrumentalization of culture for its own benefit, thereby inverting the initial mission that saw the birth of the state in the first place. But ultimately, Nietzsche diagnoses the end of that state too—its decay—and it is in this transition away from the modern nation-state, toward what we might term a postmodern state, that he will locate his political project.

My goal, then, is to argue that Nietzsche *does* offer a systematic political theory of the state, but one that is an *alternative* to the social contract tradition, which he explicitly rejects. In doing so, I intend to challenge those readings of Nietzsche that refuse any sustained or coherent thinking on politics on his behalf. Yet on the basis of his theory of the state's decay, I will also posit that Nietzsche changes the focus of his interest in politics to a new problem of political philosophy: how to reconcile as well as reestablish normative and political authority in the transition away from the modern nation-state. This shows how Nietzsche is able to adapt his political thinking to his analysis of contemporary society, thus disproving the point that Nietzsche was unconcerned with his political and social context.

It is well known that Nietzsche writes in many different styles—the aphoristic being his most famous—and that outside perhaps *The Birth of Tragedy*, *The Genealogy of Morality*, and *The Antichrist*, his books address many different themes rather than being a sustained analysis of one particular subject. But this does not mean that he did not deal with political issues, or any philosophical topoi for that matter, in a thorough manner across the range of his writings. Nor does it imply that he did not devote specific essays or chapters to political topics.[7] While my chapter will focus primarily on Nietzsche's earlier writings—"The Greek State" (1872), *Schopenhauer as Educator* (1874), and the chapter "A Glance at the State" in *Human, All Too Human* (1878) in particular—by linking these texts to later ones such as *On the Genealogy of Morality* (1887) and *Twilight of the Idols* (1888), I desire to show Nietzsche's sustained and quite-coherent interest in the state. I by no means desire to suggest that there are no breaks in the development of Nietzsche's thought; I am sympathetic to the usual tripartite division of Nietzsche's works, and Martin Ruehl has convincingly argued, to my mind, that "The Greek State" signals the start of Nietzsche's departure from his

---

[7] Note that in late 1888, Nietzsche starts to draft a "Tractatus Politicus" (KSA 13 11 [54]).

early Wagneriana.[8] Still, I do want to posit that in terms of his political reflection, especially with regard to his view of the state, Nietzsche held consistent views throughout his productive life.

Nietzsche, by theorizing three different states across his oeuvre, therefore demonstrates a sustained interest in the topic of the state throughout his corpus. Moreover, that he draws together "The Greek State" and *The Genealogy* on the subject of the birth of the state, and again *Human, All Too Human* and *Twilight of the Idols* on the matter of the modern's state decay, suggests that there are in fact strong continuities in his conceptualization of these three states over the course of his writings.

What drives the research behind this chapter is the question of identifying Nietzsche's correct place in the canon of political thought. I aim to do so by positioning Nietzsche in relation to different traditions—the social contract and theories of the decay of the state—in the history of political thought conventionally understood. My goal is to say something new about Nietzsche, not make a novel point about these traditions. Nietzsche has now became a staple of many political thought curricula, but the best manner to approach him—and certainly what best text to use, although this currently seems to have solidified around *The Genealogy*—is still a matter of contention. Through my work here I hope to begin to offer one fruitful way of doing so.

WAGNER AND SLAVERY

From the outset, Nietzsche considered political reflection to be an integral part of his work. One of the working titles of what was to become *The Birth of Tragedy* (1872) was "Tragedy and Free Spirits: Meditations on the Ethical-Political Significance of the Music Drama," and a chapter on the state and slavery was consistently planned from 1869 to 1871.[9] In early 1871, Nietzsche penned a long fragment on the theme.[10] The essay would be reproduced in near-identical form as the third of the "Five Prefaces to Five Unwritten Books," titled "The Greek State," that he offered Cosima Wagner for Christmas 1872. Yet when *The Birth* was published earlier that year, Nietzsche had been reduced to merely "noting" that "Alexandrian culture needs a slave class in order to exist" (BT 18). The chapter on state and slavery had disappeared.

---

[8] Martin Ruehl, "*Politeia* 1871: Young Nietzsche and the Greek State," in *Nietzsche and Antiquity: His Reaction and Response to the Classical Tradition*, ed. Paul Bishop (Rochester, NY: Camden House, 2004), 79–97.

[9] KSA 7 5 [22, 42, 43].

[10] KSA 7 10 [1].

Ruehl speculates that the chapter was purged at the behest of the "master," Richard Wagner.[11] Wagner's influence on Nietzsche is fully recognized, but the impact that Wagner's political thought had on Nietzsche's own political thinking has been understudied, and I wish to rectify this here. Indeed, Cosima notes in her diaries that the first oral disagreement between Wagner and Nietzsche concerned the Franco-Prussian War. Nietzsche had expressed—as he would do in a more systematic manner in his first *Untimely Meditation*—his anxiety about the threat posed to culture by the new militaristic Prussian state.[12] In response to this, Wagner, who had grown increasingly nationalistic and had moved away from some of the more radical inclinations of his youth, proclaimed that he "approves everything: the police, the soldiers, the censored press, the stifling of the parliament," in view of the Prussian victory and German unification.[13]

In his early essay *The Artwork of the Future* (1849), which Nietzsche had been given to read on his first visit to Tribschen in 1869, Wagner had argued that Greek culture had crumbled under slavery, and that the true artwork of the future could only come about through the liberation of the modern wage-laboring slave.[14] Nietzsche, however, disagreed. Drawing from his earlier fragment, he writes in "The Greek State" that "even if it were true that the Greeks were ruined because they kept slaves, the opposite is even more certain, that we will be destroyed by the *lack* of slavery" (GSt, 167). This was the "cruel-sounding truth" that he claimed to have identified in the essay: the fact that "*slavery belongs to the essence of a culture*" (GSt, 166).

These sorts of passages did not sit well with Wagner, and after a visit to Tribschen from April 3 to 8, 1871, where an early draft of *The Birth* was discussed with Cosima and Richard Wagner, the sociopolitical sections were dropped from Nietzsche's subsequent reworkings of the book.[15] It seems only someone like Wagner would have had a powerful enough influence on Nietzsche for him to change his writings, and Nietzsche's laudatory remarks about him in the conclusion to *The Birth* are well known. Yet what this episode shows is that just as Wagner's mission to create a total artwork required a total revolution of both culture and politics, Nietzsche's project

[11] Ruehl, "*Politeia* 1871," 83.

[12] Letter to Carl von Gersdorff, November 9, 1870.

[13] Richard Wagner, "Art and Revolution," in *Richard Wagner's Prose Works*, trans. William Ashton Ellis (London: Kegan Paul, 1895), 1:29. Note, however, that Wagner's Bayreuth *Festspielhaus* specifically excluded boxes and galleries from the construction of the main auditorium, which only included a uniform *parterre*. As a *Volkfest*, the festivals at Bayreuth were for the whole *Volk* equally, and in equality. The reality of the ensuing exorbitant prices put paid to this original plan. Quote as noted in Cosima's diary, from KSA 15, Basel, October 21–December 23, 1870.

[14] Richard Wagner, "The Artwork of the Future," in *Richard Wagner's Prose Works*, trans. William Ashton Ellis (London: Kegan Paul, 1895), 1:184, 69.

[15] Ruehl, "*Politeia* 1871," 83.

contained from the beginning an essential sociopolitical element, which asserted the role of slavery in the creation of high culture, but that was perhaps suppressed out of deference to Wagner. The political element was to be found in the essay on "The Greek State," which represents Nietzsche's first systematization of his early political views. That Nietzsche maintained his views on slavery, as expressed in his early draft for *The Birth*, is demonstrated by the fact that he offered an almost exact copy of the passage in question— "The Greek State"—to Cosima less than a year after the publication of *The Birth*—a poisoned gift if there ever was one.

In "The Greek State," Nietzsche also takes issue with Wagner's *On State and Religion*—another manuscript that Nietzsche read while in Tribschen— which the latter had recently composed at the behest of King Ludwig II of Bavaria.[16] There Wagner accounts for the emergence of the state as from a Hobbesian "fear of violence," which leads to a "contract whereby the units seek to save themselves from mutual violence, through a little practice of restraint."[17] While Nietzsche concurred that the state of nature was one of bellum omnium contra omnes (GSt, 170), he disagreed with the idea that the state arose through a contract. He instead saw the state as originating from a "*conqueror* with the iron hand," who "suddenly, violently, and bloodily" takes control of a yet-unformed population and forces it into a hierarchical society (GSt, 168).

Nietzsche's rejection of the social contract goes hand in hand with his affirmation of slavery: the contract would presuppose equality between pledgers and thus repudiate the slavery on which Greek culture had come about, and that would again be needed, as Wagner denied, for true culture to be re-created. Indeed, Wagner posited the social contract as a means of freeing the modern wage-laboring slave and reconciling the warring classes within the bosom of the nation under the guidance of an enlightened and Christian king (read Ludwig II).[18] This rejection of equality also sheds light on a common present-day rejection of Nietzsche as a political philosopher: as Nietzsche does not share the "egalitarian premise" of contemporary political philosophy, he is therefore excluded from its ranks, notwithstanding Nietzsche's own understanding of what politics might be.[19] And although Nietzsche's engagement with the social contract tradition emanates from a disagreement with Wagner concerning slavery, it

---

[16] The text was penned in 1864, when Wagner was summoned to the intimate companionship of the king, but only published nine years later, in 1873. Besides the disagreement over the origins of the state, Nietzsche seemed quite taken by the piece, writing to Gustav Krug on August 4 of that year that "never has one spoken to a king with such beauty and profundity."

[17] Richard Wagner, "On State and Religion," in *Richard Wagner's Prose Works*, trans. William Ashton Ellis (London: Kegan Paul, 1895), 4:11.

[18] Ibid., 4:11–15.

[19] Leiter, *Nietzsche on Morality*, 290.

also allowed him to build his own theory of the birth of the state and its justification, to which I now turn.

"THE GREEK STATE"

By referring to Hobbes, Locke, and Rousseau in his discussion of what a political philosophy ought to be, Leiter appears to have in mind the social contract tradition when he defines political philosophy in the "conventional sense of a theory of the state and its legitimacy." So at least one aspect of having a political philosophy on Leiter's terms—for the sake of this chapter, I leave aside the question of having philosophical views about liberty, law, justice, and so on, although Nietzsche clearly has a lot to say about those too—is to have a philosophy of the state that takes the form of social contract theory. The publication of Rawls's *A Theory of Justice* in 1971, with its "original position" and "veil of ignorance" that can be conceived of as being analogous to the "state of nature," has prompted a revival of the social contract tradition in the late twentieth century. But it is unfair to demand that all political philosophy, and in particular Nietzsche's political philosophy, be judged on whether it meets this criterion, which in reality was challenged as early as the notion of the social contract itself.[20] Indeed, much of what is important in political philosophy is the manner in which various thinkers have redefined the field. Hobbes notoriously did so by theorizing the modern state, a concept unknown to the ancients. We should therefore be more attentive to the terms within which Nietzsche frames his contribution to political philosophy. If we dismiss him as a political thinker because he does not match a certain predetermined criterion it not only conveniently sidelines him from the field but also misses his actual original contribution to it.

Leiter himself gets caught up in this problem. Although he criticizes Nussbaum in his work for requiring that "serious political thought" address seven precise topics that would exclude Marx from the political philosophy canon—he writes that the serious political thought that Nussbaum has in mind is in fact "'serious' academic *liberal* political theory" that "did not exist before the rise of a large class of bourgeois academics after World War II"—he nonetheless too reimposes on Nietzsche a modern understanding of political philosophy—the social contract—that would exclude someone like Plato, for whom the question of the (modern) state and its legitimacy had no meaning.[21]

---

[20] David Hume, "Of the Original Contract," in *Political Essays* (Cambridge: Cambridge University Press, 1994), 186–201.

[21] Leiter, *Nietzsche on Morality*, 293n8; Quentin Skinner, "The State," in *Political Innovation*

In "The Greek State," Nietzsche concurred with the Hobbesian view of the state of nature being a bellum omnium contra omnes. But he did not account for its birth in a contract. Instead, as we just saw, he located the birth of the "cruel tool" of the state in the iron "conquerors." Indeed, these conquerors are themselves, on Nietzsche's account, the state. Yet the "ignominious" birth of the state is justified as a means to genius and culture. "Nature"—we see the influence of Romanticism on Nietzsche's early thought here—had instilled in the conqueror the state-creating instinct so that she might achieve "her salvation in appearance in the mirror of genius."[22] The "dreadful" birth of the state, whose monuments include "devastated lands, ruined towns, savage men, consuming hatred of nations," is justified by nature because it serves as a means to genius. "The state appears before it proudly and calmly: leading the magnificently blossoming woman, Greek society, by the hand" (GSt, 169).

While Nietzsche's genealogy of the state claims to be more realistic than the "fanciful," in his own words, account of the social contract tradition, this does not imply that on his account the state cannot be justified. Of course there is a difference between normative and descriptive claims here: over the course of their writings, Hobbes and indeed Rousseau gave quite-detailed accounts of the history of the state they understood to be at odds with the normative ideals they were recommending, and the social contract theorists are often thought of as having tailored their state of nature to justify the type of state they were advocating.[23] But Nietzsche is here rejecting both their descriptive—how the state came into being—and normative claims—how the birth of the state can be justified.

The state, for Nietzsche, is justified because it opens up a space within which culture, through genius, can for the first time flourish.[24] There are a number of elements to this claim. First, that the time and energy used to defend oneself in the "war of all against all" is redirected, within a pacified society, toward more artistic and cultural pursuits. Nietzsche explains that

---

and Conceptual Change, ed. Terence Ball, James Farr, and Russell Hanson (Cambridge: Cambridge University Press, 1989), 90–131.

[22] For the Hegelian overtones of this process—Conway describes it as a "cunning of nature"—see Daniel Conway, "The Birth of the State," in *Nietzsche, Power, and Politics: Rethinking Nietzsche's Legacy for Political Thought*, ed. Herman Siemens and Vasti Roodt (Berlin: De Gruyter, 2008), 37–67. See also Lawrence Hatab, "Breaking the Social Contract," in *Nietzsche, Power, and Politics: Rethinking Nietzsche's Legacy for Political Thought*, ed. Herman Siemens and Vasti Roodt (Berlin: De Gruyter, 2008), 169–88.

[23] On this point, see Keith Ansell-Pearson, *Nietzsche contra Rousseau: A Study of Nietzsche's Moral and Political Thought* (Cambridge: Cambridge University Press, 1996).

[24] Culture predates the state in both Locke's and Rousseau's accounts. It is debatable whether it also exists in the "war of all against all"—there is space for jealousy—but it certainly was not the aim of Hobbes's state to encourage high culture in the way that Nietzsche would have wanted it, and definitely not on the basis of a slave class.

once states have been founded everywhere, the bellicose urge gets concentrated into "less frequent" yet altogether much stronger "bolts of thunder and flashes of lightning" of "dreadful clouds of war between nations." Thus, much as it was for Hobbes, the "state of nature" gets transferred to the interstate level. In the meantime, however, the "concentrated effect of that *bellum*, turned inward, gives society time to germinate and turn green everywhere, so that it can let radiant blossoms of genius sprout forth as soon as warmer days come." In other words, the energy that was used to simply stay alive in the individual war of all against all gets redirected, once encased in and protected by the new state, either collectively toward wars against other nations or, in the intermediary, toward satisfying a "new world of necessities"—namely, culture (GSt, 170).

The two interrelated justifications for the state—genius and culture—come together in the figure of the first genius—the military genius. Since the beasts of prey were organized on a "war footing," the first type of state, even the *"archetype"* of the state, is the military state, and the first genius is a military genius. The first work of art is the state itself and its constitution; Nietzsche mentions the Spartan lawgiver Lycurgus—a thought borrowed from Jacob Burckhardt.[25] As a military state, the first state therefore divides itself into hierarchical military castes, and this "warlike society" necessarily takes the form of a pyramidal structure with a large slave-class bottom stratum (GSt, 172).

Nietzsche explains how the slave comes about. As the beasts of prey are conquerors, they exercise what Nietzsche labels the "first *right*": the right of power. All rights are fundamentally "presumption, usurpation, and violence"—a notion again taken from Burckhardt. Consequently, as the Greeks saw, the defeated "belong to the victor, together with his wife and child, goods and blood"; the masses who are formed into society become the slaves of the beasts of prey because they have been conquered (GSt, 168). Nevertheless, although they are conquered, their existence also becomes justified. As they form the flesh of the state, their slavery is justified as a means to the production of the genius. For Nietzsche, true dignity is *"being acknowledged as worthy to be a means for genius"* (GSt, 172).

The slaves justify their existence as a means to genius by liberating the latter from having to physically work for their subsistence through taking on their share of the burden. This is the meaning of the cruel "truth claim" that Nietzsche makes in "The Greek State": *"slavery belongs to the essence of a culture"*:

In order for there to be a broad, deep, fertile soil for the development of art, the overwhelming majority has to be slavishly subjected to life's

[25] Jacob Burckhardt, "The State as a Work of Art," in *The Civilization of the Renaissance in Italy* (London: Penguin, 2004).

necessity in the service of the minority, *beyond* the measure that is necessary for the individual. At their expense, through their extra work, that privileged class is to be removed from the struggle for existence, in order to produce and satisfy a new world of necessities. (GSt, 166)

The extra work of the slaves liberates the artistic class from laboring for life's necessities, so that they may dedicate themselves entirely to producing great works of art that justify the existence of the state, society, slaves, and themselves as a whole. It is only a few exceptional beings—geniuses—who can produce art: the "small number of Olympian men" who produce the "world of art" by being placed on top of the "misery of men living a life of toil" (GSt, 166). Slavery, in sum, is a requisite for the existence of geniuses, who themselves are the only ones capable of producing high culture.

This account of the birth and justification of the state in "The Greek State" finds a distinct echo in the description of the state that Nietzsche offers in second essay of *The Genealogy*. In the infamous passage on the notorious blond beasts of prey, themselves perhaps "conquerors with an iron fist," Nietzsche writes:

I used the word "state": it is obvious who is meant by this—some pack of blond beasts of prey, a conqueror and master race, which organized on a war footing, and with the power to organize, unscrupulously lays its dreadful paws on the populace, which though it might be vastly greater in number, is still shapeless and shifting. In this way, the "state" began on earth: I think I have dispensed with the fantasy that has it begin with a "contract." (GM II 17)

So for Nietzsche the blond beasts of prey are themselves the state, much as were the iron conquerors; once they have conquered and enslaved a people, they become the "repressive and ruthless machinery" that shape the people into society. Later in the same section Nietzsche explains that "they arrive like fate," that "their work is an instinctive creation of forms. . . . They are the most involuntary and unconscious artists in existence. In them that terrible egoism of the artist is in control, which stares out like bronze and sees himself, in his work, eternally justified, just like a mother is in her child."

Both "The Greek State" and *The Genealogy* therefore present the same account of the birth and justification of the state, as a conquering horde that, organized on a war footing, suddenly appears to establish a hierarchical state that is its work of art, only justifiable as a whole, and within which the slaves' repressed instincts are turned inward. As "The Greek State" was never published, Nietzsche thereby gives a public endorsement to his earlier views on the state, and thus both texts should be read side by side. Moreover, that Nietzsche should reiterate fifteen years later exactly the same theory of the birth of the state suggests strong continuities between at least

Nietzsche's earlier and later periods, conventionally understood, in terms of his view of the ancient state.

We can now see Nietzsche's specific engagement with the social contract tradition, which *The Genealogy* reinforces and again makes explicit, particularly his criticism of the Hobbesian position. The main point is that while Nietzsche does share in positing a primordial war of all against all—and that, like Hobbes, this state of nature persists between constituted states—he rejects the notion that the state came about through a contract. Whereas the contractarians believe that the state arose or should arise from a contract between all members, Nietzsche sees the state as a pack of blond beasts of prey—and not some "Leviathan"—that forms the shapeless masses into a society.[26] For Nietzsche the state "begins with an act of violence" whereas the Hobbesian social contract was thought up precisely to get away from this primal hostility, and for Locke and Rousseau the state of nature was not essentially violent in the first place.[27] We might add that there is a strong methodological difference here: while Hobbes clearly wanted to make a political intervention in his time, he nonetheless offers us an abstract and legalistic contract, whereas Nietzsche provides us with a genealogical account of the rise and transformation of the state, which he only attempts to define in its different historical contexts ("only that which has not history can be defined" [GM II 13]).[28]

The fact that for Nietzsche a large slave class is created in the process also goes directly against the tradition—in which a contract was meant to guarantee some degree of freedom for everyone, and not just to the conquering few, as in Nietzsche's account. Finally, nature's intent in creating the state was, according to Nietzsche, to supply a means to genius and culture, in contrast to the social contract, which was meant to allow people to live in harmony. These justify the state's advent. But if the state is justified as a means to genius, Nietzsche takes this thought further and applies it to all aspects of life. The slaves who make up the society that the beasts of prey have formed also become justified as means to genius and culture, because it is through their extra work that the geniuses are liberated from life's "necessities" and can thereby pursue their artistic task. Not only the state but

[26] The analogy with Hobbes's "commonwealth by institution" does not hold either, given that for Hobbes this still involves a contact.

[27] Pace Hume, utility or need does not play a role here either; rather, it involves some sort of historical necessity.

[28] Another key difference is of course that while Hobbes understands life primarily in terms of self-preservation, Nietzsche conceives of it as will to power (see Paul Patton, "Nietzsche and Hobbes," in *International Studies in Philosophy* 33, no. 3 [2001]: 99–116). We can note here that the development of bad conscience, resentment and the internalisation of the instincts—the subject of much debate today—occur within a specifically *political* context, namely the birth of the state, such that Nietzsche's *moral* philosophy is determined by his *political* theory.

also humankind is justified as a means to genius. This gives a particular flavor to the famous line from *The Birth* that it is both "existence" and the "world" that are "eternally justified" (BT 5).[29]

Nietzsche can be considered to offer a "political philosophy" as Leiter would have wanted it; he has a theory of the state, which finds its origin in the blond beasts of prey, and a justification for it in being a means to genius and culture. It is, however, an *alternative* political philosophy to the social contract tradition.

THE DECAY OF THE MODERN STATE

Nietzsche had placed his reflection on the Greek state under the guise of Plato's perfect state—namely, *The Republic*.[30] There he presents Plato as being the first to have discovered "through poetic intuition" the "actual aim of the [Greek] state," which was the "constantly renewed creation and preparation of the genius, compared with whom everything else is just a tool, aid, and facilitator." In the Platonic state, we recognize the "wonderful grand hieroglyph of a profound *secret study of the connection between state and genius*," which Nietzsche believes is in "eternal need to be interpreted" (GSt, 173). So Plato is important for Nietzsche not because he offers a definition of the state as such but rather because he is the first to perceive what the ancient Greek state is truly about: the creation of genius.

Reinterpreting this secret connection is precisely what Nietzsche sets out to do in his third *Untimely Meditation*. In *Schopenhauer as Educator*, he posits his dictum that "mankind must work continually at the production of individual great men—that and nothing else is its task" (SE 6). This was, of course, the mission that nature had ascribed to the state and its slave class. But in contrast to the Greek state, where both the conquerors and slaves were simply the unconscious tools of nature—the "state-creating instinct" for the former (GSt, 168)—in the modern world mankind can arrive at a "conscious awareness of its goal": to "seek out and create the favorable conditions under which those great redemptive men can come into existence" (SE 6). Nietzsche will describe this mission Platonically, as having to institute Plato's perfect state, where the creation of the genius is the conscious aim of the state: "the promotion of philosophy as the state understands it will one day have to be inspected to see whether the state understands it *Platonically*, which is to say as seriously and honestly as though its highest objective were to produce new Platos" (SE 8).

This modern Platonic state in many ways represents *Nietzsche's* perfect state. It is a state where the conscious goal of its organization is to produce

[29] See also GM II 17: " 'meaning' with regard to the whole."
[30] In German, Plato's *Republic* is translated as *Der Staat*.

genius and culture. It should be emphasized that this agreement with Plato is a *political* agreement about how society should be structured, and not a *philosophical* one. Nietzsche rejects Plato's good in itself as philosophy's biggest error (BGE P). The political consequence of this philosophical disagreement lies in the type of genius that should be created: Nietzsche criticizes Plato for excluding the "artistic genius" from the state (although he blames that on Socrates's influence), allowing only for the "genius of wisdom and knowledge" (the philosopher-kings), whereas the genius in all his manifestations should be promoted (GSt, 168).[31]

The Greek state was not to last. While nature had instilled in the beasts of prey the "state instinct," these instincts would eventually wane such that "men placed by birth . . . outside the instinct for nation and state" would arise and come to "recognize the state only to the extent . . . [that it is] in their own interests." These men gain great power over the state because they break away from the "unconscious intention of the state" that holds sway over the conquerors, and through them the masses under their control, thereby making them "means for the state purpose." They instead come to see the state consciously for what it is: a huge war machine. As such, rejecting the role that nature had assigned to the state and themselves—of being means to genius—they selfishly start to view the state as a means for their own purposes. Nietzsche explains that "all other citizens are in the dark about what nature intends for them with their state instinct, and follow blindly; only those who stand outside this know what *they* want from the state, and what the state ought to grant them." From this, these "truly international, homeless, financial recluses" learn to "misuse politics as an instrument of the stock exchange, and state and society as an apparatus for their own enrichment" (GSt, 170).[32]

This rising self-awareness and instrumentalization of the state signals the death of the ancient state and birth of the modern one. The modern state, though, would not fulfill the Platonic mission that Nietzsche had ascribed to it. The modern Kulturstaat—meaning the state's novel and direct involvement in the promotion of cultural and education, notably through taking on the role of mass education through its public schools—is only interested in "setting free the spiritual forces of a generation just so far as

---

[31] For the parallels between Nietzsche and Plato, see Thomas Brobjer, "Nietzsche's Wrestling with Plato and Platonism," in *Nietzsche and Antiquity: His Reaction and Response to the Classical Tradition*, ed. Paul Bishop (Rochester, NY: Camden House, 2004), 241–59; Lawrence Lampert, "Nietzsche and Plato," in *Nietzsche and Antiquity: His Reaction and Response to the Classical Tradition*, ed. Paul Bishop (Rochester, NY: Camden House, 2004), 205–19; Catherine Zucker, "Nietzsche's Rereading of Plato," *Political Theory* 13, no. 2 (1985): 213–38. While the relation between Nietzsche's and Plato's philosophies has been explored, the affinities between their respective political projects less so, as I can only gesture to briefly here.

[32] We can note Nietzsche's early—still under Wagner's influence—anti-Semitism in this passage, although he would later come to describe himself as "anti-anti-Semitic."

they may be of use to existing institutions," as Nietzsche outlines in *Scho-penhauer as Educator*. "However loudly the state may proclaim its services to cultures, it furthers culture in order to further itself" (SE 6). In much the same way as the financial recluses instrumentalize the state for their own personal enrichment, the modern state applies the same logic to culture and instrumentalizes it only in order to enhance itself. This must also be understood in the context of rising nationalism, where the state instrumentalized culture as a means of furthering its own national aggrandizement. The mission to produce new Platos, then, is replaced by a complex system of reward and coercion that ensures philosophy and philosophers remain subservient to the state. "Nothing stands so much in the way of the production and propagation of the great philosopher by nature as does the bad philosopher who works for the state," Nietzsche decries, concluding with the damning accusation that the epitaph of university philosophy will read "it disturbed nobody" (SE 8).[33]

If the Greek state was not to last, nor would the modern one. In an important aphorism in *Human, All Too Human*, titled "Religion and Government," he writes that "a later generation will also see the state shrink to insignificance on various parts of the earth." The reason for this is that "modern democracy is the historical form of the *decay of the state*" (HH 472).

As Nietzsche observes, "The interests of tutelary government and the interests of religion go hand in hand together, so that when the latter begins to die out the foundations of the state are also undermined." The "belief in a divine order in the realm of politics" is of "religious origin"—the Greek state had itself arisen through some form of "magic" (GSt, 168)—so if religion disappears, then "the state will unavoidably lose its ancient Isis veil and cease to excite reverence." This is what happens when a "quite-different conception of government," democracy, begins to prevail, such that government is no longer understood as an "above in relation to a below" but merely the "instrument of the popular will." The result is that in the democratic conception of government, religion must simply follow the desires of the people, be another one of its "organs," rather than the prerogative of the priestly class. As religion can no longer provide the support to the state that it once did, the previously reinforcing relationship between the government and priests also breaks down, to be replaced by nationalism and the instrumentalization of culture.[34] Given this, "the sovereignty of the

---

[33] Cf. TI Germans 4. In his 1872 lectures "The Future of Our Educational Institutions," from which much of this material is drawn, Nietzsche explains that in view of the fact that it describes the modern state as the end point of history, Hegelianism is the philosophy that the state appropriates for itself.

[34] On this point, see Frank Cameron and Don Dombowsky, eds., *Political Writings of Friedrich Nietzsche* (New York: Palgrave Macmillan, 2008).

people serves to banish the last remnant of magic and superstition" from the state (HH 472).

In this new cold light, the "individual will see only that side of [the state] that promises to be useful or threatens to be harmful to him"—the instrumentalization theme is here continued—and so will "bend all his efforts to acquiring influence on it." But this competition will quickly become too great, resulting in the fragmentation of the political community. "Men and parties" will alternate too quickly, hurling "one another too fiercely down from the hill after barely having attained the top." "No one will feel toward the law any greater obligation than that of bowing for the moment to the force that backs up the law," while one will set out at once to "subvert it with a new force, the creation of a new majority."

Nietzsche concludes by proclaiming "with certainty" that "distrust of all government" will result from the "uselessness and destructiveness of these short-winded struggles," and will "impel men to a quite-novel resolve: the resolve to do away with the concept of the state, to abolish the distinction between public and private." Instead, an "invention more suited to their purpose than the state was will gain victory over the state." "Private companies" (*Privatgesellschaften*) will "step by step absorb the business of the state," including those activities that are the "most resistant remainder of what was formerly the work of the government": protecting "the private person from the private person."

Nietzsche seems rather unperturbed by this future development, and putting it into a historical perspective, asks, "How many an organizing power has mankind not seen die out?" mentioning the "racial clan," which was far mightier than the "family," and even "ruled and regulated long before the family existed." In reality, Nietzsche seems quietly optimistic about these future prospects. For one, "the prudence and self-interests of men" are the qualities that are best developed by this process of attempting to control the state, such that "if the state is no longer equal to the demands of these forces, then the last thing that will ensue is chaos." Yet he is not so bold as to recommend actively working for the dissolution of the state; to do so would require having a "presumptuous idea of one's own intelligence and scarcely half an understanding of history." He instead recommends that we place our trust in the "prudence and self-interest of men" who can "preserve the existence of the state for some time yet," and successfully steer humanity toward a more suitable invention. But ultimately Nietzsche contends that once the historical mission of the democratic conception of the state is accomplished, "a new page will be turned in the storybook of humanity in which there will be many strange tales to read and perhaps some of them good ones."

Human, All Too Human belongs to Nietzsche's so-called middle or critical period—conventionally seen to stretch from *Human, All Too Human* to the fourth book of *The Gay Science*—where it is often asked whether Nietzsche is in fact expressing his own views, or whether he is adopting that of an impartial and experimental spectator.[35] While in certain contexts I am sympathetic to these claims, in terms of Nietzsche's views of the state there is good reason to believe that those he expresses during this period are genuinely his. The most telling is that he explicitly quotes this section from *Human, All Too Human* in *Twilight of the Idols*, one of his last texts: "In *Human, All Too Human* (I, 472), I already characterized modern democracy (together with its hybrid forms like the '*Reich*') as the *state's form of decline*" (TI Skirmishes 39). Moreover, he also noted down the concept a number of times in his unpublished fragments between 1883 and 1885.[36] For me, the repeated insistence on this notion on Nietzsche's behalf gives it an air of finality concerning his verdict on the modern state, and suggests in this context, much as it was with his views of the ancient state developed across "The Greek State" and *The Genealogy*, a strong continuity between his earlier and later views on the matter of the modern state and its decay.

BEYOND THE MODERN STATE

Basing herself on the *Human, All Too Human* passage just discussed, Tamsin Shaw has recently argued that the reason Nietzsche does not articulate a "positive, normative political theory" is because he is a political skeptic. For her, Nietzsche's "guiding political vision" is "oriented around the rise of the modern state, which requires normative consensus in order to rule, and a simultaneous process of secularization that seems to make uncoerced consensus impossible." In secular times, the increased diversity of viewpoints results in the impossibility of locating and recognizing normative authority. While the state has the "ideological capacity" to manufacture a normative consensus, notably through arrogating to itself the instruments of education and culture, as we saw above, this consensus cannot hold in the long run: the state cannot rule through direct coercion alone; it needs to be perceived as "legitimate." Nietzsche is thus a political skeptic, according to Shaw, because he cannot see how in the modern world we can "reconcile our need for normative authority with our need for political authority."[37]

Shaw is absolutely correct in stating that for Nietzsche, the modern state in a secularized world can no longer claim the normative authority that religion once afforded it, and consequently its political authority is under-

---

[35] Ruth Abbey, *Nietzsche's Middle Period* (Oxford: Oxford University Press, 2000).
[36] KSA 10 9 [29]; KSA 11 26 [434]; KSA 11 34 [146].
[37] Tamsin Shaw, *Nietzsche's Political Skepticism* (Princeton, NJ: Princeton University Press, 2010), 2–11.

mined. Nevertheless, the passage in question should not lead us to conclude that Nietzsche is a political skeptic in the sense that he cannot see how we can "reconcile our need for normative authority with our need for political authority." Simply put, Nietzsche does believe these two authorities can be married again, but that this will happen outside the modern state structure, which, as I have emphasized above, is in decline as well as in the process of being replaced by more "innovative" and better-suited institutions.

Shaw downplays this latter point, writing that "although Nietzsche speculates, in passing, about what a world without states would be like, he accepts that political agency in the modern world is concentrated in them," noting that "in HH 472 he speculates that in the absence of religion the state as a form of political organization might die out. He warns against any rash political experiments that would hasten this process."[38] Yet the decay of the state is not something that Nietzsche speculates about in passing; it is the essential point of the aphorism. With the rise of modern democracy, the state will inevitably decay. If Nietzsche recommends that we put our faith in "the prudence and self-interest of men" to "preserve the existence of the state from some time yet," this is to ensure that the process does not descend into chaos, and that the heightened senses of the prudential men that this evolution produces are fully able to create better-suited and more innovative institutions. He is in no way suggesting that the process of the dissolution of the state be halted, or that we return to a status quo ante, where the state was in league with the priestly class. Rather, he is looking forward to reading the "strange tales" that will appear in the "storybook of humanity" once the modern state has disappeared, hoping that there will be some "good ones" (HH 472).

There is no reason to believe that political agency must solely be located in the modern state, and Nietzsche does not hold such a view. He instead locates his political project in the transition away from the nation-state. Indeed, the decay of the state signals the superseding of the modern question of political philosophy as framed by Leiter: the theory of the state and its legitimacy. The new question for Nietzsche will revolve around determining which institutions can fulfill the Platonic mission of producing the new Platos that the culture-state failed to achieve.

It is in extrastate institutions that Nietzsche believes this mission can be accomplished and that a degree of normative authority can be reestablished within them. Signaling his move to a standpoint outside the modern state structure in *Schopenhauer as Educator*, Nietzsche proposes that a "higher tribunal" should be created outside the universities, devoid of official authority, and without salaries or honors, whose "function would be to supervise and judge these institutions in regard to the education they are promoting"

[38] Ibid., 5.

(SE 8). In this way, philosophy can regain its independence and would be able to ensure that philosophy is taught at the universities with its true aim restored: to produce philosophical geniuses.

For those of the "smaller band" who will follow this path to true culture, Nietzsche explains that the institution they require would have "quite a different purpose to fulfill." It would have to be a "firm organization" that prevents them from "being washed away and dispersed by the tremendous crowd," to "die from premature exhaustion or even become alienated from their great task." This is to enable the completion of their task—preparing "within themselves and around them for the birth of the genius and the ripening of his work"—through their "continual purification and mutual support," and their "sense of staying together" (SE 6). Nietzsche insists that "one thing above all is certain: these new duties are not the duties of a solitary; on the contrary, they set one in the midst of a mighty community held together, not by external forms and regulations, but by a fundamental idea. It is the fundamental idea of *culture*" (SE 5). His insistence on the community—as opposed to the individual—in carrying out the mission of culture seriously challenges the view put forward by Kaufmann, Leiter, and Williams, among others, that Nietzsche's writings are destined solely for the solitary thinker cut off from the rest of the world.

This new institution that will defend culture is the intellectual counterpart to the private companies that will slowly start taking over the role of the state. Here we see Nietzsche adapting his continued goal of producing genius and high culture—new Platos—to his analysis of the decline of the modern state, thereby demonstrating his grasp contra Leiter of the sociopolitical context of the time and ability to draw out the consequences of this understanding for his cultural ideal. It is to this group that Nietzsche will ascribe the "expert normative authority" that Shaw doubts can appear. The question of how to combine expert normative authority with political authority remains unresolved for now, but I will argue in chapter 6 that the best way to think about this is through Nietzsche's reconceptualization of the notion of great politics, particularly his call in his last writings and notes for the foundation of a party of life, which will fight a war of spirits against its opposing party of Christianity to establish a sufficient space within a democratic society for those who are called to this path of culture to pursue their mission.

In this chapter, I have endeavored to bring to the fore what to my mind is the underexplored influence Wagner had on Nietzsche's political thinking, and that issue arises again here. While previously I underlined how Nietzsche diverged from Wagner's account of slavery in ancient Greece, the impact that Wagner's own account of the decay of the modern state had on Nietzsche's thinking on the matter is patent. Returning to *The Artwork of the Future*, one of Wagner's earlier writings and thus permeated by his then more anarchistic leanings, Wagner had opposed the modern state, which he saw as a "most unnatural unions of fellow men," called into existence by mere "external caprice, e.g., dynastic interests" that yoked together a certain number of men "*once and for all*." Against this, he proposed a vision of a more fluid society in which people would come together in "special unions" to carry out certain projects—unions to be disbanded once the task was completed. These unions will "ever shape themselves anew, proclaim more complex and vivacious change, the more do they proceed from higher, universal, spiritual needs." The only lasting union that Wagner envisages is of the "material sort"—rooted in the "common ground and soil"—that arise to satisfy the needs that all men have in common, the sum total of which represents "the great association of *all* Mankind." The driving force behind these special unions for Wagner is the "*Volkish Want*."[39]

In his "Religion and Government" passage from *Human, All Too Human*, Nietzsche, also rejecting the modern state, transforms this *Volkish Want* into a democratic will, which sounds the death knell of the modern state, and Wagner's notion of special unions, grounded in both material and spiritual needs, is recast as the private companies that will take over the work of the state. Perhaps of most interest is that Wagner gives an image of how the cultural version of his special unions are to be organized, and from this we can infer how Nietzsche's own spiritual new institutions might work. The key is understanding the relationship that the *Darsteller* entertains with the "fellowship of all the artists" (note again the communal aspect of the enterprise): all the "lonely one" can do is "prefigure [the artwork of the future] to himself," but it will remain an "idle fancy" if it is not brought to life by the fellowship, the only entity able to do so through a common striving.[40] Once the *Darsteller* is invested with an idea, he raises himself to the position of poet, or the "artistic legislator," by convincing the other free members of the fellowship of his idea and thereby takes on its "dictatorship" until the completion of the project. Wagner emphasizes that once the project is completed, the poet-dictator—a position open to anyone in the congregation—must return to the fold of the fellowship: the function of the lawgiver is always "*periodic*," and his rule can never be extended to "*all* occasions."[41]

CONCLUSION

Wagner allows us to put into place the final piece of the jigsaw that is Nietzsche's theory of the birth and decay of the state. I think the correct way of

[39] Wagner, "The Artwork of the Future," 203–10.
[40] Ibid., 88.
[41] Ibid., 201–2.

conceptualizing this transition is not to see it as the death of the state tout court but rather as going through a number of different transformations—or revaluations, to use a more Nietzschean term—from ancient state where its role was to serve as a means to culture, to the modern nation-state that appropriated culture for its own sake, to finally a much more decentralized, minimalist, regulatory, postnational one. The key here is to keep in mind that Nietzsche differentiates the state from that which he calls the business of the state—that is, the work of government, which for him includes "protecting the private person from the private person," which private contractors will take up.[42] This new entity will retain a relationship to the coercion that gave birth to it, although certainly in a less direct, more regulatory way. With Wagner, we can also see that it will have a European or indeed worldwide scope—"the great association of *all* Mankind," which chimes well with Nietzsche's notion of the good European and his rejection of the *nationalist* modern state (BGE 254)—but it will still be rooted in the need for material cooperation, allowing for a freer play of different institutions within this framework. In sum, Nietzsche's postmodern state will take the form of a European-wide decentralized and regulatory state, within which different institutions will be allowed freer rein to pursue their respective activities, some—the private companies, probably the vast majority—for private gain within a broader economic and material framework, while others—the new institutions, a select few—their cultural goals.[43]

Nietzsche was not the only one to prophesize the state's decay in the second half of the nineteenth century. But the originality of his theory is twofold. First, his idea of the decay of the state is linked to his later, more infamous statement about the death of God (GS 125): once the religious foundation of the state was called into question, the state can no longer support itself, and this will lead to its inevitable dissolution. Here we see Nietzsche relating his philosophical insights to an account of modern society. Second, Nietzsche sees democracy, or the democratic will, as the catalyst for the fragmentation and final disintegration of the state. Thus, in contrast to Marxism where democracy is the result of the proletariat overthrow of the state, in Nietzsche's account democracy is the cause of the state's "withering away."[44] That being said, we might draw an analogy between the idea of a permanent material union and the notion of the "administration

[42] Needless to say, the contrast here with Weber is intriguing.

[43] On this European dimension, see Stefan Elbe, *Europe: A Nietzschean Perspective* (London: Routledge, 2003); Daniel Conway, "Whither the 'Good Europeans'? Nietzsche's New World Order," *South Central Review* 26, no. 3 (2009): 40–60.

[44] For Nietzsche's (lack of) knowledge of Marx, see Thomas Brobjer, "Nietzsche's Knowledge of Marx and Marxism," *Nietzsche-Studien* 31 (2002): 298–313. Nietzsche's knowledge of socialist thought was often mediated through Wagner.

of things," although in Nietzsche's case this union is not as democratic as the Marxists would have wanted, as I will now turn to.[45] Nor would Nietzsche have had any sympathy with Herbert Spencer's Social Darwinist theory of the collapse of the state into political economy through a gradual self-disciplining of society, as elaborated in *Social Statics*, which he saw as the victory of the herd.[46]

In Nietzsche's postmodern state, future political hierarchy will still be a fact of life, much as it was in the Greek state and his perfect Platonic state—both in the internal structuring of the new institutions, as we saw with the poet-dictator, and the relationship that these institutions entertain with the outside world, which will demand a transfer of resources to them so that they may fulfill their cultural mission, much in the same way that the slaves provided for the Olympian men in "The Greek State," although on a new basis.[47] Indeed, for Nietzsche hierarchy is a fundamental and inescapable aspect of society. In *Beyond Good and Evil* (1886) he writes that "as long as there have been people, there have been herds of people as well, and a very large number of people who obey comparatively few who command." He continues: "So considering the fact that humanity has been the best and most long-standing breeding ground for the cultivation of obedience so far, it is reasonable to suppose that the average person has an innate need to obey as a type of *formal conscience* that commands" (BGE 199). Zarathustra (1885) echoes this sentiment: "Wherever I found the living, there too I heard the speech of obedience. All living is obeying. And this is the second thing that I heard: the one who cannot obey himself is commanded. Such is the nature of the living" (Z II Self-Overcoming).

While the modern state may have lost its legitimacy, it is through this more ancient idea of an enduring instinct of commanding and obeying that Nietzsche desires to see authority restored. First, the intellectual authority in the new institutions he proposes must be restored. Then these institutions, metamorphosed into the party of life, must secure political authority through the same means of commanding and obeying as well as through fighting a war of spirits against its opposing party of Christianity (EH Destiny 1). The future, according to Nietzsche, lies with those bold enough to

---

[45] I am aware that in its original Saint-Simonian formulation, it is not democratic either.

[46] See J. W. Burrow, *The Crisis of Reason: European Thought, 1848–1914* (New Haven, CT: Yale University Press, 2000), 73–77. On Nietzsche's knowledge of Darwinism, see John Richardson, *Nietzsche's New Darwinism* (Oxford: Oxford University Press, 2008). TI Skirmishes 14, "Anti-Darwin": "Assuming . . . that there is such a struggle for existence . . . its result is unfortunately the opposite of what Darwin's school desires. . . . The species do *not* grow in perfection: the weak prevail over the strong again and again, for they are the great majority."

[47] In modern parlance we might think of this as something like an independent arts council that is allocated its resources through some form of state taxation.

attempt to command peoples again as they were in the past, and as they have always been. "Who can command, who must obey—*here it is tried*!" Zarathustra proclaims. "Human society: it is an experiment, this I teach—a long search: but it searches for the commander!—an experiment, oh my brothers! And *not* a 'contract!'" (Z III Tables).[48] If for Nietzsche the state did not arise through a contract, neither will his postmodern state ideal.

---

[48] See also GM II 17: "He who can command, who is naturally a 'master[,]' . . . what has he to do with contracts!"

CHAPTER 3

DEMOCRACY

A common refrain in the contemporary scholarship is that during his so-called middle period, commonly understood as spanning both books of *Human, All Too Human* (1878–80), *Daybreak* (1881), and the first four books of *The Gay Science* (1882), Nietzsche demonstrates a favorable disposition toward democracy.[1] Writers such as William Connolly, Owen, Paul Patton, and Schrift offer up *The Wanderer and His Shadow* 293 (1880), titled "Ends and Means of Democracy," as typifying Nietzsche's allegedly prodemocratic sentiment.[2] There, Nietzsche explains that "democracy wants to create and guarantee as much *independence* as possible: independence of opinion, of mode of life, and of employment." So far, one might be tempted to say, so good from a democratic point of view, although Nietzsche has yet to give reasons for desiring such independence in the first place. This is consistent with the view that in his middle period, Nietzsche demonstrates a more "neutral" or "scientific" approach, adopting democracy's own point of view ("to that end") and trying to think through its logical consequences. But he has yet to endorse it.

---

[1] On Nietzsche's middle period, and how it differs from his earlier and later periods in this vein, see Ruth Abbey, *Nietzsche's Middle Period* (Oxford: Oxford University Press, 2000); Paul Franco, *Nietzsche's Enlightenment: The Free-Spirit Trilogy of the Middle Period* (Chicago: University of Chicago Press, 2011). Not everyone agrees with this periodization. Leiter, for instance, claims that Nietzsche's mature work starts with *Daybreak*; see his *Nietzsche on Morality* (London: Routledge, 2003), 26.

[2] See William Connolly, "Nietzsche, Democracy, Time," in *Nietzsche, Power, and Politics: Rethinking Nietzsche's Legacy for Political Thought*, ed. Herman Siemens and Vasti Roodt (Berlin: De Gruyter, 2008), 118; David Owen, "Nietzsche, Ethical Agency, and the Problem of Democracy," in *Nietzsche, Power, and Politics: Rethinking Nietzsche's Legacy for Political Thought*, ed. Herman Siemens and Vasti Roodt (Berlin: De Gruyter, 2008), 159. See also Alan Schrift, "Nietzsche's Contest: Nietzsche and the Culture Wars," in *Why Nietzsche Still? Reflections on Drama, Culture, and Politics*, ed. Alan Schrift (Berkeley: University of California Press, 2000), 195–97; Paul Patton, "Nietzsche, Genealogy, and Justice," in *Nietzsche and Political Thought*, ed. Keith Ansell-Pearson (London: Bloomsbury, 2013), 16.

The discussion surrounding *The Wanderer and His Shadow* 293 takes place within a broader debate about the role that Nietzsche is to play in contemporary democratic theory. A number of different thinkers, such as Bonnie Honig, Wendy Brown, Dana Villa, Connolly, and Warren, among others, along with more specifically Nietzsche scholars such as Lawrence Hatab, Schrift, and Owen, have seized on Nietzsche's alleged decentering of the human being as a means of revitalizing (American) democracy on a radicalized, postmodern basis, moving away from a conception of democracy too stuck, in their minds, in a religious and naturalistic vision of man now considered obsolete.[3] Much of this literature has been articulated through the theme of agonistic democracy, and finds as its springboard Nietzsche's writings on the agon in his early, unpublished essay "Homer's Contest" (1872).[4] In this account, Nietzsche is often paired with Weber, Carl Schmitt, and Arendt, among others—with the latter offered as the whiggish democratic end point of a story to which the others frequently do not seem to immediately fit.[5] For this group, many different ways in which Nietzsche's thinking could be made congenial to democracy have been suggested, including Connolly's idea of "agonistic respect," Owen's concept of "agonistic deliberation," with a view to "ennobling democracy," Hatab's "adversarial system," or even Arendt's "robust public sphere," which has also been linked to Nietzsche's idea of the agon.[6]

Against this view other authors, such as Detwiler, Peter Berkowitz, Peter Bergmann, Fredrick Appel, and Dombowsky, have emphasized Nietzsche's aristocratic leanings.[7] It is important to note here that as most scholars—I

[3] See variously Bonnie Honig, *Political Theory and the Displacement of Politics* (Ithaca, NY: Cornell University Press, 1993); William Connolly, *Identity/Difference* (Ithaca, NY: Cornell University Press, 1991); Mark Warren, *Nietzsche and Political Thought* (Cambridge, MA: MIT Press, 1991); Lawrence Hatab, *A Nietzschean Defense of Democracy: An Experiment in Postmodern Politics* (Chicago: Open Court, 1995); Alan Schrift, ed., *Why Nietzsche Still? Reflections on Drama, Culture, and Politics* (Berkeley: University of California Press, 2000); David Owen, *Nietzsche, Politics, and Modernity* (London: Sage, 1995).

[4] Owen and Herman Siemens have argued that the agonistic theme is pervasive in Nietzsche's later work. See David Owen, "Nietzsche's Freedom: The Art of Agonic Perfectionism," in *Nietzsche and Political Thought*, ed. Keith Ansell-Pearson (London: Bloomsbury, 2013).

[5] For an example of this view, see Tracy Strong, *Politics without Vision: Thinking without a Banister in the Twentieth Century* (Chicago: University of Chicago Press, 2012).

[6] For articles from the authors mentioned here, see Herman Siemens and Vasti Roodt, eds., *Nietzsche, Power, and Politics: Rethinking Nietzsche's Legacy for Political Thought*, ed. Herman Siemens and Vasti Roodt (Berlin: De Gruyter, 2008).

[7] Bruce Detwiler, *Nietzsche and the Politics of Aristocratic Radicalism* (Chicago: University of Chicago Press, 1990); Peter Berkowitz, *Nietzsche: The Ethics of an Immoralist* (Cambridge, MA: Harvard University Press, 1995); Peter Bergmann, *Nietzsche: "The Last Antipolitical German"* (Bloomington: Indiana University Press, 1987); Fredrick Appel, *Nietzsche contra Democracy* (Ithaca, NY: Cornell University Press, 1999); Don Dombowsky, *Nietzsche's Machiavellian Politics* (Basingstoke, UK: Palgrave Macmillan, 2004).

think Hatab is alone in claiming that Nietzsche *should* have been a democrat—agree on the fundamentally aristocratic—that is, hierarchical or slave-based—nature of Nietzsche's political thought, the question was always going to be whether Nietzsche's political thinking *could* be used for democratic purposes, or at least in what manner.[8] Rejecting the former group's approach, this latter group has been more interested in portraying Nietzsche as the arch antidemocrat of our times, whose sole role is to serve as the main argumentative opponent against which budding democratic theorists need confront their ideas. The telltale sign of this approach is in the presentation of Nietzsche as an Emersonian "provocateur," or again the attempt to link him to more liberal thinkers such as John Stuart Mill and sometimes Alexis de Tocqueville (in France, Nietzsche is often depicted as *"un Tocquevillien enragé"*).[9] The aim here is to isolate Nietzsche's critique of democracy from his other, more positive pronouncements about what should be done about democracy—pronouncements that will be the subject of this chapter. In this account, Nietzsche's critique of democracy as herd morality is equated to Mill or Tocqueville's "tyranny of the majority."

Both schools of interpretation are thus guilty of wanting to "domesticate" Nietzsche.[10] The agonists, by simply picking and choosing elements of Nietzsche's thought that fit their project without seriously engaging with his fundamentally aristocratic thinking, have transformed Nietzsche into an unlikely cheerleader for their cause.[11] On the other hand, the antidemocrats, by corralling Nietzsche's critique of democracy from his broader vision, have made Nietzsche "safe for liberal democracy" by lining him up with less threatening liberal critiques of democracy such as Mill and Tocqueville that have already been tamed by contemporary democratic theory. By this is meant that while Mill and Tocqueville are thought to have offered a more

[8] Here I follow Tracy Strong, "In Defense of Rhetoric: Or How Hard It Is to Take a Writer Seriously: The Case of Nietzsche," *Political Theory* 41, no. 4 (2013), 507–32. Strong argues that Nietzsche's use of rhetoric gives his readers the impression that he is writing *for them*, which can help explain why he appears to be appropriated by so many diverging causes. Strong's point is that a close reading of Nietzsche's texts forces us to develop a self-critique of ourselves, which I will return to in conclusion of this chapter.

[9] This is prominent in Appel, *Nietzsche contra Democracy*, 8; Detwiler, *Nietzsche and the Politics of Aristocratic Radicalism*, 8; Warren, *Nietzsche and Political Thought*, 221; Owen, "Nietzsche's Freedom," 80. Ansell-Pearson also approaches Nietzsche in this way; see the epigram from Ralph Waldo Emerson in Keith Ansell-Pearson, *An Introduction to Nietzsche as Political Thinker* (Cambridge: Cambridge University Press, 1994). See also Alan Kahan, *Aristocratic Liberalism: The Social and Political Thought of Jacob Burckhardt, John Stuart Mill, and Alexis de Tocqueville* (New Brunswick, NJ: Transaction Publishers, 2001).

[10] See Ruth Abbey and Fredrick Appel, "Domesticating Nietzsche: A Response to Mark Warren," *Political Theory* 27, no. 1 (February 1999): 121–25.

[11] Quentin Skinner nicely calls this "playing tricks on the dead"; see his "Meaning and Understanding in the History of Ideas," in *Visions of Politics, Volume I: Regarding Method* (Cambridge: Cambridge University Press, 2002), 65.

"internal" critique of democracy that aimed at ameliorating democratic politics within its own structure, Nietzsche might best be understood as supplying an "external" critique of democracy that had no particular truck in the preservation of democracy at all. Indeed, if in Nietzsche's description of the irresistible democratization of Europe in *The Wanderer and His Shadow* above we hear an echo of Tocqueville's "providential fact" of democracy, the latter's aim was to reconcile what he took to be the virtues of the aristocratic system within a democratic context, whereas for Nietzsche the relation that the two entertain with one another was thought of in a much more external manner, as I will explore. So Nietzsche must not solely be understood as a critique of democracy, as this line of interpretation suggests, but his theories of the future development of democracy must also be taken seriously.

In many ways, then, this debate represents two sides of the same coin. Both groups of thinkers take democracy as we now understand it as their starting point and then try to figure out what Nietzsche has to say to it, either positively in that Nietzsche offers stimulating resources with which to think through a refounding of democratic legitimacy, or negatively, as someone who provides the sharpest critique of democracy that democratic theorists must endeavor to refute. The aim of this chapter is to move away from this dichotomy with the goal not of refuting it; instead, it wishes to ask first and foremost what Nietzsche himself understood by democracy *during his time*, and from that point try to think about how his perspective can help us better conceptualize our understanding of democracy today. I thus posit two moments of interpretative work—first historical and then contemporary—as opposed to immediately asking for Nietzsche's contemporary relevance. This cuts to the heart of the methodological disagreement that I have with much of the secondary literature on Nietzsche in general and this debate in particular: that instead of coming to Nietzsche with predetermined categories to commit an anachronism, we must *start* with the historical Nietzsche, to see how he thought about the topic at hand and what he had to say about it, before drawing conclusions (if any) about how it relates to our own world over a century later.[12]

My goal is twofold. On the one hand, it is to show that a more detailed engagement with Nietzsche's writings on democracy can allow us to overcome the opposition between the so-called gentle (proto-democratic) and bloody (the politics of domination) Nietzsche, so as to better see the role that both democracy and aristocracy play in his vision of the European future.[13] To do so, this chapter will pay special attention to the political,

[12] I should say that in this I insert myself more in the line of Bergmann's *Nietzsche*, which is sensitive to and enlightening about Nietzsche's historical context.

[13] See Warren, *Nietzsche and Political Thought*, 224. For the original discussion set in these terms, see also Crane Brinton, *Nietzsche* (Cambridge, MA: Harvard University Press, 1948).

intellectual, and cultural contexts within which Nietzsche's thought evolved—namely, Bismarck's relationship to the new German Reichstag, the philological discovery of an original Aryan race, and Nietzsche's encounter with Gobineau's racist thought through his frequentation of the Wagner circle. It will reveal Nietzsche to be a particularly astute guide to understanding the politics of his time. On the other hand, I wish to argue that what should be Nietzsche's most lasting contribution to democratic thinking is not to be found in the different ways he may or may not be used to buttress certain contemporary ideological positions; rather, it is illustrated in how his notions of herd morality, misarchism, and the genealogical method, alongside his critique of majoritarianism, provide us with the conceptual tools to better understand the political world we inhabit today. I do not mean to suggest that mining Nietzsche for thinking about contemporary democratic politics might not yield stimulating results—quite the contrary—or that the hierarchical nature of Nietzsche's thought is not something that needs to be reemphasized, which is something I wish to do too. Mine is not, as such, a purely critical enterprise. But I do want to argue that the richest legacy Nietzsche provides us with in thinking about democracy is precisely those intellectual tools he fashioned for himself to understand democracy as he experienced it. These tools are as needful today as ever.

DEMOCRACY IN THE *KAISERREICH*

Nietzsche's political coming-of-age coincided with the birth of the German Empire, the Kaiserreich. His productive life spanned the gradual democratization of Germany, in which he retained a close, if critical, interest. Notwithstanding his "untimely" pose, Nietzsche kept much abreast of politics, admitting in his older age that he was an avid reader of the *Journal des débats*, which reported on French parliamentary politics, along with the *Journal de Goncourt* and *Revue des deux Mondes*.[14] For three years Nietzsche would have participated directly in a democratic election. In 1867, the first free elections were organized in northern Germany, but the age threshold had been set at twenty-five; Nietzsche was then twenty-two. There is every reason to believe, however, that if he could have voted he would have done so, and he followed the elections closely with his friends.[15]

---

[14] See letter to Jean Bourdeau, December 17, 1888, KSB 8; letter to Heinrich Koeselitz, December 30, 1888, KSB 8.

[15] Thomas Brobjer, "Critical Aspects of Nietzsche's Relation to Politics and Democracy," in *Nietzsche, Power, and Politics: Rethinking Nietzsche's Legacy for Political Thought*, ed. Herman Siemens and Vasti Roodt (Berlin: De Gruyter, 2008), 214–15. See also, more generally, Bergmann, *Nietzsche*.

The next general election was held after unification, on March 3, 1871, but by that time Nietzsche was already in Basel and had renounced his German citizenship. There he became acquainted with Swiss democracy. Although he commended it for its tolerance, he was ultimately critical.[16] Burckhardt had entered his intellectual orbit by this time too, and Burckhardt, who had experienced firsthand revolutionary movements, served as a reactionary influence on Nietzsche's view of democracy. In fact, in September 1869, four months after Nietzsche had given his inaugural lecture, the First International held its Fourth Congress in Basel. One of its attendees was Mikhail Bakunin.[17]

The view that Nietzsche had no experience of democracy, and that if he had such experience, he would have been much more sympathetic to it, thus must be accepted with considerable reserve.[18] It is certainly the case that nineteenth-century German democracy looked quite different from democracy as we know it today, but returned to its historical context, the German suffrage was actually one of the most extensive of its time. Margaret Anderson, a leading scholar of this period, describes Germany during this epoch as a "suffrage regime."[19] So Nietzsche did have an experience of certain democratic practices—and indeed perhaps one of the fullest that one could have had at the time—yet that experience is somewhat removed from what we would know today. But being present "at the birth" of the rise of democracy in Germany, Nietzsche is a privileged witness to the general "transition to democracy" that was taking place in Europe in the latter part of the nineteenth century. Given this, his commentary is especially valuable since he was alive to the historical context of such a development. Moreover, the world he inhabited contained a much larger diversity of political systems, allowing him to compare and contrast lived experiences; we can think of his travels to Switzerland, Italy, and France. Finally, he did not suffer from "hindsight bias" in the sense that there was no predetermined path to democracy, meaning that his political horizon remained clear.

Nietzsche appears to have an acute grasp of what democracy in his time amounted to (or not). In *The Wanderer and His Shadow* 293—to return to the opening aphorism and period I identified as Nietzsche's first sustained engagement with the topic—Nietzsche concludes the passage in question with

[16] Letter to Erwin Rohde, November 20–21, 1872, KSB 4. "One can be cured of republicanism here" (letter to Sophie Ritschl, May 10, 1869, KSB 7).

[17] Martin Ruehl, "*Politeia* 1871: Young Nietzsche on the Greek State," in *Nietzsche and Antiquity: His Reaction and Response to the Classical Tradition*, ed. Paul Bishop (Rochester, NY: Camden House, 2004), 79–97.

[18] See Brobjer, "Critical Aspects." See also, more broadly, Hatab, *A Nietzschean Defense of Democracy.*

[19] Margaret Anderson, *Practicing Democracy: Elections and Political Culture in Imperial Germany* (Princeton, NJ: Princeton University Press, 2000), 13.

the line: "That which now calls itself democracy differs from the older forms of government solely in that it drives with *new horses*: the streets are still the same old streets, and the wheels likewise the same old wheels." The implication is that while there is a new political institution—the Reichstag (the new horses)—politics has changed little in the new Reich; Bismarck and the Junkers still rule (the same old wheels of power) behind the parliamentary facade, and continue to implement their nationalist realpolitik (the same old [policy] streets). "Have things really got less perilous because the well-being of nations now ride in *this* vehicle?" Nietzsche rhetorically asks, questioning the purported superiority and pacific nature of the new regime.[20]

Nietzsche also was able to develop criticisms of democracy in his time that were to become staple critiques of modern democratic regimes. He was, for one, quite alive to the dangers of majoritarian rule. In "The Right of Universal Suffrage," he explains that "a law that decrees that the majority shall have the decisive voice in determining the well-being of all cannot be erected on a foundation that is first provided by that law itself" (WS 276). To secure its foundation, it requires in the first place the unanimous consent of all: "Universal suffrage may not be an expression of the will merely of the majority; the whole country must desire it." This it fails to achieve: "As hardly two-thirds of those entitled to vote, perhaps indeed not even a majority of them, come to the ballot box, this is a vote *against* the entire suffrage system." Democracy never founds itself, and continual nonparticipation implies a rejection of the regime as a whole: "*nonparticipation* in an election constitutes precisely such an objection and thus brings about the downfall of the entire voting system." As a significant minority does not participate in voting, then the system never succeeds in marshaling the foundation it needs, thereby simply becoming the unassented and undemocratic rule of a majority.[21]

Earlier in "Permission to Speak!" in *Human, All Too Human* (1878), Nietzsche had argued for minorities' right of secession. Accommodating himself—continuing in the "realist" mode of his middle period—to democracy as one "accommodates oneself when an earthquake has displaced the former boundaries and contours of the ground and altered the value of one's

[20] We might note that the extension of the suffrage in Germany was Bismarck's way of extending his control and power. During the Schleswig-Holstein crisis, he threatened the Austrians with being forced to extend the suffrage if they did not give in, and after they did, nonetheless extended the suffrage. I thank Tracy Strong for this observation.

[21] While he toys with the idea of the "absolute veto" of the individual, Nietzsche is not facetious, and so as to not "trivialize" the problem, concludes that "the veto of a few thousand hangs over this system as a requirement of justice." This takes on its full importance when we consider that Nietzsche sees the Renaissance, a movement that he would like to rekindle, as being "raised on the shoulders of just a band of a hundred men" (HL 2, 10).

property," Nietzsche accepts that if the majority want to rule themselves with their "five or six ideas" through "self-determination," then so be it; but on the same account, those few who do not want "all of politics" to be understood in this way should be able to "step a little aside" (HH 438). Taken together with his exposure of democracy's failing to ground itself through the consent of all, Nietzsche here pinpoints one of the major criticisms of the ideal of popular sovereignty—its application to minorities, who are either subsumed within a larger majority that may deny their interests and values (as above), or else must be allowed, on the same basis of self-determination, to constitute smaller sovereign communities of their own.[22]

DEMOCRACY AND ARISTOCRACY

In *The Wanderer and His Shadow* 293, to return to the aphorism with which I opened, Nietzsche explains—and alarmingly so for those who want to see in him a positive disposition toward democracy—that the logic of democratic independence dictates that "it needs to deprive of the right to vote both those who possess no property and the genuinely rich . . . since they continually call its task into question." Congruently, "it must prevent everything that seems to have for its objective the organization of parties. For the three great enemies of independence in the above-names threefold sense are the indigent, the rich, and the parties." The poor are dependent on others, and therefore likely to be swayed; the rich are simply too powerful; and political parties stifle independent thought in the name of the party line. Although Nietzsche qualifies such statements with the claim that he is speaking of democracy as "something yet to come"—which might play into the hands of the postmodern democratic agenda—this is a rather inauspicious start for a modern understanding of democracy premised on universal political equality and mediated through political parties.

What the authors who interest themselves in this passage are right to highlight is that this period represents one of Nietzsche's first attempt to theoretically grapple with the rising tide of democracy in Europe. Yet it is not clear that this analysis issues in a defense of democracy instead of its critique. Indeed, in the aphorism with which he opens his reflections on democracy in *The Wanderer and His Shadow*, "The Age of Cyclopean Building," Nietzsche ultimately conceives of it as a means to a new form of aristocracy: "The democratization of Europe is a link in the chain of those tre-

---

[22] While I think Nietzsche has his "cultural few" in mind more than anyone else in particular, we might remind ourselves here of the context of the Kulturkampf against the German Catholics, whom now cut off from Austria, had become a permanent minority in the new Reich, thereby giving a certain texture to his thoughts.

mendous *prophylactic measures*[,] . . . only now is it the age of cyclopean building!" (WS 275). Continuing to adopt his more neutral standpoint, Nietzsche in this passage also shows his realism, explaining that "the democratization of Europe is irresistible: for whoever tries to halt it has to employ in that endeavor precisely the means that the democratic idea first placed in everyone's hands." The means in question here are those Nietzsche associated with the aims of democracy that he identified in the section above: independence. In Nietzsche's eyes, the logic of democracy in creating and guaranteeing as much independence as possible is in the end to provide—involuntarily so—the foundations on which a new aristocracy will come about. Furthermore, the only way to oppose this democratization is to create barriers to remain independent from it—barriers that democracy is precisely creating in the first place—hence speeding up the process even more.

Nietzsche expresses anxiety about those who engage in this democratic work of building protective stone dams and walls; they appear "a little purblind and stupid," there is something "desolate and monotonous in their faces, and gray dust seems to have got even into their brain." But posterity will judge them kindly, since it is thanks to their efforts in building the stone dams and protective walls that guarantee independence that the "orchards of culture" will no longer be destroyed overnight by the "wild senseless mountain torrents" of "barbarians" and "plagues." It is they who lay the foundations for the new 'highest artist in horticulture, who can only apply himself to his real task when the other is fully accomplished!'. Because of the time that lies between means and end, those who build the walls and trellises think they themselves are the ends, but that is because "no one yet sees the gardener or the fruit trees *for whose sake* the fence exists."

The vision of democracy that Nietzsche provides in *The Wanderer and His Shadow*—one in which democracy supplies the building blocks for the appearance of a new aristocracy, the "highest artist in horticulture," of the future—is strikingly similar to that found in *Beyond Good and Evil* 242, where Nietzsche observes that what he is "trying to say is: the democratization of Europe is at the same time an involuntary exercise in the breeding of *tyrants*—understanding that word in every sense, including the most spiritual" While the logic of these passages is different—although complementary, as I will argue—the conclusion that Nietzsche draws from his study of democracy in both these periods is remarkably congruent: it is a stepping-stone toward a new form of aristocracy. This puts pressure on the idea of the exceptional nature of Nietzsche's middle period, which would render it more pliable to a positive democratic reading, and consequently, on the notion that there are no strong continuities in Nietzsche's political reflection, in this instance, when it comes to democracy.

MISARCHISM, CHRISTIANITY, AND HERD MORALITY

Beyond Good and Evil (1886), along with its "annex" *The Genealogy of Morality* (1887) and book 5 of *The Gay Science* (1887), also penned around this time, represents Nietzsche's second major moment of grappling with democracy after *The Wanderer and His Shadow*, with which it entertains strong links, as we saw above. During this period, Nietzsche makes three of his most famous claims about democracy: the "democratic movement is the heir to Christianity," which is itself linked to herd morality (BGE 202); it is a form of misarchism, the democratic mind-set that is opposed to all forms of authority (GM II 12); and it represents a form of political and physiological degeneration (BGE 203). I now turn to these three assertions.

In *Beyond Good and Evil*, Nietzsche declares that *"morality in Europe these days is herd morality"* (BGE 202). Later in the text Nietzsche will explain that there are two types of morality, a master and slave morality, corresponding to a view of the world as either differentiated by "good and bad" or "good and evil," respectively, which he will go on to explore in a more systematic manner in the first essay of *The Genealogy*. There he notes that it is slave morality, through a revaluation of all values, which has come to rule over Europe. It is Christianity that brings herd morality into politics: "This morality is increasingly apparent in even political and social institutions: the *democratic* movement is the heir to Christianity" (BGE 202).

The problem is not herd morality as such but rather its belief that it is the *only* morality possible, and that this morality should be imposed on everyone else. Yet herd morality "stubbornly and ruthlessly declares 'I am morality itself and nothing else is moral!' "[23] In the preface to *Beyond Good and Evil*, Nietzsche describes dogmatism as one of the "worst, most prolonged, and most dangerous of errors" that philosophy has ever made (BGE P). This is evident in herd morality's dogmatic claim that it is the only morality possible, and thus its view should be imposed on the rest of the population. More specifically, Nietzsche associates this dogmatism with Plato's the good in itself, but unlike modern herd morality, Plato only believed these pure forms were accessible to an initiated few. What makes modern Europeans believe they now know the answer to Socrates's question of what good and evil is, is Christianity (BGE 202), which democratizes Plato's teaching: "Christianity is Platonism for the 'people' " (BGE P).

Against this, Nietzsche writes that "as we understand things," herd morality is "only one type of human morality beside which, before which, and

---

[23] On herd morality's universalizing claims, see also Raymond Geuss, "Nietzsche and Morality," in *Morality, Culture, and History: Essays on German Philosophy* (Cambridge: Cambridge University Press, 1999), 167–97.

after which many other (and especially *higher*) moralities are or should be possible" (BGE 202). But herd morality fights "tooth and nail" against such a "possibility." Indeed, already in *Human, All Too Human* Nietzsche had explained that he had nothing to object to those of the herd, with their "five or six ideas," who want to "forge for themselves their own fortunes and misfortunes," although he warns that they should be prepared to bear the "calamitous consequences of their own narrow-mindedness" (HH 438). The problem is that believing they and only they are and can be right, they desire to impose their ideas about ruling on everyone else, whereas Nietzsche demands that those who do not share these ideals be allowed to "step a little aside."[24] So Nietzsche wants a space within which those who desire to pursue their cultural calling can do so according to the morality that befits such a situation, which herd morality, in claiming it is the only type of morality possible, violently opposes.[25]

In *The Genealogy*, Nietzsche uses misarchism to describe democracy, to "coin a bad word for a bad thing," as he puts it (GM II 12). Misarchism is the "democratic idiosyncrasy of being against everything that dominates and wants to dominate."[26] The democratic mind-set is thus against all types of authority. This relates back to how herd morality came to power in the first place—the "slave revolt in morality" (GM II 7)—through opposing the institutions of master morality. "Slave morality from the start says No to what is 'outside,' 'other,' 'a nonself'" (GM I 10).

There is a strong link here to the question of independence that Nietzsche identified as one of the hallmarks of democracy in *Human, All Too Human*, which aimed to promote "independence of opinion, mode of life, and employment." In terms of misarchism, it is the democratic mind-set of refusing any type of intellectual authority that is most prominent, and consequently a desire to be able to form one's own opinion. But the element of independence of mode of life and employment also comes to the fore. In the past men felt predestined to their line of work, and this led to the establishment of the "broad-based social pyramids" that are medieval "estates, guilds, and inherited trade privileges." In democratic societies, however, where people have unlearned this faith, "the individual is convinced he can do just about anything *and is up to playing any role*" (GS 356). This means that anyone feels they can exercise certain professions—namely, those relating to culture and education—that were not open to them before, and to

---

[24] For minorities' right of secession, see the previous section.

[25] Leiter, in his *Nietzsche on Morality*, explores this idea well.

[26] We can discern the germs of this thought already in GSt, 171, where Nietzsche comments that the aim of the "liberal-optimistic worldview," which has its roots in the French Revolution, is to "dissolve the monarchical instincts of the people" through the spread of universal suffrage.

which Nietzsche does not believe they are up to.[27] "On deeper consideration," Nietzsche concludes, "the role has actually *become* character; and artifice, nature"; men actually end up becoming the role they gave themselves.

The predominance of the actor comes at the price of the "great 'architects,'" those who have the "strength to build," the "courage to make far-reaching plans," who dare to undertake works that would require "millennia to complete" (GS 356). Modern man's ever-shifting nature means that

> what is dying out is that fundamental faith on the basis of which someone could calculate, promise, [and] anticipate the future in a plan on that grand scale. . . . [T]he basic faith that man has worth and sense only insofar as he is *a stone in a great edifice*; to this end he must be *firm* above all, a "stone" [and] . . . above all not an actor!

"From now on will never again be built, *can* never again be built," Nietzsche concludes, "a society in the old sense of the term. . . . "To build that, everything is lacking, mainly the material."

This passage as a whole has given rise to much debate. On the one hand, there are those who submit this section as an example of how Nietzsche does not have a positive political vision (no possibility of a new society being built), and on the other hand, there are those who offer Nietzsche's reflections on the democratic figure of the actor as an illustration of his prodemocratic views.[28] Both are, to my mind, mistaken. In terms of this section, it is most important to emphasize that a society in the old sense of the word—that is, a medieval guild one—can no longer be built. But pace those who do not see a positive political program in Nietzsche, the democratization of Europe offers the opportunity to build a society in a new sense of the word, and this society, contra those who want to construe Nietzsche as a proto-democrat, will not be egalitarian, as we will now see.

DEGENERATION AND THE GOOD EUROPEAN

A strong theme within Nietzsche's discussion of democracy is its association with physical degeneration.[29] In *Beyond Good and Evil* 203, Nietzsche remarks that for him the "democratic movement is not merely an abased

---

[27] See TI Germans 5: "'Higher education' and *horde*—that are in contradiction from the outset. Any higher education is only for the exception: you have to be privileged to have the right to such a high privilege."

[28] See Owen, "Nietzsche, Ethical Agency, and the Problem of Democracy"; William Connolly, "Debate: Reworking the Democratic Imagination," *Journal of Political Philosophy* 5, no. 2 (1997): 201.

[29] Not be confused with its cultural counterpart, decadence.

form of political organization but rather an abased (more specifically diminished) form of humanity, a mediocritization and depreciation of humanity in value." Democracy finds its social and anthropological origin in the "democratic mixing of classes and races" (BGE 224), the "mixing of blood between masters and slaves" (BGE 261). This mixing of master and slave morality occurs through intermarriage between different castes, and the resulting conflict between the two value systems—without either getting the upper hand—that is incarnated in their offspring results in a general indecision and slowness in the population at large:

> The different standards and values, as it were, get passed down through the bloodline to the next generation where everything is in a state of restlessness, disorder, doubt, [and] experimentation. The best forces have inhibitory effects; the virtues themselves do not let each other strengthen and grow; both body and soul lack a center of balance, a center of gravity and the assurance of a pendulum. (BGE 208)

"What is most profoundly sick and degenerate about such hybrids is the will." Nietzsche adds, "They no longer have any sense of independence in decision making or the bold feeling of pleasure in willing."[30] Democracy is the political manifestation of this enfeeblement.

This ethnographic study of democracy's origins takes a seemingly unsavory turn in *The Genealogy of Morality*, when Nietzsche equates master morality with an "Aryan conquering race," and slave morality with the "dark-skinned and especially the dark-haired man" (GM I 5). While in *Beyond* Nietzsche saw democracy as emanating from an unresolved and detrimental conflict between master and slave morality, in *The Genealogy* he appears to suggest it is not solely the moral but also the physiological victory of the slaves over the masters. There he asks:

> To all intents and purposes the subject race has ended up by regaining the upper hand in skin color, shortness of forehead, and perhaps even in intellectual and social instincts: Who can give any guarantee that modern democracy . . . [is] not in essence a huge *throwback*—and that the conquering *master race*, that of the Aryans, is not physiologically being defeated as well? (GM I 5)

If from our perspective this makes for uncomfortable reading, during Nietzsche's own time this language was common currency, and the theories he expresses were acceptable scientific ones. Andreas Retzius had classified Europeans into two categories: "dolichocephalic"—that is, "long-headed"

---

[30] For Paul Bourget's and Charles Féré's influence on Nietzsche's idea of the degeneration of the will, see Gregory Moore, *Nietzsche, Biology, and Metaphor* (Cambridge: Cambridge University Press, 2004), 126.

Nordic Europeans who were meant to be blond and blue eyed; and "brachycephalic"—that is, the "round-headed" Mediterraneans whom Nietzsche is referring to here.[31] Antiquarians had just discovered that Sanskrit was related to all European languages, and this gave rise to the myth of an original *ur-Volk*, whom Friedrich Schlegel christened the Aryans, who had emigrated from India and conquered Europe in prehistoric times—hence Nietzsche's view of the Aryan conquering master race.[32] It was philologists who had led the way in the discovery of the Indo-European link, and this explains why Nietzsche, himself trained as a philologist, takes an etymological perspective when it comes to explaining the origins of good and bad in *The Genealogy* (GM I 4), and why he deduces that the Celts were blond: "The word *fin* (for example, in the name *Fin-Gal*), the term designating nobility, and finally the good, noble, and pure, originally referred to the blond-headed man" (GM I 5).

Nietzsche thus accepts this theory of the Aryan race as historical fact, and builds his own theory of master and slave morality on it. In reality, Nietzsche appears to be more interested in delineating the different moralities than the exact physical attributes that these moralities manifest themselves through; he is more interested in *values* than he is in *race*. He lists "Roman, Arabian, Germanic, Japanese nobility, Homeric heroes, Scandinavian Vikings" as examples of these blond beasts of prey (GM I 11), of which one at minimum—depending on where one places the Arabs (Berbers?)—could never have been fair headed. In this sense, then, the blond beast is a metaphor for a lion, the noble king of the jungle, and the Aryan and Celtic races just so happen to be the historical conquering races of Europe, but may take on other non-Aryan attributes in other circumstances (Arabian or Japanese). There is therefore both a literal and figurative aspect to Nietzsche's account of the blond beasts of prey: while historically the European conquerors were blond (literal), Nietzsche then uses this theory and applies it to the rest of the world (figurative).[33]

One of the key figures in the development of these ideas is the self-styled count, Gobineau, who was an intellectual companion to Wagner when Nietzsche frequented his circle in the late 1860s and early 1870s.[34] Gobineau's

---

[31] J. W. Burrow, *The Crisis of Reason: European Thought, 1848–1914* (New Haven, CT: Yale University Press, 2000), 105.

[32] Ibid., 106.

[33] Both Gregory Moore and Nicholas Martin emphasize the figurative aspect of the blond beasts, and that it mainly refers to being "noble." I agree that it is the value in question that is key, but want to underline here that this value first finds its roots, at least in the European setting, in a direct physical appearance. See Moore, *Nietzsche, Biology, and Metaphor*, 157; Nicholas Martin, "Breeding Greeks: Nietzsche, Gobineau, and Classical Theories of Race," in *Nietzsche and Antiquity: His Reaction and Response to the Classical Tradition*, ed. Paul Bishop (Rochester, NY: Camden House, 2004), 43.

[34] The extent of Gobineau's influence on Nietzsche is subject to debate, but it certainly

successor, the Englishman Houston Stewart Chamberlain, became Wagner's son-in-law, and his *Foundations of the Nineteenth Century*, published in 1899, added the anti-Semitic dimension to Gobineau's thought that had not been particularly prevalent in the latter's. Gobineau's theory, as expressed in *On the Inequality of the Human Races*, published between 1853–55, and only translated in German a decade later, attributed a purer German—that is, Frankish and ultimately Aryan—stock to the French aristocracy.[35] The view at the time was that the purer the line, the closer one was to the original Aryan conquering races and all the benefits that went with that; the Teutons, Goths, and Celts were thought to be the closest. But the decline and elimination of the French aristocracy, so Gobineau thought, which was brought about through interbreeding, led to a generally mongrelized and plebeian leveling, of which democracy was the political expression. For Gobineau, racial purity was key to all civilization and human history, leaving him desperately pessimistic about the future prospects of France and Europe.[36]

Many of Gobineau's theories find an echo in Nietzsche's view of democracy: that it is the political manifestation of a general decline in human physiology, brought about through the interbreeding of different classes. But already Nietzsche distinguishes himself by placing the emphasis on morality, while Gobineau underlined race. Indeed, if Nietzsche often seems to conceive of the world in racialized terms, this is habitually in a rather vague or generic manner instead of the more precise meaning it might have today, or the word is used as a stand-in for other terms: Nietzsche speaks of the "French" or "English" race (versus nation/people), or again of a master or slave race (versus class/caste).[37] It is part of the language that people used at the time to express themselves; what is important to see is what use Nietzsche himself made of it. Ultimately, Nietzsche would not fall for Gobineau's darkly pessimistic view of where this was all leading us. Instead, he would

---

seems to be the case that Nietzsche would have encountered his thought through his frequentation of the Wagner circle, for which there was some enthusiasm. See Martin, "Breeding Greeks," 42; Moore, *Nietzsche, Biology, and Metaphor*, 124.

[35] This idea of the German roots of the French aristocracy can be traced back to Charles de Montesquieu, with his notion in *The Spirit of the Laws* of liberty emerging from the "German woods."

[36] We can note that for Nietzsche, there are "no pure races but only races that have become pure, even these being extremely rare.... The Greeks offer us the model of a race and culture that has become pure, and hopefully we will one day achieve a pure European race and culture" (D 272). For a commentary on this aphorism, see Martin, "Breeding Greeks," 40. See also John Richardson, *Nietzsche's New Darwinism* (Oxford: Oxford University Press, 2004), 199.

[37] On how Nietzsche uses *Rasse* (race) and *Stand* (estate, class, or caste) interchangeably, highlighting the more ambiguous use of the term, see Moore, *Nietzsche, Biology, and Metaphor*, 125. Richardson (*Nietzsche's New Darwinism*, 199) also writes that when Nietzsche says race, he means a large human group.

draw the exact opposite conclusion—as optimistic as Gobineau's was pessimistic: that the leveling of the modern European would lead to a new, interracial European aristocracy.

Previously in *The Wanderer and His Shadow* we saw how for Nietzsche the independence-inducing institutions of democracy laid the foundation on which a new aristocracy could come into being. In *Beyond Good and Evil*, he adds the more physiological aspect to this development:

> Behind all the moral and political foregrounds that are indicated by formulas like [Europe's *democratic* movement], an immense *physiological* process is taking place and constantly gaining ground—the process of increasing similarity between Europeans, their growing detachment from the conditions under which climate- or class-bound races originate, their increasing independence from that *determinate* milieu where for centuries the same demands would be inscribed on the soul and the body—and so the slow approach of an essentially supranational and nomadic type of person who, physiologically speaking, is typified by a maximal degree of the art and force of adaptation. (BGE 242)

What Nietzsche is talking about here is the *"European in becoming"*—that is, the good Europeans (BGE 241), who will arise through multinational unions and will become the new European nobility. Nietzsche, somewhat ironically given the uses that he was subsequently put to, actively encourages the union of Jews and Junkers for the breeding of his new ruling caste, explaining that it would be extremely interesting to see whether the genius for money, patience, and intellect (with the latter especially missing in the Junkers) could be productively married to the "hereditary art of commanding and obeying" (BGE 251).

I can add that there are institutional, economic, and cultural facets to this European coming together. Already in *The Wanderer and His Shadow*, and specifically in the aphorism "The Victory of Democracy," Nietzsche describes that once the people are able to gain power through "great majorities in parliament," they will "attack with progressive taxation the whole dominant system of capitalists, merchants, and financiers, and will in fact create a middle class" (WS 292). So through universal suffrage and the Reichstag, a middle class will be developed on the basis of redistributive taxation. "The practical result of this increasing democratization," Nietzsche continues, will be a "European league of nations, in which each individual nation, delimited by the proper geographic frontiers, has the position of a canton with its separate rights." Because of the democratic "craze for novelty and experiment," echoing the discussion above, Nietzsche thinks that "small account will be taken of the historical memories of previously existing nations," but instead the "correction of frontiers" will be carried out to serve the *"interest* of the great cantons and at the same time of the whole federation." These corrections will be the task of future diplomats, who will be backed not by armies but rather by "motives and utilities," of who will be students of "civilization, agriculturists, and commercial experts."

Along with this institutional move toward unity, Nietzsche, in his notes at the time of *Beyond Good and Evil* (1885), sees an economic reason for this Europeanization. There he explains that what he is concerned with, and what he sees preparing itself slowly and hesitatingly, is a "United Europe":

> [With] the need of a new unity there comes a great explanatory economic fact: the small states of Europe, I refer to all our present kingdoms and "empires," will in a short time become economically untenable, owing to the mad, uncontrolled struggle for the possession of local and international trade. (Money is even now compelling to European nations to amalgamate into one power). (KSA 11 37 [9])

Finally, in the work of Napoléon, Goethe, Ludwig von Beethoven, Stendhal, Heinrich Heine, Schopenhauer, and even Wagner, Nietzsche discerns in *Beyond* the preparation for a new cultural synthesis as well as the groundwork for the European of the future. *"Europe wishes to be one,"* he concludes (BGE 256).

These passages shed light on a section discussed above—namely, that a general enfeeblement that manifests itself through democracy ensues from intermixing. While it might be the case that such an intermixing results in a general enfeeblement of the population at large, those who are able to master their conflicting natures are able to transform themselves into something more: "Then arise those marvelously incomprehensible and inexplicable beings, those enigmatic men, predestined for conquering and circumventing others," of which Nietzsche offers Alcibiades, Julius Caesar, and those he considers to be the first Europeans, Friedrich II and Leonardo da Vinci, as examples (BGE 200). It is in this double movement—toward enfeeblement and strength—that gives rise to two different types that we must understand how the new European master race is due to come about. As Nietzsche puts it,

> Future Europeans will be exceedingly garrulous, impotent, and eminently employable workers who will feel the *need* for masters and commanders like they need their daily bread. The democratization of Europe in effect amounts to the creation of a type prepared for *slavery* in the most subtle sense: the strong man will need to be stronger and richer than he has perhaps ever been before—thanks to the lack of prejudice in his schooling, to an enormous diversity in practice, art, and masks. What I'm trying to say is: the democratization of Europe is at the same time an involuntary exercise in the breeding of *tyrants*— understanding that in every sense of the word, including its most spiritual. (BGE 242)

CASTE SOCIETY

The aforementioned quotation calls on two themes in Nietzsche that I will now turn to: caste society and slavery. From the onset of his thinking, Nietzsche held that a caste society was a prerequisite for the development of high culture, and he held this thought continuously throughout his active life. What evolved over the course of his work was the ever-subtler relationship that the two spheres should entertain with one another. So in "The Greek State," Nietzsche writes that

> in order for there to be a broad, deep, fertile soil for the development of art, the overwhelming majority has to be slavishly subjected to life's necessity in the service of the minority, *beyond* the measure that is necessary for the individual. At their expense, through their extra work, that privileged class is to be removed from the struggle for existence, in order to produce and satisfy a new world of necessities. (GSt, 166)

Later in the text Nietzsche will recast this division into "*military castes*, out of which rises, pyramid shaped, on an exceedingly broad base of slaves, the edifice of a 'martial society'" (GST, 173). Here the higher class is placed firmly and directly above the lower class: the lower class provides the upper class its means of existence so that it can freely devote itself to its artistic pursuits.

In *Human, All Too Human*, his more "critical" phase, Nietzsche reiterates the claim that "a higher culture can come into existence only where there are two different castes in society: that of the workers and that of the idle" (HH 439). But he also suggests in the previous aphorism that in view of the democratization of politics, those who do not share that understanding should be allowed, as we saw previously, to "step a little aside" (HH 438). Nietzsche seems to be suggesting here that the two spheres should be separated—that there should no longer be any link between the two castes, so as to protect the latter from the all-engrossing herd morality of the former. Yet he concludes the passage with the anticipation that there will come a time when "these few" will "emerge from their silent isolation and test the power of their lungs again: for then they call to one another like those gone astray in a wood in order to locate and encourage one another." The higher class will in the future come together again and challenge the democratic mass: "whereby much becomes audible, to be sure, that sounds ill to ears for which it is not intended."

Leaving aside *Beyond Good and Evil* for now, to which I will return to more fully over the course of this and the next section, Nietzsche continues his discussion of caste society in *The Antichrist* through the Laws of Manu.

There he restates the claim that "a high culture is a pyramid: it needs a broad base, its first presupposition is a strong and healthily consolidated mediocrity," which he defines as "crafts, trade, farming, *science*, [and] most of art—in a word, *employment*" (AC 57). "Mediocrity is needed *before* there can be exceptions: it is the condition for a high culture."

There has been much debate as to whether the Laws of Manu represent a political ideal for Nietzsche. Thomas Brobjer has argued that they do not, and should best be understood as a means solely through which Nietzsche engages in a cultural critique of Christianity.[38] It is certainly the case that Nietzsche presents the Laws of Manu as fundamentally different from "every type of Bible,' and that it would be a "sin against *spirit* even to mention its name in the same breath as that of the Bible" (AC 56). He also writes a "Critique of the Laws of Manu" in his notes (KSA 13 15 [45]). But this critique occurs within a discussion of the "holy lie."[39] In the published text, Nietzsche concludes this discussion with the view that "in the end, it comes down to the *purpose* the lie is supposed to serve" (AC 56): whether it is "in order to sustain or to *destroy*" (AC 58). The Laws of Manu, in opposition to Christianity, sustain a thriving life; they are a "form of religious legislation whose goal was to 'eternalize' the supreme condition for a *thriving* life, a great organization of society; Christianity, by contrast, saw its mission as bringing this sort of an organization to an end." As such, seen through the prism of the holy lie, Nietzsche's evaluation of the Laws of Manu is quite positive.

Nor do the Laws of Manu appear to be simply an empty political contrast with Christianity. When the Laws of Manu are put together with the other historical moments that Nietzsche refers to as his ideal types over the course of his writings—the Greek state, the Renaissance, and India—a certain pattern seems to emerge. This pattern shows Nietzsche to prefer a two-caste system, with the higher caste itself divided into a spiritual and physical aristocracy, as it was in the distinction between the historical priestly and warrior nobles in the first essay of *The Genealogy*.[40] The parallel with Plato's

[38] Thomas Brobjer, "The Absence of Political Ideals in Nietzsche's Writings: The Case of the Laws of Manu and the Associated Caste Society," *Nietzsche-Studien* 27 (1998): 300–318. Leiter (*Nietzsche on Morality*, 294) cites this article in support of his contention that Nietzsche has no political philosophy. See also the debate with Don Dombowsky in his "A Response to Th. H. Brobjer's 'The Absence of Political Ideals in Nietzsche's Writings,'" *Nietzsche-Studien* 30 (2001): 387–93. See also Brobjer's reply: "Nietzsche as Political Thinker: A Response to Don Dombowsky," *Nietzsche-Studien* 30 (2001): 394–96.

[39] See KSA 13 15 [45]: "the whole book is founded on the holy lie"; "A Critique of the Holy Life," KSA 13 15 [42].

[40] See R. Lanier Anderson, "On the Nobility of Nietzsche's Priests," in *Nietzsche's* On the Genealogy of Morality: A Critical Guide, ed. Simon May (Cambridge: Cambridge University Press, 2011), 24–55. On the tripartite division of *The Genealogy*—people, warriors, and priests—and the priests' leading role in the revaluation of good and bad into good and evil,

Republic—Plato's perfect state, as Nietzsche puts it in his conclusion to "The Greek State"—with its philosopher-kings and guardians is patent. In *The Antichrist*, Nietzsche explains this as letting the "*noble* classes, the philosophers, and the warriors stand above the crowd" (AC 56). The first group (the philosophers) is made up of "predominantly spiritual people," the second (the warriors) consists of those characterized by "muscular and temperamental strength," while the last group (the crowd) is composed of those who are "not distinguished in either way—the mediocre." Moreover, the Laws of Manu provided a template of how the two factions of the higher class, the priests and warriors, should interact.

> The ones who are second: these are the custodians of the law, the guardians of order and security, these are the noble warriors, this is above all the *king*, as the highest formula of the warrior, judge, and preserver of the law. The ones who are second are the executive of the most spiritual people; they are closest to them, belong to them, and take over everything *crude* in the work of ruling. (AC 57)

This is in tune with what Nietzsche had already written of the Brahmins in *Beyond Good and Evil*, where they "assumed the power to appoint kings for the people, while they themselves kept and felt removed and outside" from the "turmoil and tribulations of the *cruder* forms of government," retaining "purity in the face of the *necessary* dirt of politics" (BGE 61). So the role of the spiritual class is to appoint a king, who is the leader of the guardians, along with providing the legal framework that it will be the duty of the warrior class to uphold, and in general engaging in the day-to-day activities of ruling as the executive arm of the priestly class.

Although this might not be the most truthful reconstruction of the Laws of Manu—there is a strong element of ideological appropriation in Nietzsche's rendering of the Laws of Manu, perhaps not helped by the dubious scholarship of Louis Jacolliot, whose edition he used—Nietzsche, much like his "interpretation" of the Greek state (GSt, 173), seems more interested in extracting what he takes to be the timeless elements that the Laws of Manu provide.[41] As such, he makes a point of underscoring, as it was with "The

---

see Christopher Janaway, *Beyond Selflessness: Reading Nietzsche's Genealogy* (Oxford: Clarendon Press, 2009). Nietzsche clearly identifies most with the priestly class, despite all its faults; it was responsible for establishing the rich inner lives that form, for him, the basis of all cultural achievement. Williams (*Shame and Necessity* [Berkeley: University of California Press, 2008], 12) was quick to see the importance of Christianity in Nietzsche's thought for the development of culture as we know it today.

[41] See Koenraad Elst, "Manu as a Weapon against Egalitarianism: Nietzsche and Hindu Political Philosophy," in *Nietzsche, Power, and Politics: Rethinking Nietzsche's Legacy for Political Thought*, ed. Herman Siemens and Vasti Roodt (Berlin: De Gruyter, 2008), 543–82. The Laws of Manu in fact accounted for four different castes: the priestly, the martial, the merchant, and the laboring class (note that the chandala were not a class at all but rather outcasts, the

Greek State," that it is "nature, *not* Manu," that endorses the caste order: "Caste *order*, the most supreme, domineering law, is just the sanction of a *natural order*, natural lawfulness par excellence," and later repeats: "In all this, to say it again, there is nothing arbitrary, nothing 'contrived.' . . . Caste-order, *order of rank*, is just a formula for the supreme law of life itself" (AC 57).[42] As Nietzsche portrays it, caste society is something historically objective and natural, and not simply a subjective projection of his own desires.

So far Nietzsche has only provided us with historical examples of what his (idealized) two-tiered caste system looks like, but how is this meant to be adapted to his present time? In an important note of 1887 titled "The Strong of the Future," which was destined for his planned magnum opus, "The Will to Power," Nietzsche gives the clearest indication of what form his future caste system might take. There he posits that the higher class must not be "merely a master race that will exhaust itself in ruling, but a race with its *own sphere of life*" (KSA 12 9 [153]). Again, two spheres are postulated in this vision of the future, with both having their own spheres of existence. As Nietzsche puts it in another note of around this time, which refers back to *The Genealogy*, "The spirit of the herd should rule within the herd—but not beyond it; the leaders of the herd require a fundamentally different valuation for their own actions, [and] the same applies to the independent ones, or the 'beasts of prey'" (KSA 12 7 [6]). This view is echoed in Nietzsche's account of the Laws of Manu, where he explains that there each "physiological type separate[s] out and gravitate[s] in different directions, each having its own hygiene, its own area of work, its own feelings of perfection and field of mastery" (AC 57). But beyond this separating out of spheres of existence, Nietzsche posits a *degree* of ruling by the masters ("not exhaust itself in ruling"), and to understand that degree, we must now turn to the issue of slavery.[43]

SLAVERY

The two most important elements to grasp in Nietzsche's view of slavery are, on the one hand, surplus, in the sense that it is from the surplus that the

---

untouchables; see TI Improvers 3). Nietzsche conflates the last two, and deems the first pair to be two elements of the noble class, to fit his two-caste ideal.

[42] "If the state now is actually viewed enthusiastically as the aim and goal of the sacrifices and duties of the individual, then all this indicates how enormously necessary the state is, without which *nature* might not succeed in achieving, through society, her salvation in appearance" (GSt, 169; emphasis added).

[43] For a similar assessment of Nietzsche's view of the relation between the elite and the herd, and their respective roles, see Richardson, *Nietzsche's New Darwinism*, 206.

slaves produce that a higher class can be relieved of its necessity to cater for itself and therefore can engage in artistic creation; and on the other hand, justification, in the sense that the slave's existence—indeed all life—needs to be justified. In "The Greek State," as we saw previously, it was the "extra work" of the slaves that allowed the "privileged class to be removed from the struggle for existence, in order to produce and satisfy a new world of necessities" (GST, 166). "The misery of toiling men must still increase in order to make the production of the world of art possible to a small number of Olympian men." But it is in being means to these geniuses that the slaves acquired, according to Nietzsche, their dignity. And not just the slaves: "Every human being, with his total activity, only has dignity insofar as he is a tool of the genius." It is thus the art that the geniuses produce that justifies the slave and the society as a whole, including, of course, the masters themselves. As Nietzsche's refrain in *The Birth of Tragedy* has it, "Only as an *aesthetic phenomenon* is existence and the world eternally *justified*" (BT 5); both the existence of the slaves and the world needs to be justified.

In the sections explored previously, both in *The Wanderer and His Shadow* and more specifically *Beyond Good and Evil*, we saw how Nietzsche thought the democratization of Europe would gradually lead to the creation of slaves who would call on the existence of a new spiritual aristocracy "like they need their daily bread" (BGE 242). In the notes in preparation for "The Will to Power" that I started to examine, Nietzsche elaborates on this thought. In "The Strong of the Future," he explains that society is "in a state of transition," and that "sooner or later *it will no longer be able to exist for its own sake* but only as a means in the hands of a stronger race" (KSA 12 9 [153]). "As soon as it is attained, this *leveled-down* species requires *justification*; its justification is that it serves a higher and sovereign type, which stands on it and can only thus rise to its task," and which will be able to take on its task through a "draining of forces" from society.

The new European democratic man, once his leveling is complete, will call on a new form of higher type to justify his existence. While Nietzsche may have abandoned his artist's metaphysics of *The Birth* after his split with Wagner, his concern about life needing to be justified remains whole. In *The Genealogy*, he writes that "man, the boldest animal and the one most accustomed to pain, does *not* repudiate suffering as such; he *desires* it, he even seeks it out, provided that he has been shown a *meaning* for it, a *reason* for suffering" (GM III 27). So the logic of the movement is thus: once modern democratic man has arrived at the end point of his development, he will look around to try to find a meaning for his existence. Having failed to find one, he will call on a new higher being who will provide him with one— there is every reason to believe this will still be an aesthetic one—to which he will transfer the surplus of his work so that such cultural creation can freely take place. Indeed, the failure of democracy to supply meaning for existence can be considered Nietzsche's fourth great critique of democracy, adding to his views about the link that democracy entertains with herd morality, misarchism, and degeneration.

It is in this lack of justification for their suffering that makes the modern wage-working slaves experience their lives as one of distress. Already Nietzsche had opened "The Greek State" with the claim that while the terms "dignity of man" and "dignity of work" had been invented to assuage the misery of the modern worker, these ring hollow because what the workers truly need, as the Greeks had understood, is to serve as a means to something greater than themselves. In *The Gay Science*, Nietzsche offers an analysis of modern commercial society. He concludes that workers are just exploited until exhaustion—to be replaced once this point is achieved rather than being maintained as it was with the ancient slaves—for the sole sake of profit. The other difficulty is that modern workers cannot conceive of any difference between themselves and captains of industry beyond the good luck of the latter (GS 40). They are "undistinguished and uninteresting persons," or worse still, "crafty, blood-sucking dogs of men," speculating on everything with their "vulgar, red, fat hands," and "whose name, form, [and] character reputation are altogether indifferent to them." From this the workers' ressentiment toward their employers grew, as did their desire for socialism.

There is a clear sense that for Nietzsche, no doubt influenced by Wagner, slavery in some form will always exist; in *Human, All Too Human*, he writes that "he who does not have two-thirds of his day to himself is a slave; let him be what he may otherwise be: statesman, businessman, official, [or] scholar" (HH 283), which might make us reflect on our respective professions—and that one class will forever live off the surplus of the other. The crucial questions, then, are: How is this exploitation justified, and whom does it benefit? In Nietzsche's terms, if all life is fundamentally exploitation, as he puts it in *Beyond Good and Evil* 259, then what and who gives this suffering meaning? (GM III 27).

This helps explain Nietzsche's reaction to the "labor question," which he dismisses as a "piece of stupidity" (TI Skirmishes 40). The reason for this is that if slaves are made to believe to be something they are not, then they will come to regard their existence as an injustice: "If we want slaves, then it is foolish to educate them to be masters." Instead, Nietzsche proposes that the position of the modern wage laborer should be perceived through the prism of a military organization: "Soldiers and their leaders have always a much higher mode of comportment toward one another than workers and their employers" (GS 40). In a note of 1887, Nietzsche writes, "Workers should learn to feel as *soldiers* do. Remuneration, an honorarium, but no salary! No relationship between payment and *effort*! Rather, the individual should, *according to his kind*, be so placed as to *achieve* the *highest* that is compatible with his power" (KSA 12 9 [34]). The move from a salary to an honorarium represents the move from an employment-type economy where the worker is paid for his efforts to a slave-based one where remuneration is based solely on the existence of the worker. Consequently, the basis of a slave class is given through the permanence of the slave's position, in contrast to the worker's continual precarious selling of his labor to his various capitalist employers. Slaves, in Nietzsche's view, are often much happier than modern workers: "The slaves live more securely and happily than the modern workers in all regards, and that slave labor is very little labor compared to that of the 'worker'" (HH 457). In view of the master's desire to preserve the slave, a degree of *"equalization"* occurs between the two, where "rights exist between the slaves and master. . . . [I]n this regard even the weaker of the two has rights, though they are more modest" (HH 93).

So far, not only has the worker been told he is something that he is not but his exploitation for the purposes of commercial society also has been, in Nietzsche's eyes, a complete waste: "The *exploitation* of the worker was, as we now understand, a piece of folly, a robbery at the expense of the future, a jeopardizing of society" (WS 286). In the future, this exploitation will be put in the service of a new *"superior race,"* to which the masses are ready to "submit to *slavery* of every kind, provided that the superior class above them constantly shows itself legitimately superior and *born* to command" (GS 40).

Nietzsche believes this demand for a new cultural aristocracy will be inevitable, as it arises from a universal need to have one's life (aesthetically) justified. In another note destined for "The Will to Power," he expresses his desire to show that a *"countermovement is inevitably associated* with any increasingly economical use of men and mankind," describing this countermovement as the *"separation of the luxurious surplus of mankind"* from which a new higher type will come into existence, of which the parable for this type is the overman (KSA 12 10 [17]). The exploitation of mankind "presupposes the existence of those for whom such an exploitation would have some *meaning*": a "higher form of *aristocracy* of the future."

As such Nietzsche—perhaps surprisingly—wants the great process of European leveling to be accelerated, and not slowed down, so as to prepare the way for this new aristocracy: "The necessity of *cleaving gulfs, of distance*, of the *order of rank*, is therefore imperative, *not* the necessity of retarding the process above mentioned" (KSA 12 9 [153]). "He is equally in need of the *enmity* of the masses, of those who are leveled down.' He requires that feeling of distance from them. He stands on them; he lives on them" (KSA 12 10 [17]). We should not understand this leveling down as an economic impoverishment but rather as an intellectual and physiological one, as described above. On the contrary, Nietzsche writes in another note of around this time that the worker of today will "one day live like the bourgeoisie."[44] This is in line with what he had written concerning a "solid mediocrity" in *The Antichrist*. Indeed, Nietzsche is quite willing to accept that the sphere of the workers is materially richer than that of the new masters, but that *"above them, distinguishing itself by its lack of needs, [is] the higher caste*—that is, poorer and simpler, but possessing power," which is reminiscent of what Nietzsche says of the Brahmin class, which while keeping itself at a distance from the everyday dirt of politics and somewhat less concerned with material wealth, ruled through its superior intellectual and spiritual power along with its ability to legislate values.

This brings us to Nietzsche's concept of the pathos of distance. The crucial passage is *Beyond Good and Evil* 257:

> Without the *pathos of distance*, such as grows out of the incarnated difference of classes, out of the constant looking out and looking down of the ruling caste on subordinates and instruments, and out of their equally constant practice of obeying and commanding, of keeping down and keeping away—that other more mysterious pathos could never have arisen, the longing for an ever widening of distance within the soul itself, the formation of ever higher, rarer, further, more extended, more comprehensive states, in short, just the elevation of the type "man," the continued "self-overcoming of man."

This section has recently been the subject of much attention, and there has been a strong move in the secondary literature to detach the physical and political aspect to the pathos from its more psychological or internal ones. The story often told is one of dissolution: although the pathos may have originally come about in a hierarchical society, this society has come to pass, but the inner striving for the pathos can remain within a democratic setting.[45]

There are good reasons to resist such an interpretation, at least in the way that Nietzsche thinks about it. For one, Nietzsche opens the section in question with the line: "*Every* elevation of the type 'man' has so far been the work of an aristocratic society and *so it will always be*—a society believing in a long scale of an order of rank and differences of worth among human be-

[44] See Steven Aschheim, *The Nietzsche Legacy in Germany, 1890–1900* (Berkeley: University of California Press, 1994), 182.

[45] See Paul van Tongeren, *Die Moral von Nietzsches Moralkritik: Studie zu "Jenseits von Gut und Böse"* (Bonn: Bouvier, 1989). See also Thomas Fossen, "Nietzsche's Aristocratism Revisited," in *Nietzsche, Power, and Politics: Rethinking Nietzsche's Legacy for Political Thought*, ed. Herman Siemens and Vasti Roodt (Berlin: De Gruyter, 2008), 299–318.

ings, and requiring slavery in some form or other." As the emphases on "every" and "so it will always be" attest to, it is only within a caste and slave society that the pathos of distance will arise in the first place—not just arise, but also be *maintained*. As has been suggested, a pathos of distance can *only* exist in a hierarchical society, and not in a modern democracy.

There is thus a strong *structural* link between the external and internal pathos, such that the one cannot exist without the other, although in the chronology of things the external must necessarily come first. Nietzsche underscores the *"constant* looking out and looking down of the ruling caste on subordinates and instruments"—again "their equally *constant* practice of obeying and commanding"—and that these class differences are "incarnated," indicating that the inner pathos of distance develops within the confines of a caste society. To put it another way: without the constant looking down that is inherent in a caste society, the inner pathos of distance could never have developed in the first place ("that other more mysterious pathos could never have arisen"), such that, inversely, it would disappear if a caste society were also to disappear, having no legal structure to sustain the external pathos of distance in which it roots and constantly renews itself.

Nietzsche preserves this separation over the course of his next publications. In *The Genealogy*, Nietzsche posits that "the pathos of distance *should* keep the task of the two groups forever separate" (GM III 14), thereby confirming that the pathos exists only in a caste society, and also stressing "the rule that the political concept of rank always transforms itself into spiritual concept of rank" (GM I 6). In *Twilight of the Idols*, Nietzsche explains that the "chasm between man and man, class and class, the multiplicity of types, the will to be oneself and to distinguish oneself—that, in fact, which I call the *pathos of distance*, is proper to all *strong* ages" (TI Skirmishes 37). Speaking of strong ages, we saw that in the future society Nietzsche advocates he insists on the necessity of cleaving gulfs, of distance, and this takes place within a caste society comprised of democratic slaves and a new aristocracy of the future (KSA 12 9 [153]).

It thus seems that at least for Nietzsche, the external and internal pathos of distance cannot be separated. And while there have been suggestions in the secondary literature that something like an "economy of esteem" might replace the need for an external pathos of distance, this strikes me again as relying on a division of labor that is constitutive of a hierarchical society, so that an intellectual and cultural hierarchy—esteeming highly paid professionals and even artists—is still anchored in an unequal political and economic framework—precisely Nietzsche's point.[46]

[46] Owen, "Nietzsche, Ethical Agency, and the Problem of Democracy," 143–68.

CONCLUSION

We are now in a good position to fully piece together Nietzsche's vision of Europe's democratic future. His thesis is that the general leveling of mankind will necessarily lead to the demand for a new cultural aristocracy, whose role it will be to provide this homogenized mass a(n) (aesthetic) meaning to their life. Two spheres will come into existence: on the one hand, the mass, whom Nietzsche is quite happy for it to rule itself democratically, and in fact allows it to be the richer of the two, on the condition that it does not demand that the other, much more restricted sphere of the cultural elite fall under its purview. While the two spheres are mostly separated out and rule themselves according to their own moralities, there remains a twofold relationship between the two that permits us still to talk about a degree of slavery, understood in the Nietzschean sense.[47] First, there is a transfer of resources from the larger sphere to the smaller, in the sense that is it from the surplus that the new democratic slaves produce that the select few can be liberated from having to provide for themselves and can pursue their cultural mission. Second, thanks to the two spheres being kept separate, a pathos of distance can still develop between the new cultural nobility and leveled mass, which is in effect routed in a caste system, underlining how for Nietzsche the two—external and internal pathos of distance—are inseparable.[48]

By caste system in Nietzsche's future vision is meant first and foremost the existence of two separate spheres that have their own modes of existence; the issue of inequality arises only as a secondary and instrumental consideration. In sum: in the Greek state the smaller sphere is placed vertically, directly above the larger one, with a line drawn between the center of the larger sphere to the center of the smaller one to represent the direct exploitation of the slaves by the masters; in *Human, All Too Human*, the two spheres are completely separate, with no line linking them, since the masters and slaves live in mutual ignorance; in Nietzsche's future, the larger and smaller spheres are placed horizontally, side by side, with perhaps a horizontal line (Nietzsche would think of the smaller sphere as being as powerful as the larger one) linking the top extremity of the larger sphere to the top extremity of the smaller sphere, to represent the transferal of resources from one to the other—maybe mediated through the postnational regulatory

[47] This is how I understand Nietzsche's comment about a "new type of slavery" (GS 377) should be read.

[48] Richardson (*Nietzsche's New Darwinism*, 212) explains that what the elite needs is economic independence and the capacity to direct the values of the herd accordingly.

state that I explored at the end of the last chapter—without the directly exploitative element present in the Greek state.

Even though Nietzsche believes that a countermovement to the democratization of Europe is inevitable, this does not lead him to think that the ideal society he posits is inevitable. This is what Zarathustra learns in his first speech in the marketplace, where the assembled crowd cries out for the last man and not the overman who Zarathustra had been advocating. In chapter 6, with the notions of great politics, war of spirits, and the party of life, I will further explore Nietzsche's ideas on how to bring these two spheres about, how they are to govern themselves, and what relationship they are to entertain with one another. In the meantime, we can see how this democratic future goes hand in hand with that of the state's future, analyzed in chapter 2, which was instigated in the first place by the democratic decay of the modern state: the private companies and their freer play belong to the democratized sphere, while the new nobility will locate itself in the new cultural institutions. I already evoked the transfer of resources here within a broader framework, which will be one of the elements that will make up the relationship the two spheres have with one another, as I will discuss later.

In his *Introduction to Nietzsche as Political Thinker*, Ansell-Pearson writes that as Nietzsche "seeks to legitimate aristocratic rule through the notion of *culture*," rather than through a social contract, he fails to "address the question of legitimacy on the level of social justice and the 'right of subjectivity,'" which was how "Hegel described the right of the modern individual to self-determination." The result is a "politics of domination," as "it is difficult to see how aristocratic rule as conceived by Nietzsche could be maintained except through ruthless forms of political control." Nietzsche's aristocrats, Ansell-Pearson believes, would have to rule with recourse to "highly oppressive instruments of political control and manipulation." As such, Nietzsche's "new aristocratic order, which institutes itself through compulsion and violence, must give rise to permanent class conflict, to a politics of pride and glory, on the one hand, and one of envy and resentment, on the other."[49] It is not immediately clear—beyond its putative association with democracy—why Nietzsche needed to frame his project within the boundaries of Hegelianism. But if, however, as I have explored in this chapter, Nietzsche's future society is comprised of two spheres, each ruling itself according to its own desires, with only a degree of resources being channeled from one sphere to another, perhaps even voluntarily if it is these new slaves that call on the creation of a new artistic class, then the politics of such a society need not be as ruthless as Ansell-Pearson thinks it to be.

[49] Ansell-Pearson, *An Introduction to Nietzsche as Political Thinker*, 154–55, 41–42.

In *Beyond Good and Evil*, Nietzsche explains that it is in the space between master and slave that "pity and similar sentiments can find a place" (BGE 260), and in his discussion of the Laws of Manu he observes that "when an exceptional person treats a mediocre one more delicately than he treats himself and his equals, this is not just courtesy of the heart—it is his duty" (AC 57). I therefore find myself more in agreement with Ansell-Pearson's alternative view of what Nietzsche's society could become: a "peaceful coexistence between different human types (say, between the over-human and human), in which the former pursues artistic self-creation and self-discipline, and the latter preoccupy themselves with mundane and material pursuits."[50] I do so, however, with one caveat: the relationship between the two spheres that I have sketched above has to be retained—there remains a degree of slavery and pathos between the two spheres—instead of Ansell-Pearson's more completely separate, and consequently apolitical, vision.[51]

As mentioned in the introduction, an old debate in the scholarly literature has been between a tough or bloody (the politics of domination) Nietzsche, as opposed to a gentler (proto-democratic) one. In my study so far I have brought to the fore the fact that both tendencies are present in Nietzsche: tough in the sense of the inevitability of slavery, and gentle in its possible reconciliation with democracy. Instead of choosing to emphasize one or the other, as the participants of the debate are wont to do, to match their own position, I think the best approach is to follow Nietzsche himself—through his interpretation of different historical periods. The Greek state certainly sees Nietzsche in his bloodier phase, with his stress on violence and slavery in a crude sense. But as we move toward what Nietzsche starts to think of as the future, a much gentler Nietzsche appears. Hence, there might be a difference between a historically bloodier Nietzsche and a gentler, more predictive one—one perhaps not as democratic as some would like, but certainly, as I will examine more fully in chapter 6, one who has theorized the "spiritualization" of hostility, and has come to conceive slavery on a subtler basis and recalibrated what might be meant by the pathos of distance. As such, the question is less whether Nietzsche himself was tough or not, but what conclusions he draws for the different periods he is investigating; whether the periods themselves, and not Nietzsche, are tough or not. There are certainly different facets to Nietzsche's thinking, and while he does toy—consciously—with a number of different controversial ideas throughout his life, and has a taste for provocations, when it comes to elaborating his future, I would assert that the gentle side dominates.

[50] Ibid., 158. John Richardson, in his *Nietzsche's System* (Oxford: Oxford University Press, 2002), comes to such a view too.

[51] Yet this does not imply that conditions within the higher cultural sphere itself should not be "tough" (cf. BGE 44, 262) but rather the relationship that the two spheres are meant to entertain with one another.

Arguing against those agonistic interpreters of Nietzsche who want to found their agon on the notion of agonistic respect, Herman Siemens has—correctly, to my mind—put forward the view that the relationship between the two spheres that I have been discussing should be understood through the prism of "agonal hatred."[52] The agon, as Nietzsche theorizes it in "Homer's Contest," does grow out of "envy, jealousy, ambition, [and] hatred," but hatred in the Zarathustrian sense of the word—that is, in taking *"pride in one's enemy and the successes of one's enemy,"* instead of contempt toward an inferior one would be willing to eradicate. This brings us to the topic of the agon in Nietzsche's thought. We will see later in the book how the agon can be used internally by the artistic class to further its own activities, but for now the agon helps to underscore three key thoughts in Nietzsche's vision of the future. First, within this agon the new nobles have no desire to destroy the other party; quite the contrary, since Nietzsche clearly understands the value in "having enemies": "every party grasps that its interest in self-preservation lies in the opposition party not losing its power" (TI Morality 3). The destruction of one party would render the other, like Miltiades in "Homer's Contest," a base tyrant. Second, there is necessarily a degree of equality between the two spheres, or otherwise the agon would give way to domination, which is why the larger and smaller spheres are at the same vertical height in the diagram that I attempted to sketch earlier. Finally, the agon must take place within a caste society, without which the external aspect, having nothing to struggle against, could not exist.

This emphasis of the agonistic struggle being *between* different spheres, alongside an internal one, is at odds with how those agonistic Nietzscheans want to utilize Nietzsche's theory of the agon, seeing it as taking place only *within* the democratic sphere itself. Placing "Homer's Contest" back beside its other preface—both were part of a unpublished collection by Nietzsche titled "Five Prefaces to Five Unwritten Books"—reminds us that for Nietzsche, the agon took place within a slave society: ancient Greece. Even though it is true that the "contest" extends to all—"even potters harbor grudges against potters" (HC, 176)—the specifically political and indeed cultural aspect of the struggle that the contemporary theorists of the agon have in mind requires slavery in the sense that contestants need free time to be able to engage in such activities. The question that those who want to appropriate Nietzsche's theory of the agon for contemporary use must therefore address is that of slavery within a democratic setting. Can we moderns conceive of ourselves as having sufficient free time that we might engage again in such agonistic politics? Or will this be reserved, as it was in the past, for the select few who have the time and resources to do so? On Nietzsche's

---

[52] Herman Siemens, "Reassessing Radical Democratic Theory in the Light of Nietzsche's Ontology of Conflict," in *Nietzsche and Political Thought*, ed. Keith Ansell-Pearson 92–93.

view, at least, the answer to the first question appears to be "no," as only a class freed of the necessity to work would have sufficient time to engage in such pursuits, which are in fact constitutive of its cultural task.

What is striking is that the contemporary agonists do not take any heed of Nietzsche's emphatic and polemical claim in "The Greek State" that if the "Greeks perished through their slavery," we moderns "shall perish through the lack of slavery" (GSt, 167); the agon is only possible with some form of slavery. This lends credence to the charge that the contemporary agonistic literature is rather elitist, not willing to engage with the fact that the majority of people do not have the leisure to participate in the political or cultural agon. Moreover, while the project to "ennoble workers" so that they may fully participate in democracy on an equal footing with the rest of the population—of which we find a strong echo in the works of the democratic Nietzscheans—has been a staple of European left-wing politics since the beginning of the twentieth century, and the Jeffersonian ideal of "every man an aristocrat" has a long legacy in the United States, the emphasis on "struggle," however, as the foundation of politics has been until recently the preserve of the continental (antidemocratic) Right, not to mention the Far Right, and the relationship that today's left-wing Nietzscheans entertain with that legacy has been, to my mind, insufficiently accounted for.[53] If the contest is at the heart of politics, this does not make the contest and politics automatically democratic; quite the contrary. So while certain authors that the postmodern Nietzscheans call on to bolster their position might prove more amenable to their task—Arendt, from the list I drew up in the opening, with her more democratic reading of the agon, should be—Nietzsche, because of his fundamentally aristocratic conception of the contest, is not.

Bernard Crick has offered three ways of thinking about democracy: as a "principle or doctrine of government"; as a "set of institutional arrangements or constitutional devices"; and as a "type of behavior," which he helpfully defines as "the antithesis of both deference and unsociability."[54] Nietzsche, in short, is opposed to democracy as a principle or doctrine of government, because he understands it as the coming to power of herd morality. But he is more ambiguous when it relates to democratic mores and behavior; he is opposed to misarchism, the democratic mind-set of being against all forms of authority, and sees physiological degeneration behind the rising tide of democratization, yet he also perceives the germs of a new multiracial European nobility in this movement. Lastly, Nietzsche views the institutional aspect of democracy in a generally positive light, as it

---

[53] See Aschheim, *The Nietzsche Legacy in Germany*, 164–200.

[54] Bernard Crick, *Democracy: A Very Short Introduction* (Oxford: Oxford University Press, 2002), 5.

mounts bulwarks to defend culture and ultimately provides the foundations on which this new aristocracy can come into being.

I have highlighted the privileged position that Nietzsche occupied as a commentator on the rise of democracy in Germany due to his historical location, and how he was quick to identify problems with democracy that would become staples of political theory in the subsequent century.[55] His analysis of democracy maps itself particularly well onto Anderson's *Practicing Democracy*, one of the leading historical studies of the period. Anderson's main thesis is that it is through the *practice* of democracy that the people were gradually able to acquire more rights and liberties from what was originally intended simply as a ratification of the powers that be. The logic of party competition meant that citizens were afforded more and more political rights—secret ballots, voting booths, and so on—and this chimes well with Nietzsche's view that democracy's aim is to foster independence—independence of opinion, mode of life, and employment. In fact, in his "The Victory of Democracy" aphorism in *The Wanderer and His Shadow*, Nietzsche explains that in their desire to combat socialism, the German political parties are forced to appeal more and more to the masses: "In the long run democracy alone gains the advantage, for *all* parties are now compelled to flatter the 'people,' and grant them facilities and liberties of all kinds, with the result that the people finally become omnipotent" (WS 292). Part of the process of claiming these new rights was to challenge established authority itself, and Anderson is alive to the fact that "it was the nature of the imperial franchise to turn every contest into a challenge to authority." Or, to put it in Nietzsche's words, democracy gives rise to misarchism.[56]

When Nietzsche's conceptualizing of democracy as herd morality is coupled with Plato's view of democracy as mob rule in *The Republic*, we can see how Nietzsche offers an intriguing link between ancient and modern critiques of democracy. In this sense Nietzsche may be one of the most acute commentators on democracy we have, although we cannot conceive of him simply as its opponent, as the antidemocratic reading of Nietzsche has tended to do, but also need to investigate where he thought such a development would lead, as I have tried to do over the course of this chapter. Aside from his discussion of degeneration—although as I have argued he ultimately transforms this into a question of morality, which is where his novelty lies—Nietzsche's view of the increasing mixing of Europeans, aided

[55] To these latter, I can add that Nietzsche saw the links between democracy and fragmentation ("establish large bodies of *equal importance* with mutual safeguards" [GSt, 171]); how democratic politics is extremely short-term and unstable (the monkeys scrambling over a throne of mud in Z I Idol); and how in democracies, politics becomes an increasingly disingenuous game (the "moral hypocrisy of the commanding class" [BGE 199]).

[56] Anderson, *Practicing Democracy*, 415.

and abetted by cultural, intellectual, institutional, and economic factors leading to a unified Europe, seems rather prescient in terms of the Europe we know today.

Nietzsche, on the one hand, serves as a good guide to the democratization of late nineteenth-century Germany and Europe, aspects of which—political parties and secret voting—we would recognize as features of our own political system. On the other hand, he remains one of the sharpest critics of the birth of democracy he experienced firsthand, due to pinpointing key criticisms—problems of majoritarianism and democratic legitimacy—that were to become staples of democratic debates in the subsequent century, alongside connecting with a long arc of antidemocratic thought stretching back to Plato. But his main contribution to democratic thought, I contend, is in the conceptual tools he affords us in trying to understand democracy through his notions of herd morality, misarchism, and the genealogical links it entertains with Christianity, all of which still provide us with powerful prisms through which to analyze democracy today. The term misarchism, for instance, in revealing the antiauthority foundations of the democratic mind-set, might allow us to better recognize the continuing—and from this perspective, irreversible—erosion of trust in public institutions. Such a mind-set is part and parcel of democracy, and to see this allows us to better understand what can and cannot be done about it.

Nietzsche is quite singular in the nineteenth century in denouncing democracy and Christianity as one—we can easily think of examples of thinkers rejecting one but not the other—particularly the absolutist claims that both make. While some studies of the relationship that Christianity entertains with democracy do exist, none, to my knowledge, have approached it from the genealogical perspective that Nietzsche is advocating here, and such an approach would undoubtedly shed light on our contemporary political system.[57] Indeed, for non-Christians the strong link that Nietzsche posits between democracy and Christianity might prove a little unsettling, or at least might force a rethink of the basis of their commitment to democracy. If God is dead, then the question is whether democracy is part of the "shadows of God" that Nietzsche decried (GS 125, 108): though we no longer believe in its religious underpinning, we still adhere to the same worldview. We are no longer Christians, but we will live according to Christianity's values. Can one be a democrat if one is no longer a Christian? Does the

---

[57] See Charles Taylor, *A Secular Age* (Cambridge, MA: Harvard University Press, 2007); Emile Perreau-Saussine, *Catholicism and Democracy: An Essay in the History of Political Thought* (Princeton, NJ: Princeton University Press, 2012). With its idea of Christianity as the "religion of the end of religion," the closest might be Marcel Gauchet, *The Disenchantment of the World: A Political History of Religion* (Princeton, NJ: Princeton University Press, 1997).

realization of the Christian origins of democracy, if Nietzsche is right, compel a reconsideration of one's commitment to democracy?[58]

The force of Nietzsche's analysis was to expose how such a worldview is ultimately grounded in some sort of herd morality; the secularized lives we live today have their roots not simply in Christianity but in slave morality too. And herd morality still captures something fundamental about how we do live our lives presently: we no longer appeal to a divine transcendence to orient our lives, but lacking another point of reference, we model ourselves on the behavior of the people around us. What Nietzsche shows us is how that reflex was the ground on which Christianity took root in the first place, and how we have yet—against our best atheistic protestations—to overcome it, to found new values as well as live our lives beyond good and evil. Do we want our political system and how we live our lives to be rooted in herd morality? These are some of the insights and challenges that Nietzsche's critique of democracy offers us.

---

[58] In this I agree with Strong ("In Defense of Rhetoric," 522–24) that reading Nietzsche forces us to formulate a self-critique of ourselves.

CHAPTER 4

PHILOSOPHY AND POLITICS

Much has been written about Nietzsche's notions of the will to power, eternal return, and overman, and I do not mean to offer a comprehensive interpretation of each one of them here; that would require another three separate studies in their own right.[1] Instead, I wish to concentrate on the ethical and political dimensions of these concepts, dwelling on the philosophical aspects solely to draw out these points. So for the will to power, I want to link that idea strongly to Nietzsche's theory of the agon, especially how it is articulated in his early, unpublished essay "Homer's Contest," which was, along with "The Greek State," one of the "Five Prefaces to Five Unwritten Books." That study allows us to see that if it is correctly channeled through certain institutions of the ancient Greek agon, including ostracism, the will to power can lead to positive outcomes both ethically—in pushing the participants to individually excel through a healthy competition—and politically, in that competition is marshaled for the benefit of the whole polis.[2] I will present the so-called doctrine of the eternal return as a selective device for *politically* separating out those who are strong enough to carry through Nietzsche's great politics, and are thereby suitable to join his party of life, from those who are not, and *ethically* as a means of liberating oneself from the politics of ressentiment.[3] Finally, the controversial topic of the Über-

---

[1] A good place to start here would be, in a more "continental" vein, Gilles Deleuze, *Nietzsche and Philosophy*, trans. Hugh Tomlinson (London: Continuum, 2006); Pierre Klossowski, *Nietzsche and the Vicious Circle* (London: Continuum, 2005); Jacques Derrida, *Spurs: Nietzsche's Styles / Eperons: Les Styles de Nietzsche*, trans. Barbara Harlow (Chicago: University of Chicago Press, 1979). See also Walter Kaufmann, *Nietzsche: Philosopher, Psychologist, Antichrist* (Princeton, NJ: Princeton University Press, 1974); Wolfgang Müller-Lauter, *Nietzsche: His Philosophy of Contradictions and the Contradictions of His Philosophy*, trans. David Parent (Champaign: University of Illinois Press, 1999); Alexander Nehamas, *Nietzsche: Life as Literature* (Cambridge, MA: Harvard University Press, 2002).

[2] On this point of the agon, see also Bernard Reginster, *The Affirmation of Life: Nietzsche on Overcoming Nihilism* (Cambridge, MA: Harvard University Press, 2009).

[3] On the ethical interpretations of the eternal return, see R. Lanier Andersen, "Nietzsche

mensch, which as noted earlier, I render as the overman, has provided a segue into debates about perfectionism, and while I contend that an Emersonian ethical perfectionist reading of Nietzsche leads to the dreaded last man rather than to the overman, a moderate version of Rawls's political perfectionism might not be such a bad way of characterizing Nietzsche's politics.

THE WILL TO POWER

In "What I Owe to the Ancients" in *Twilight of the Idols*, Nietzsche states that it is the study of the Greeks that gave him his first insight into his philosophical notions of the eternal return, will to power, and overmen. The will to power, he writes, is the "Greek's strongest instinct" (TI Ancients 3). They "trembled in the face of the tremendous force of this drive," such that "all their institutions grow out of the preventative measures they took to protect each other against their inner *explosives*." One way in which these explosives channeled themselves was in the continuous warfare between the ancient Greek city-states. "This tremendous inner tension vented itself outwardly in terrible and ruthless hostility; the city-states tore each other apart so that the citizens in each one were able to find peace from themselves." This passage, written at the end of Nietzsche's intellectual life, harks back to the scene that Nietzsche had depicted of antiquity in his early essay "The Greek State," where the bellum omnium contra omnes is redirected, once encased within a state society, in a much less frequent but altogether much more ferocious war between nations (GSt, 170).

Another early, unpublished essay, "Homer's Contest," provides another, more positive account of the institutions that the Greeks invented to protect themselves from their tremendous will to power and channel it into something constructive. In it, Nietzsche explains that the Greeks' "terrible impulse"—what he later identifies, as we just saw in *Twilight*, as the will to power—is best captured in Hesiod's metaphor of the two Eris goddesses. The first, the eldest, is "wicked," born to the "Black Night," promotes "wicked war and feuding," and leads men into a "hostile struggle to the death" (HC). It is this one that leads men to the violent and destructive wars between city-states. But the younger Eris, with Zeus's blessing, is "good"; here, "jealousy, grudge, and envy goads men into action, not however, the action of a struggle to the death but the action of the *contest*." This agon

on Redemption and Transfiguration," in *The Re-Enchantment of the World: Secular Magic in a Rational Age*, ed. Joshua Landy and Michael Saler (Stanford, CA: Stanford University Press, 2009), 225–58; Nadeem Hussain, "Honest Illusion: Valuing for Nietzsche's Free Spirits," in *Nietzsche and Morality*, ed. Brian Leiter and Neil Sinhababu (Oxford: Clarendon Press, 2007), 157–91.

"drives even the unskilled man to work; and if someone lacking property sees someone else who is rich, he likewise hurries off to sow and plant and set his house in order; neighbor competes with neighbor striving for prosperity." Even though both Eris goddesses rely on envy, the former makes envy into something destructive (destroying one's neighbor), while the latter uses it as a stimulus toward self-betterment (being more prosperous than one's neighbor by one's own work).

Seen from the perspective of "The Greek State," the "older" wicked Eris represents the original state of nature and the bellum omnium contra omnes that continues between nations once they are formed, while the younger Eris represents how violence is positively channeled toward art and genius once society is created by the blond beasts of prey. We can see here the parallels between the two goddesses and a positive and negative conception of the will to power. The first wicked Eris represents the reactive forces that in the state of nature have mankind wage a war of all against all. Once societies are formed, it transposes this war between all into a war between city-states, continuing its aim of separating and destroying mankind. The second and good Eris—the active forces—initially commands men, through the conquering horde, into forming societies. Once these are created, she drives them to better themselves and their surroundings through the agon.[4]

If wars between nations were a means to redirect the natural war of all against all so that peace could reign within the confines of the city-states, on the domestic level the Greeks invented other institutions to channel such violence. Although the war between states takes its cue from the wicked Eris who leads men into a hostile struggle to the death, these institutions have as their patron the good Eris who drives men to better themselves. The institutions that the Greeks developed to protect each other against their inner explosives are those of the contest, but not simply to protect. The contest also has a positive aim: "the well-being of the whole, of state society. . . . [E]very Athenian was to develop himself, through the contest, to the degree to which this self was of most use to Athens and would cause least damage" (HC). Thus the will to power can take on a positive ethical and political meaning—ethical in the sense that the ethos of the contest provides the impetus and guidance to individuals so that they may improve themselves within a healthy context. They do so to bring glory to their cities, which is the political element.

What is key is how the institutional setup of the agon preserves its positive ethos, thereby directing it toward the good of the community. Siemens is thus correct in arguing that the spirit of the contest is preserved by its

[4] On active and reactive forces, see Gilles Deleuze, "Active and Reactive," in *The New Nietzsche: Contemporary Styles of Interpretation*, ed. David Allison (Cambridge, MA: MIT Press, 1985), 80–106.

institutional setup. Without its institutions, the forces of the agon, as we will see below, would revert to the destructive bad Eris type. This is against those radical democratic readings, examined in the last chapter, of Nietzsche's agon that focus exclusively on the ethical aspect of the contest while disregarding its political and deeply hierarchical makeup, which is only made possible through the existence of a slave class, as the links to "The Greek State" attest to.[5] Much like the pathos of distance, the agon necessitates a political structure for its positive, ethical role to be fulfilled. Without that structure, only a destructive will to power would exist.

Perhaps one the most famous institutions of the Greek agon that Nietzsche does not mention is the Olympics, where the negative warmongering Eris is transformed into a peaceful athletic contest. The other institution that Nietzsche discusses is that of ostracism, to which he gives a novel interpretation. He explains:

> The original function of this strange institutions is, however, not as a safety valve [of removing tyrants] but as a stimulant—the preeminent individual is removed to renew the tournament of forces: a thought that is hostile to the "exclusivity" of genius in the modern sense, but assumes that there are always *several* geniuses to incite one another into action, just as they keep each other within certain limits too. That is the kernel of the Hellenic idea of competition: it loathes a monopoly of predominance and fears the dangers of this; it desires, as *protective measure* against genius—a second genius. (HC)

If a genius were to achieve such a glorious deed that makes him *"hors de concours,"* like Miltiades's success at Marathon, he would be destroyed by hubris, forced to commit a lowly deed because he could no longer vent and give positive direction to his force within the confines of the agon. Having no longer an equal with whom to spar against, he would revert to the evil Eris and commit an act of destruction that would ultimately lead to his own self-destruction. Hubris, Nietzsche writes, also explains the downfall of Athens and Sparta: having subjugated their opponents, they oppressed them in such a manner that when the Persians attacked, the Greek allies were too weak to help them repel the Persian threat. In oppressing their opponents, the Athenians and Spartans destroyed the balance of power that

---

[5] See Herman Siemens, "Nietzsche's Political Philosophy: A Review of Recent Literature," *Nietzsche-Studien* 30 (2001): 509–26. As Nicholas Martin reminds us in "Breeding Greeks: Nietzsche, Gobineau, and Classical Theories of Race" (in *Nietzsche and Antiquity: His Reaction and Response to the Classical Tradition*, ed. Paul Bishop [Rochester, NY: Camden House, 2004], 46), "Freed from daily toil, a small number of Greeks (approximately one-fifth of the population) was driven by this same energy to rivalry with one another and to the highest cultural achievements."

makes for a constructive agonistic space. This lack of competition results in both weaker antagonists and, correspondingly, a weaker central power.

Hubris in Nietzsche's thinking is thus the idea that if one becomes too powerful for the agon, if there no longer exists a sufficiently strong counter-power, then the victor's excess force will search for other ways to discharge itself. No longer structured by the institution of the contest into a positive force, this excess will return to the fold of the reactive, wicked Eris, looking to completely annihilate the enemy. But in doing so one opens oneself to attack from other, even more powerful entities (the Gods or the Persians). Having destroyed the means of making oneself stronger (the agon), one's previous actions will impede one from resisting these other entities. The significance that Nietzsche gives to ostracism is that if someone or some entity begins to be too dominant within the agon, then this force must be removed to restore a healthy competition. The removed force can then measure itself against something stronger, hopefully forming a new contest with a new, external force.

The agon provides the institutional setup within which a positive will to power can both grow and be channeled toward positive outcomes rather than destructive, negative ones. Through a wholesome contest, one premised on bettering your adversaries instead of destroying them, athletes or artists can measure themselves against other athletes and artists, and in competing, can improve their own abilities. The agonistic ethos, its ethical facet, is maintained through the (political) institutions of the gymnasium, palaestra, and city-state more widely, along with the institution of ostracism. Without such institutions, the will to power would revert to a war of all against all as was the case in the state of nature, underlining how political institutions are necessary for the will to power to express itself in an active, creative way.

This destructive aspect of the agon as conceived by Nietzsche is overlooked by the democratic reading, which perceives agonistic (democratic) politics in a purely constructive light. It is not alive to the fact that such a politics can become destructive too, as many examples of recent politics attest to, and hence fails to address the possible dangers that Nietzsche had identified. Moreover, the need for a certain structure to direct the agon toward positive outcomes highlights the fact that the institutional setup is key, and a reflection on what institutions are needed today to fulfill this role is often lacking in the literature. In the same manner that art justified the whole in *The Birth of Tragedy*, what the agon produces is for the benefit of the whole community, which can share in its successes. Although those successes might be individual, much like the art that is produced by the few ultimately justifies the existence of the whole, whose labor made such successes possible in the first place, those successes reflect positively on the polis as a whole, thereby recompensing all those who made them possible, even if indirectly.

THE ETERNAL RETURN

It is Heraclitus whom Nietzsche most associates with the institution of the agon in his early lectures on "Philosophy in the Tragic Age of the Greeks." He is the one who identified Hesiod's good Eris as the cosmic principle of the contest—"the contest idea of the Greek individual and the Greek state, taken from the gymnasium and the palaestra, from the artist's agon, from the contest between political parties and between cities" (PTAG 5). Heraclitus is also the key figure when it comes to Nietzsche's notion of the eternal return. Quoting directly from the "What I Owe to the Ancients "section from *Twilight of the Idols*, which is where Nietzsche claims he unearthed his philosophical theories of the will to power, eternal return, and overman, Nietzsche writes in his review of *The Birth of Tragedy*—his first revaluation, as we saw in chapter 1—that the "doctrine of the 'eternal return' . . . this is Zarathustra's doctrine, but ultimately it is nothing Heraclitus couldn't have said too" (EH BT 3).[6] There he describes Heraclitus's philosophy as one that affirms "passing away *and destruction*," along with saying "yes to opposition and war, *becoming* along with a radical rejection of the very concept of 'being.'"[7] As Nietzsche recognizes, these ideas have a crucial influence on his own "Dionysian philosophy," in particular the eternal return. In "Philosophy in the Tragic Age of the Greeks," Nietzsche elaborates on Heraclitus's philosophical position. He explains that "the strife of the opposites gives birth to all that comes to be; the definite qualities that look permanent to us express but the momentary ascendancy of one partner. But this by no means signifies the end of the war; the contest endures in all eternity" (PTAG 5).

While Nietzsche's understanding of the world is fundamentally influenced by his interpretation of Heraclitus, he transforms this theory into an ethical and political doctrine. This is the doctrine of the eternal return, and it will be Zarathustra's task over the course of the work, especially the first three parts, to reveal and teach this doctrine.

---

[6] See also: "Nobody had ever turned the Dionysian into a philosophical pathos before: *tragic wisdom* was missing; I could not find any sign of it, even among the *eminent* Greek philosophers, those from the two centuries *before* Socrates. I had some doubts in the case of *Heraclitus*" (EH BT 3).

[7] This seems in line with how Nietzsche had presented Heraclitus in his lectures on him. See PPP Heraclitus: "He knows only Becoming, the flowing"; PTAG 5: "'Becoming' is what I contemplate."

The political purpose of the lie is to serve as a selection criterion between ascending and descending life, and therefore whether one is strong enough to pursue great politics.[8] Ultimately, it also serves as a tool to determine what caste one should belong to in Nietzsche's positing of his future two-sphere political ideal. Nietzsche first introduces the doctrine of the eternal return in his published work in the penultimate section of book 4 of *The Gay Science*, the original ending to the book, with book 5 being a later addition, and just before Zarathustra makes his entry, underscoring the links between the two. Importantly, he opens the presentation of the doctrine with the qualifier "what if"—the hypothetical nature of the question suggesting that Nietzsche is aware that this is not actually a true representation of reality.[9] It serves as a thought experiment, a litmus test, to distinguish affirmative life forces from negative ones. So if the doctrine affirms a cosmological view of the world, that everything will happen/return/recur again, the hypothetical nature of the question suggests that Nietzsche does not believe that cosmological view to be true but rather is using it as a way of getting a certain reaction out of those subjected to it.[10]

The infamous question is,

> What if some day or night a demon were to steal into your loneliest loneliness and say to you: "This life as you now live it and have lived it

---

[8] See EH BT 2: "The real opposition:—the *degenerate* instinct that turns against life with subterranean vindictiveness . . . and a formula of the *highest affirmation* born out of fullness"; AC 2: "What is good?—everything that enhances people's feeling of power, will to power, power itself. What is bad?—everything stemming from weakness." For the eternal return as selective, see Gilles Deleuze, *Nietzsche and Philosophy*, ed. Hugh Tomlinson (London: Continuum, 2006).

[9] In his notes, Nietzsche does appear to toy with the idea that the (cosmological) doctrine of the eternal return is true, but it strikes me here that Nietzsche is thinking about the different ways one might present the theory—whether presenting it as a true theory of the world might be more convincing. Yet the fact that these musings remain in his notes suggests to me that he did not actually believe it. See KSA 12 5 [71]: 6: the "most scientific of all theories."

[10] For the purposes of this study, I don't make a theoretical differentiation between translating the term as either return or recurrence. For an overview of the different interpretations of the eternal return, see Paul Loeb, *The Death of Nietzsche's Zarathustra* (Cambridge: Cambridge University Press, 2010), 2: "that we should look instead in Nietzsche's unpublished notes (Heidegger 1982); that Nietzsche intended eternal recurrence only as a useful fiction, mythical image, hypothetical thought experiment, as-if story, or practical postulate (Clark 1990, 245ff.; Schacht 1991, 232ff.; Gooding-Williams 2001, 213); that he conceived of eternal recurrence as an incommunicable esoteric or mystical insight (Salaquarda 1989; Stambaugh 1994); that he had no single, univocal doctrine in mind (Winchester 1994, 9–33; Gooding-Williams 2001, 183ff.); he designed eternal recurrence as an exoteric noble lie that would conceal his true esoteric views (Levine 1995, 122ff.; Rosen 1995, x–xvi, 10–17; Waite 1996, 315ff.); or even that he intended us to notice that eternal recurrence is flawed, incoherent, or self-consuming thought (Berkowitz 1995, 207–10; Magnus 1999)."

you will have to live once again and innumerable times again; and there will be nothing new in it, but every pain and every joy and every thought and sigh and everything unspeakably small or great in your life must return to you, all in the same succession and sequence—even this spider and this moonlight between the trees, and even this moment and I myself. The eternal hourglass of existence is turned over again and again, and you with it, speck of dust!" (GS 341)

Nietzsche presents a choice: "Would you not throw yourself down and gnash your teeth and curse the demon who spoke thus? Or have you once experienced a tremendous moment when you would have answered him: 'You are a god, and never have I heard anything more divine?'" Depending on whether one answers positively (ascending) or negatively (descending), then one will be deemed to be a member of the corresponding higher or lower caste.[11]

The doctrine of the eternal return has a strong *ethical* function too.[12] It has a dual aim: to redeem the past and prepare for the future coming of the overmen. Its first purpose is to fight against the spirit of revenge, to redeem the past. Zarathustra says that *"mankind be redeemed from revenge*: that to me is the bridge to the highest hope and a rainbow after long thunderstorms" (Z II Tarantulas). The spirit of revenge is the thought of "it was": that the will is unable to will backward (Z II Redemption).[13] What brings about spitefulness is the inability to change one's past. Nietzsche proposes to redeem the negativity associated with this past by changing the "it was" into a "thus I willed it" through the doctrine of the eternal return. Zarathustra does so by affirming the present "Moment" (Z III Vision and Riddle 2): if one accepts and is willing to eternally relive the present moment, then one redeems all one's past. One will proclaim "thus I willed it" (Z II Redemption) concerning one's past, as this past makes possible the present that one affirms. It is redeemed because if one is happy with the present, than one must accept all the past that made it possible, including all its joys and pain. Zarathustra asks: "Have you ever said Yes to one joy? Oh my friends, then you also said Yes to *all* pain" (Z IV Sleepwalker Song 10).

[11] For an earlier version of this notion, see SE 3: "Genius, the highest fruit of life, can perhaps justify life as such; the glorious, creative human being is now to answer the question: 'Do you affirm this existence in the depths of your heart? Is it sufficient for you? Would you be its advocate, its redeemer? For you have only to pronounce a single heartfelt Yes!—and life, though it faces such heavy accusation, shall go free.'—What answer will he give?—The answer of Empedocles."

[12] For the individual strengthening capacities, the eternal return is meant to engender in the positive types; see John Richardson, *Nietzsche's New Darwinism* (Oxford: Oxford University Press, 2004).

[13] We might remember that Nietzsche wrote *Zarathustra* after Lou Andreas-Salomé refused him.

The reason why all the past, including all its ups and downs, must be accepted is that if one single aspect of it were changed, then the present moment would not be the same. As Nehamas explains, "To want to be different in any way is for Nietzsche to want to be different in every way. . . . [T]o want anything about oneself to change is for one to want to cease to be who one is."[14] One would therefore not be affirming the same moment, and would remain trapped in the spirit of revenge that wants to change the past. This is why the doctrine of the eternal return must be the "unconditional and infinitely repeated cycle of *all* things" (EH BT 3; emphasis added). Once the past is redeemed, one can rediscover the innocence of becoming and creating, like Heraclitus's child at play or the final metamorphosis of Zarathustra's first speech: "The child is innocence and forgetting, a new beginning, a game, a wheel rolling out of itself, a first movement, a sacred yes saying" (Z I Metamorphoses).

Nietzsche presents this idea of redeeming the past by affirming the present through his "vision" of a young shepherd "writhing, choking, [and] twitching, his face distorted, with a thick black snake hanging from his mouth" (Z III Vision and Riddle 2). Zarathustra tries to pull the snake out of his throat, but in vain. This would be to want to change the past, for the snake not to have bitten the shepherd in the first place. But to rid himself of the snake, the shepherd must "bite down" on the head of the snake. He does so, and as such is transformed into an "illuminated, *laughing* being!" In this affirmation of the present he redeems the past pain of the snakebite and transforms it into the joy of his accomplishment. The overmen are prefigured in this transformed, laughing shepherd. Nietzsche asks, "*What* did I see then as a parable? And *who* is it that must someday come?" Here we get the first hint at what the overmen are supposed to represent: they are those who overcome the ressentiment spirit of revenge of the last men through the doctrine of the eternal return.

"Biting off the head" epitomizes what Nietzsche identifies as the "pessimism of strength"—one of the discoveries that he associates with *The Birth of Tragedy* (BT P 1). This pessimism of strength is the Dionysian state: "saying yes to life, even in its strangest and harshest problems" (TI Ancients 5)—that is, the doctrine of the eternal return. As "nobody had ever turned the Dionysian into a philosophical pathos before: *tragic wisdom* was missing," Nietzsche declares himself "the first *tragic philosopher*" (EH BT 3). That is to say, while the Greeks had discovered tragedy, they expressed it through drama, but had not theorized it philosophically, which Nietzsche claims to be the first to do.

But if the aim is to redeem the past, the affirmation of the present also has a forward-looking dimension. As Nietzsche puts it in *Twilight of the*

---

[14] Nehamas, *Nietzsche: Life as Literature*, 156.

Idols, "[It is] the eternal return of life; the future promised by the past and the past consecrated to the future" (TI Ancients 4). One can put this aspect of the doctrine in the following way: "What future aim would successfully redeem the pain I am currently experiencing?" Or again: "What future achievement would make my current pain worthwhile?" In this manner the doctrine offers a forward-looking dimension too. Indeed, in his notes of 1881 Nietzsche had stated that "my doctrine affirms: your duty is to live in such a manner that you must *desire* to live anew" (KSA 9 11 [163]). The imperative contains two related aspects, as seen above. First, one desires to relive all one's current pain as a necessary means to the moment that redeems all such past pain. This pain is necessary because without it success in one's endeavor could not be achieved. To will that success without the past pain, second, would be to will a different past, and thus a different, defeated present, thereby remaining trapped in the spirit of ressentiment.

While the doctrine can be conceived of as an imperative, it differentiates itself from the Kantian moral imperative.[15] It does so because Nietzsche, the first "immoralist," does not desire his doctrine to be a universal moral category applicable to all people in all circumstances. For one, the doctrine, in its political guise, is meant to exclude those who represent descending life forces. Building on the basis that people are thereby fundamentally unequal, Nietzsche does not believe that every person should behave universally in the same manner when faced with the same situation. As Nietzsche observes in *The Antichrist* 11, resuming much of what has been argued so far,

> One more word against Kant as a *moralist*. A virtue needs to be our *own* invention, our *own* most personal need and self-defense: in any other sense, a virtue is just dangerous. Whatever is not a condition for life *harms* it: a virtue that comes exclusively from a feeling of respect for the concept of "virtue," as Kant would have it, is harmful. "Virtue," "duty," "goodness in itself," goodness that has been stamped with the character of the impersonal and universally valid—these are fantasies and manifestations of decline, of the final exhaustion of life, of the Königsberg Chinesianity. The most basic laws of preservation and growth require the opposite: that everyone should invent his *own* virtues, his *own* categorical imperatives. A people is destroyed when it confuses its *own*

---

[15] Kaufmann (*Nietzsche: Philosopher, Psychologist, Antichrist*, 322–25) writes that "the suggestion that the eternal recurrence is to be construed as essentially similar to Kant's Categorical Imperative is misleading." But Deleuze ("Active and Reactive, 89–100), who seems closer to the mark, explains that the doctrine of the eternal return is a "half-avowed and half-hidden rival" to the Kantian imperative. In fact, his positing of the doctrine of the eternal return as "whatever you will, will it in such a manner that you also will its eternal return" seems quite apposite.

duty with the concept of duty in general. Nothing ruins us more profoundly or inwardly than "impersonal" duty, or any sacrifice in front of the Moloch of abstraction. To think that people did not sense the *mortal danger* posed by Kant's categorical imperative![16]

With Nietzsche's doctrine, one has to come up with one's own virtues, one's own values, find one's own way. As Zarathustra puts it, " 'This—it turns out—is *my* way—where is yours?'—That is how I answered those who asked me 'the way.' *The* way after all—it does not exist!" (Z III Spirit of Gravity 2). The values will depend on both the given circumstances and the individual's or group's constitution. In fact, the only way to silence the spirit of gravity incarnated in the mole and the dwarf who say "good for all, evil for all" is to declare "this is *my* good and evil." As such, the doctrine of the eternal return not only redeems the past but in providing a newly found innocence also actively encourages the creation of new, positive, and nonuniversal values.

There is a clear link here between the doctrine of the eternal return and the insight Nietzsche gained from his study of the Greeks that a healthy culture is a precondition to a genuine philosophy; the doctrine's aim is to restore precisely the healthy instincts that are the bedrock to a healthy culture, and that has given way to the decaying moralism of the post-Socratic ancient Greeks. This is done through the political and ethical functions of the doctrine of the eternal return. Moreover, that the doctrine of the eternal return affirms the existence as well as eternal return of the last man (Z III Convalescent 2) brings to the fore the necessity of a caste society—one sphere devoted to the production of the overman, and the other to the perpetuation of the last man—and the necessary pathos of distance that the former must maintain with regard to the latter for their goal to be attained.

THE OVERMAN

In the passage "On Self-Overcoming," life reveals its secret to Zarathustra. It explains that it is "that *which must always overcome itself.*" Zarathustra adds: "Truly I say to you: good and evil that would be everlasting—there is no such thing! They must overcome themselves out of themselves again and again." Were the values of good and evil to cease to perpetually overcome themselves, this would mean the end of "life." It would lead to the last values; it would lead, as Zarathustra proclaims in the prologue, to the last men (*den letzten Menschen*) (Z P 5).[17] The last men are those who claim to have

---

[16] For an earlier engagement with Kant's categorical imperative, see GS 335.

[17] For Nietzsche, values are embodied, such that the last men incarnate the last values. As Zarathustra says, "Body am I through and through, and nothing besides; and soul is just a

invented happiness and who live the longest. They believe that they have found the best way to live—in a happy mediocrity—and hence resist their overcoming. Having no aim beyond their self-satisfaction, they have neither the means nor desire to strive for a type of life beyond their own, and in doing so perpetuate life. They want, in effect, the "end of history."[18]

From this perspective, the overmen are those who overcome the values of the last men, thereby creating a new type of existence and in this way continuing life.[19] Zarathustra opens his speech in the marketplace claiming to teach the overman. He says, *"I teach you the overman (Ich lehre euch den Übermenschen). Man (Der Mensch) is something that must be overcome. All creatures so far created something beyond themselves; and you want to be the ebb of this great flood and would even rather go back to animals than overcome man?"* (Z P 3). The overmen are those who overcome man in the same manner that man overcame the ape: "What is the ape to man? A laughingstock or a painful embarrassment. And that is precisely what man shall be to the overmen: a laughingstock or a painful embarrassment." "Man" is Zarathustra's contemporaries on the marketplace—modern man.

What Zarathustra is offering is an alternative: either man can continue on his current path that leads to the last men, or he can overcome those values and try for a new type of existence. He says,

> It is time that mankind set itself a goal. It is time that mankind plant the seed of its highest hope. Its soil is rich enough for this. But one day that will be poor and tame, and no tall tree will be able to grow from it anymore. . . . Beware! The time of the most contemptible human is coming, the one who can no longer have contempt for himself. Behold! I give you the *last man (der letzte Mensch)*. (Z P 5)

---

word for something on the body. . . . [B]ehind your thoughts and feelings, my brother, stands a powerful commander, an unknown wise man—he is called self. He lives in your body, he is your body" (Z I Despisers).

[18] See Francis Fukuyama, *The End of History and the Last man* (London: Penguin, 1993). Note the often-overlooked second part where Fukuyama criticizes the end of history as leading to the last man.

[19] While there has been a move to translate *mensch* as "human" or "human being," leading to "overhuman," I think Nietzsche would have used the gender-biased "man." For a critique of Nietzsche's sexist views and language, see C. Heike Schotten, *Nietzsche's Revolution: Décadence, Politics, and Sexuality* (New York: Palgrave Macmillan, 2009). For my review of it, see Hugo Drochon, "Nietzsche, Politics, and Gender," *Nietzsche-Studien* 39 (2010): 678–81. Nonetheless, I think the overmen can be understood as both male or female figures when we consider in how high a regard he held both Lou Andreas-Salomé and Cosima Wagner, describing the latter as Ariadne, Dionysus's lover (See KSB 8, letter to Cosima Wagner, January 3, 1889). When Nietzsche depicts the parents he deems fit to procreate in order to produce the overmen, while he gives traditional attributes to man ("fit for war") and woman ("fit for bearing children"), he does say he wants both to be "fit to dance in head and limb" (Z III Tables, 23), establishing some degree of parity between the two.

Mankind is at a turning point, according to Zarathustra, and faces a choice: either it can continue on its current path, which will lead to the last men, or it can plant the seeds now—while its soil is still rich enough—for a new type of being. The crowd of the marketplace hail the arrival of the last men—"give us these last men, oh Zarathustra!" they cry, suggesting that the majority of modern men desire to be last men—so Zarathustra turns to look for companions, a minority, whom he would "lure away from the herd," and with whom he would write "new values on new tablets" (Z P 9). It is these companions that Zarathustra will put on the path of producing the overmen. Mankind would thus, at least for the time being, split into two: the majority (represented by the crowd of the marketplace) would continue on the path toward the last men, while a small minority (Zarathustra's companions) would separate from this group to attempt a new type of existence, a new type of evaluation in opposition to those of modern man, as a means of attaining the overmen. In doing so they perpetuate life.

In *Nietzsche and the Political*, Daniel Conway offers a political reading of the overman, centered on the notion of perfectionism.[20] He writes that "Nietzsche's perfectionism attains its apotheosis in his enigmatic conception of the *Übermensch*, or 'over-man.' . . . He thus conceives of the *Übermensch* as embodying the perfection, rather than the transcendence, of humankind." For Conway, the overman "constitutes Nietzsche's general answer to the founding question of politics," which Conway had identified in his introduction as "*what ought humankind to become*." Nietzsche's answer, according to Conway, is that "'we' should undertake to breed a type of individual whose pursuit of self-perfection contributes to the enhancement of humankind and thereby justifies our own existence."[21]

I am sympathetic to Conway's claim that for Nietzsche, the fundamental question of politics revolves around the issue of political legislation, of "what ought humankind to become," in the sense that the aim of Nietzsche's philosophical project is to make possible the appearance of the overmen. If the overmen undeniably constitute an ideal for Nietzsche, I am less convinced that this is best captured through his notion of perfectibility; there is a tension between the *over*man—defined, as we saw above, by over-

[20] Stanley Cavell was the first to read Nietzsche as an Emersonian perfectionist; see his "Aversive Thinking: Emersonian Representations in Heidegger and Nietzsche," in *Conditions Handsome and Unhandsome* (Chicago: University of Chicago Press, 1990), 33–63. Conway expresses his debt to Nietzsche; see Daniel Conway, *Nietzsche and the Political* (London: Routledge, 1997), 144n2. See also James Conant, "Nietzsche's Perfectionism: A Reading of *Schopenhauer as Educator*," in *Nietzsche's Postmoralism: Essays on Nietzsche's Prelude to Philosophy's Future*, ed. Richard Schacht (Cambridge: Cambridge University Press, 2001), 181–257; Vanessa Lemm, "Is Nietzsche a Perfectionist? Rawls, Cavell, and the Politics of Culture in Nietzsche's 'Schopenhauer as Educator,'" *Journal of Nietzsche Studies* 34 (2007): 5–27.
[21] Conway, *Nietzsche and the Political*, 20, 3, 26.

coming—and the pursuit of self-perfection—a tension that Conway elides. There are two main reasons why Conway's idea of perfectionism does not match up with Nietzsche's concept of the overman, as I will develop over the course of this section. For one, if man is perfected as he is now, in his modern "human, all too human" incarnation, the end result will be the last man, not the overman. It is instead another type that must be perfected—one removed from the values of the herd, and who thereby contain the seeds of the overmen. Second, Nietzsche's advocacy of the "immoral" methods to attain the overman is at odds with Conway's more democratic and individual ethical perfectionism, and presupposes a degree of institutional organization—the party of life—that Conway denies.

Conway writes that the "task of 'great politics' is neither to destroy nor to transcend the all-too-human within us, but to bring the all-too-human to completion and perfection."[22] But what Zarathustra is saying during his first speech on the marketplace is that the completion of the values of his contemporary modern man as they are currently constituted—the crowd of the marketplace—leads to the all-too-human last man, not the overman. Man is placed on a continuum between the ape and the overman: "Mankind is a rope fastened between animal and overman" (Z P 4). To perfect man, to accept his values as they now stand, is to achieve the last man, not the overman. They will be the last beings to exist, and no overmen will come to life: "The time approaches when human beings will no longer give birth to a dancing star" (Z P 5). This is why Zarathustra emphasizes how the modern last man must first be overcome, that at least a small number revalue his values, so that a new type of being can come into existence within that group. Only once this last man is overcome by a minority can we start to concentrate on perfecting a new type of being away from the values of the herd, and one whose relation to man is parallel to man's relation to the ape, with the one growing out of the other, but in this way producing a new type of being.

In *Ecce Homo*, Nietzsche returns to the figure of the overman to refute certain contemporary interpretations of the term, and there he presents his ideal as a "type that has the highest constitutional excellence" (EH Books 1), which might go in the direction of a "perfectionist" reading. But here again Nietzsche stresses how this "excellence" is diametrically opposed to anything that might pass as excellence in his contemporary, modern man. He explains that his "type" of the overman is "in contrast to 'modern' people, to 'good' people, to Christian and other nihilists," which we can identify as last men. Nietzsche continues: "This word *'overman'* is understood almost everywhere with complete innocence to mean values that are the *opposite* from the ones appearing in the figure of Zarathustra, which is to say the

---

[22] Ibid., 13.

'idealistic' type of the higher sort of humanity, half 'saint,' half 'genius.'" Later, quoting directly from *Thus Spoke Zarathustra*, Nietzsche adds that Zarathustra "does not conceal the fact that *his* type of person . . . is an overman specifically when compared to the *good*; that the good and just would call his overmen *devils*" (EH Destiny 5), reinforcing the view that for Nietzsche, Zarathustra's overmen are the direct opposite of the Christian "good" last men. By addressing the overmen's opposition to the last men in terms of good and evil, Nietzsche also draws the link that the overmen entertain with the revaluation of all values. So if there is a perfection to be attained, it is to be found in another type of human being who has overcome the values of the modern last man.

That the figure of the overman reappears in Nietzsche's later writings refutes the commonly held notion that it is a theme that only features in *Zarathustra*, yet drops out of all later works. Indeed, the overman features not only in *Ecce Homo* but also in *The Genealogy*, where Napoléon is presented as a "synthesis of *Unmensch* and *Übermensch*" (GM I 16), and again in *Twilight of the Idols*, where Cesare Borgia is considered to be a "higher man," as a type of Übermensch (TI Skirmishes 37). Crucially, the overman also appears in *The Antichrist*, and at a rather central juncture. In the third aphorism, part of the "We Hyperboreans" section that Nietzsche planned as the introduction to his magnum opus, Nietzsche poses his "problem," which serves as the *problématique* to the work, of "what type of man (*Mensch*) should be *bred*, should be *willed* as having greater value, as being more deserving of life, as being more certain of a future." He explains that "this more valuable type has appeared often enough already: but only as a stroke of luck, as an exception, never as *willed*" (AC 3). In the following aphorism, Nietzsche describes this *"higher type"* as a "type of overman in relation to humanity in general," claiming that such "successes" are "real strokes of luck" (AC 4). It is therefore quite clear that the new type of man that Nietzsche is advocating should be bred and willed is in fact the overman. Again the overman is opposed to another last man type of "the domestic animal, the herd animal, the sick animal: man—the Christian," and it is this "opposing" type that has so far been "willed, bred, [and] *achieved*" (AC 3). "You should not beautify Christianity or try to dress it up," Nietzsche writes. "It has waged a *war to the death* against this *higher* type of person" (AC 5).

It is interesting to note that Nietzsche explains that such types have already existed in the past, and certainly might continue in the future, though not, he is quick to emphasize, as willed.[23] "There is a continuous series of

[23] This apparently jars with Zarathustra's claims to the contrary—that "never yet has there been overmen" (Z II Priests). Yet there are two mitigating factors, both of which have to do with the context of the work (Z), suggesting that these two statements can be reconciled. First, Nietzsche's audience: in the sense that neither the people of the marketplace nor his companions have ever encountered such a figure, perhaps Zarathustra himself, who seems to

individual successes in the most varied places on earth and from the most varied cultures," Nietzsche writes. "Successes like this, real strokes of luck, were always possible and perhaps will always be possible. And whole generations, families, or peoples can sometimes constitute this sort of bull's eye, *right on the mark*" (AC 4). The notion of strokes of luck harks back to Nietzsche's descriptions of the Greek philosophers as chance wanderers in "Philosophy in the Tragic Age of the Greeks," and we might conceive of Nietzsche's whole generations, families, or peoples as a reference to the ancient Greeks. The fact that these bull's eyes appeared "in the most varied places on earth and from the most varied cultures" reminds us that the blond beasts of prey of *The Genealogy* hailed equally from "Roman, Arabian, Germanic, Japanese nobility, Homeric heroes, [and] Scandinavian Vikings" (GM I 11).[24] What I mean to suggest is that while the figure of the overman is only explicitly present in *Zarathustra, Ecce Homo*, and *The Antichrist*—not to mention *The Genealogy* and *Twilight of the Idols*, making it already four more works than is usually credited—the profile of such a figure is already anticipated in the figure of the Greek philosophical genius, along with the beasts of prey. Moreover, if it is the case that *Zarathustra* represents in a certain manner the summit of Nietzsche's philosophical teaching, as I will explore in the following chapter, then it is coherent that the overmen, the end point of Nietzsche's project, should appear principally—though not uniquely—there.

Given this, there appears to be two levels of overcoming in Nietzsche's conception of the overmen: the individual level and the species level. The first relates to the continuous attempt at self-overcoming that certain individuals engage in within the species, while the second relates to the overcoming of a certain type of species—in Nietzsche's understanding, from ape to man—and—or so he hopes—from man to overman. Even though perfectionism as Conway understands it is perhaps most aligned with the first notion of (self-)overcoming—particularly when it is linked, in a positive sense, to the notions of giving one's character "style," or again "becoming who one is," where one attempts to get the best out of oneself—it also has a role to play in the second—species-level—overcoming, as we will see.[25] Although perfectionism, as I have argued above, can only take place

---

be more of a preparatory figure in any case. Second is the use of rhetoric in *Zarathustra*, in the manner in which Zarathustra often speaks in parables as well as how he uses the overman figure as an exhortation for the last men and his companions to overcome themselves.

[24] We can conceive of the blond beasts of prey as overmanly types, because they represent a new value—namely, the state-creating instinct—that did not exist before their appearance.

[25] See GS 290: "giving 'style' to one's character"; GS 270, 335; EH P: "becoming who one is." On "becoming who you are," see Aaron Ridley, introduction to *Nietzsche: The Antichrist, Ecce Homo, Twilight of the Idols, and Other Writings*, trans. Judith Norman (Cambridge: Cambridge University Press, 2005), vii–xxxiv; more generally, Nehamas, *Life as Literature*.

within a given species, it is when this species starts to attain its natural end that a tipping point is reached from which a new form of species becomes possible. As Nietzsche explains in *Schopenhauer as Educator* 6,

> When a species has arrived at its limits and is about to go over into a higher species, the goal of its evolution lies not in the mass of its exemplars and their well-being, let alone in those exemplars who happen to come last in point of time, but rather in those apparently scattered and chance existences that favorable conditions have here and there produced.

Nietzsche had just described these existences as the "more uncommon, more powerful, more complex, [and] more fruitful." So when a certain species, modern man, begins to attain its natural end, its goal is not to be found in the perfection of those who come last in point of time—the last men—but instead in the perfection of those scattered and chance existences—that is, those who have started to overcome the last men and sow the seeds for a new type of being.

Nietzsche's admiration of the Greeks is well known, and in chapter 1 one of the reasons suggested for this esteem was the fact that they were the first—and so far only, perhaps outside the Renaissance—to have achieved a healthy culture, where philosophy and culture are in harmony. Another reason may be because the appearance of the figure of the philosopher represents one type of overcoming that Nietzsche is especially interested in. In this it provides us with a model of how Nietzsche might have understood overcoming, at the individual and species levels. As Nietzsche observes in his introductory remarks to his lectures on the "Pre-Platonic Philosophers," the philosopher had to overcome in particular the poet, among others, before finding his true vocation (PPP 2–5).[26] Even this transition was a little hazy: "In itself it is arbitrary to say that so-and-so is the first [philosopher], and that before him there was no philosophers, for a type does not come to exist all at once" (PPP 2). This transition, or transformation, of poet into philosopher gives us a model for understanding overcoming and its linked notion of the overman. We see that perfectionism plays a role too, in the sense that it is only with the perfection of the Greek poet that a new type— the philosopher—was able to come into existence. That the philosopher had to build on the poets is highlighted by Socrates's, and especially Plato's,

[26] PPP 2: "The *poet*, who represents a preliminary stage to the philosopher, was to be overcome. . . . Thales overcomes (1) the mythical preliminary stage of philosophy, (2) the sporadic-proverbial form of philosophy, and (3) the various sciences—the first by thinking conceptually, the second by systematizing, and the third by creating one [unified] view of the world. Philosophy is therefore the art that presents an image of universal existence in concepts; this definition fits Thales first."

wrestling and rivalries with them.[27] Yet while building on that type of existence (the poets), philosophers represent an overcoming of that type and thus a new type of being.

One might suggest that Nietzsche's mission is the perfection of this new type of existence that is the philosopher, who took a wrong turn, as I developed in chapter 1, with the advent of Socrates's moralism and Plato's adoption of it.[28] The modern world as Nietzsche knew it was a child of this error, with the last men representing the final—perfect—exemplar of Christianity, understood as "Platonism for the 'people'" (BGE P). This world, however, also contained within itself the seeds to its own overcoming, notably in the figure of the philosopher. Nietzsche's aim is to re-create the conditions—a hierarchical society—on which a pure culture could come into existence, which in turn would be the soil from which healthy philosophers could grow. In short, he wanted to re-create the conditions that made possible Plato, so that he could correct Plato's mistake (moralism) and lead philosophy to its natural end. This is to prepare for the appearance of another overman, who in turn would overcome the philosopher, in the same way that the philosopher overcame the poet.[29] It is therefore not surprising that it is his new philosophers who are tasked with legislating a new society into existence, whose goal will be the creation of new overmen.

This does not make the overmen, to my mind, a teleological ideal, because no end point is ever determined. The precise "content" of the overmen is never given, although Nietzsche does posit some noble contours. But it cannot be predicted what form the overmen will take, even if that is the posited aim. In the same way one could not predict that the overcoming of the poet would lead to the figure of the philosopher, what precise form the overcoming of the philosopher would take is also unpredictable, beyond the fact that they will have antecedents in the philosopher in the same manner that the philosopher had antecedents in the poet. Furthermore, what Nietzsche is aiming for are new overmen—ones who would overcome modern man. Other overmen (philosophers and blond beasts of prey) have existed in the past, overcoming more ancient forms of being. Yet the time will

---

[27] See HC: "What, for example, if of particular artistic importance in Plato's dialogues is mostly the result of a competition with the art of the orators, the sophists, [and] the dramatists of his time. . . . Only the contest made me a poet, a sophist, and orator!"

[28] See also BGE 191: "Ever since Plato, all theologians and philosophers have been on the same track. Which is to say: in matters of morality, it has been instinct, or (as the Christians say) 'faith,' or (as I say) 'the herd' that has had the upper hand so far."

[29] In "Nietzsche's Minimalist Moral Psychology"(in *The Sense of the Past: Essays in the History of Philosophy*, ed. Miles Burnyeat [Princeton, NJ: Princeton University Press, 2006], 299–310), Bernard Williams speculates, referring to both Nietzsche and Ludwig Wittgenstein, about a world that no longer had need for philosophy or theory. Perhaps this is what he had in mind.

come for these new overmen to be in turn overcome by yet another overman-like figure in relation to themselves, so as to continue life's perpetual self-overcoming.

Although the overcomings detailed so far have been primarily "unconscious," driven by either Nature or Eris, Nietzsche believes that mankind is at a stage where it can "arrive at a conscious awareness of its goal" (SE 6). For him, "mankind ought to seek out and create the favorable conditions under which such great redemptive men can come into existence"—that is, the willed breeding of new overmen. This "consciousness" has unfortunately been used so far, at least in Nietzsche's eyes, rather negatively, with the state being transformed into a means to personal enrichment, or again as a crux for popular culture, in contrast to its original mission of being a means to higher culture, as I discussed in chapter 2. It wasn't just the state that became a conscious tool for man but also humanity itself. The priests of Christianity decided on a project of "domestication," of "improving" the human race, which was two pronged. First they set about hunting down and caging the blond beasts, those who represent the opposite of their ideal, taming them so as to make them docile, much like wild animals once they are imprisoned in a zoo (TI Improving 2).[30]

As Nietzsche puts it in *The Antichrist* 5,

> You should not beautify Christianity or try to dress it up: it has waged a *war to the death* against this *higher* type of person, it has banned all the basic instincts of this type, it has distilled "evil" and "the Evil One" out of these instincts—the strong human being as reprehensible, as "depraved." Christianity has taken the side of everything weak, base, failed, [and] it has made an ideal out of whatever *contradicts* the preservation instincts of a strong life; it has corrupted the reason of even the most spiritual natures by teaching people to see the highest spiritual values as sinful, as deceptive, as *temptations*."

One of the most effective methods that the priests used to achieve this domesticating project is their revaluation of the noble values of good and bad into good and evil, as Nietzsche explores in the first essay of *The Genealogy*. Next they bred a new type of man, the last men representing the perfection of this domesticating project. It is they that were "willed, bred, *achieved*: the domestic animal, the herd animal, the sick animal: man—the Christian" (AC 3).

Nietzsche notes that "in the methods they have employed, the morality of *breeding* and the morality of *domestication* are fully worthy of each

---

[30] On taming, domestication, and breeding, see Richardson, *Nietzsche's New Darwinism*, 191–93.

other. . . . Boiling this down to a formula, you could say: *all the methods* that have been used so far to try make humanity moral have been thoroughly *immoral*" (TI Improving 5). If Nietzsche's aim is to perfect a type of being that represents the overcoming of the last man, the immoral breeding methods he advocates to do so seem different from Conway's and the other perfectionists' notion of an individually highly stylized and democratized self-creation. Using a Rortyan language, Conway writes that "the *Über-mensch* is any higher human being whose "private" pursuit of self-perfection occasions an enhancement of the species as a whole, thus contributing to the perfection (rather than the transcendence) of the all-too-human." He later admits that Richard Rorty's own position is indebted to Nehamas's reading of Nietzsche as the prophet of self-creation.[31]

We see here the links that this type of perfectionism entertains with the notion of (democratic) self-creation. Conway is of the opinion that while Nietzsche is interested in what he labels the macropolitical (the institutional) in his early work, with the realization of the decadence of modernity he moves his center of attention to the micropolitical (the "infrainstitutional"), which he defines as "those relations between a people and its representative exemplars that are *not* mediated by social institutions." He explains, "We might think of the political microsphere on an organic model, as the vital core that engenders the signature legislations of a people or community, from which the political macrosphere extends outward as an involuntary, spontaneous outgrowth," citing as examples of these "vital resources" "autochthonous folkways, tribal rituals, ethnic customs and memory traces, familial habits and mores, [and] hieratic regimes of diet and hygiene."[32] In short, Conway is saying that Nietzsche moves from the political to the ethical.

Part of the reason Conway believes that Nietzsche changes his focus to the microsphere is due to his own lonely, nomadic existence: "Nietzsche's immersion in the political microsphere thus reflects the experimental nature of his own life and work."[33] In doing so, Conway rehearses the view of Nietzsche as a solitary figure—a view I have challenged over the course of the book. Conway also follows the thesis that if Nietzsche "usually associates [the] *pathos* of distance with the aristocratic regimes he expressly admires, its existence is not dependent on any particular form of political regime," because it is essentially ethical. Therefore, a "diminished" pathos of

---

[31] Conway, *Nietzsche and the Political*, 25, 128: "Explicitly building on the narrative model of self-creation that Alexander Nehamas attributes to Nietzsche, Rorty enlists Nietzsche to galvanize the ethical life of contemporary liberal democratic societies."

[32] Ibid., 48. Beyond the slightly parochial—perhaps patronizing—element to this description, many would consider this list to be precisely a representation of social institutions, with their own rules and conduct, which Conway denies.

[33] Ibid., 50.

distance can be preserved in the microsphere, having been lost to the decadence of modern institutions in the macrosphere, once those individuals within this microsphere continue to perfect themselves. But as I have argued in the previous chapter, at the very least for Nietzsche, the pathos of distance in the microsphere is dependent on a hierarchical macrosphere.[34]

Conway's view of Nietzsche's move from the macropolitical to the micropolitical isn't, however, without its merits. It is certainly the case that Nietzsche rejects the institutions of his day, from the modern state to the entire education system. As I have asserted in chapter 2, he thus locates his project beyond the nation-state as it is currently constituted for him. Yet at the same time this does not mean that he gives up on institutions altogether, as Conway would have us believe. In *Schopenhauer as Educator*, Nietzsche suggests that those who take the path to true culture, and therefore the new overmen, should set up a new institution to protect themselves (SE 6), as explored above. Nietzsche will later systematize this institution as the party of life, as I will look at further in chapter 6, thereby also giving it an explicitly political function, and this captures Nietzsche's attitude toward institutions: new ones with different functions need to be set up, not done away with completely.

To defend his view that Nietzsche gives up on institutions, Conway relies on a final commonplace in the secondary literature—one that I discussed in chapter 3; it presents *The Gay Science* 356 as indicative of Nietzsche's abandonment of institutions due to his claim that "we are no longer material for society." As I maintained above, though, it is a society in the "old sense of the word"—made up of medieval guilds—which we are no longer material for, but we might still be material for a society "in a new sense" of the word. In *Twilight of the Idols*, Nietzsche echoes this point, as Conway picks up on, stating,

> Our institutions are no good anymore; people are unanimous on this count. But this is *our* fault, not the fault of the institutions. After we lose all the instincts that give rise to institutions, we lose the institutions themselves, because *we* are not suited to them anymore. . . . For there to be institutions, there needs to be a type of will, instinct, [and] imperative that is antiliberal to the point of malice: the will to tradition, to authority, to a responsibility that spans the centuries, to *solidarity* in the chain that links the generations, forward and backward ad infinitum. (TI Skirmishes 39)

[34] Ibid., 39–49. There is a remarkable echo of MacIntyre's use of Nietzsche in *After Virtue*, where MacIntyre states that Nietzsche's critique of modernity is valid, and hence we should retreat to microcommunities to preserve what is left of culture in the new dark ages that are already on us, and wait for a new Saint Benedict. MacIntyre's influence on Conway seems confirmed in his discussion of him in the final chapter of the book (see ibid., 123–25).

Drawing from his studies of the Greeks, Nietzsche sets about restoring a healthy society that would bring it and philosophy back into harmony. To do so, he desires to resuscitate healthy instincts, notably through the doctrine of the eternal return—instincts that would lead to the re-creation of purposeful institutions. Conway is quite right to highlight that Nietzsche's first move toward re-creating such instincts is to attempt to lure the still-worthy few from the herd and set up a microcommunity to prepare for the coming of the overmen. And while an ethical transformation is unquestionably part of Nietzsche's plan, this does, however, take place within certain necessarily *political* institutions, similar to those of the Greek agon.

CONCLUSION: POLITICAL PERFECTIONISM

Nietzsche is an ethical perfectionist in the sense that he desires to perfect a certain type of being, away from the values of the herd, as a means to the overmen. He is also a political perfectionist in the sense that he believes that society should be organized in a way that makes the coming of these overmen possible—that the overmen should be bred, should be collectively *willed*. Indeed, the question of Nietzsche's political perfectionism is what sparked the debate regarding Nietzsche's perfectionism in the first place. In "Aversive Thinking: Emersonian Representations in Heidegger and Nietzsche," Stanley Cavell set about disputing Rawls's claim in *A Theory of Justice* that Nietzsche is a *political* perfectionist, defending instead an Emersonian *moral* perfectionism that he attributes to Nietzsche. The debate revolved around Nietzsche's claim in *Schopenhauer as Educator* 6 that "mankind must work continually at the production of individual great men—that and nothing else is its task," which Rawls takes as encapsulating the notion of political perfectionism. In section 50 of *A Theory of Justice*, titled "The Principle of Perfection," Rawls writes that "the absolute weight that Nietzsche sometimes gives the lives of great men such as Socrates and Goethe is unusual. At places he says that mankind must continually strive to produce great individuals. We give value to our lives by working for the good of the highest specimen."[35] Cavell responds with "this sounds bad. Rawls takes it straightforwardly to imply that there is a separate class of great men (to be) for whose good, and conception of good, the rest of society is to live."[36] Cavell, of course, is more interested in interpreting Emerson than Nietzsche.[37] Yet this image of the overmen as Epicurean figures, not interested in,

[35] John Rawls, *A Theory of Justice* (Cambridge, MA: Harvard University Press, 1999), 325.
[36] Cavell, "Aversive Thinking," 146. Cavell criticizes Rawls for mistranslating "*die Entstehung der Exemplars*" as "the production of specimens" instead of "the emergence of exemplars." I thank Tracy Strong for this note.
[37] Conway (*Nietzsche and the Political*, 25) writes that "Nietzsche's meditation on Schopen-

nor indeed needing, politics, is persistent throughout the literature.[38] While it is certainly the case that the overmen would not be interested in participating in everyday politics, this does not mean that they would have no interest in politics *at all*, as I have started to explore in chapter 3 and will continue to do so in chapter 6.

Rawls identifies two variants in his definition of political perfectionism. The first, which can perhaps be labeled as the more "extreme" version, holds that the "sole principle of a teleological theory directing society [is] to arrange institutions and to define the duties and obligations of individuals so as to maximize the achievement of human excellence in art, science, and culture."[39] The second, more "moderate" one, as Rawls claims, is where the "principle of perfection is accepted as but one standard among several," being "balanced against others." Both variants can be stronger or weaker, depending on how much weight is accorded to culture. For the first variant Rawls writes, "The principle obviously is more demanding the higher the relevant ideal is pitched," and it is this highly demanding perfectionism that he attributes to Nietzsche, noting that "the absolute weight that Nietzsche sometimes gives the lives of great men such as Socrates and Goethe is unusual." That is to say, the sole principle that has any value is the production of Socrates and Goethe. For Rawls, in short, Nietzsche is the most extreme of the extreme first variant of perfectionism. For the second variant, Rawls observes that "the extent to which such a view is perfectionist depends, then, on the weight given to the claims of excellence and culture" over other claims. He offers the illustration of the ancient Greeks: "If for example it is maintained that in themselves the achievements of the Greeks in philosophy, science and art justified the ancient practice of slavery (assuming that this practice was necessary for these achievement), surely the conception is highly perfectionist." It is highly perfectionist within the moderate strand because while there are a number of different standards—philosophy, science, and art—the demands placed on these are high, and are justified by rather extreme forms of inequality (slavery).

I argue throughout this book that Nietzsche sees the necessity of having two castes in society, but in chapter 3 I also looked at the evolving relationship that the two spheres might entertain with one another, and how Nietzsche comes to posit two separate, if intertwined, spheres, each with their

hauer is, to an as yet undisclosed extent, a transcription and elaboration of Emersonian passages." He suggests that Nietzsche models the overman on Emerson's "representative men," who "in their own private pursuits of self-reliance, display (and thereby represent) the potentialities for perfection resident within the human soul."

[38] See Richard Roos, "Nietzsche et Épicure: l'idylle héroïque," in *Lectures de Nietzsche*, ed. Jean-François Balaudé and Patrick Wotling (Paris: Le Livre de Poche, 2000), 283–350.

[39] Rawls, *A Theory of Justice*, 325. On the "extreme" label, see Cavell, "Aversive Thinking," 49.

own duties and responsibilities. Thus, although Nietzsche is still interested in producing new Socrates and Goethes—or more to the point, more Platos—this is not the only standard that holds in his vision of a future European society. On Rawls's scale, Nietzsche therefore might not appear to be as extreme as Rawls makes him out to be. That the two spheres Nietzsche posits should have different aspirations—that the spirit of the herd rules within the herd, and the "independent ones" have their own different valuation—reveals that there are balances to Nietzsche's desire for society to be organized in such a way as to make the overmen possible.

This brings him closer to the second, more moderate variant that Rawls identifies. Indeed, it brings him closer to the Greek society that Rawls discusses—a society from which Nietzsche drew great inspiration. Yet in accepting that the herd can have its own valuation, and the less extreme form slavery in this account takes, Nietzsche's society appears in fact less perfectionist within this second strand than ancient Greece.[40] Even though Nietzsche's ends are undeniably the organization of society so as to produce the overmen, the means he suggests to do so are more mixed. This makes his perfectionism, to my eyes, more interesting. If Rawls is correct that Nietzsche is a political perfectionist, he is a more moderate perfectionist than Rawls presents him to be. That is, he is not an extreme perfectionist, as Rawls depicts him, who desires everything to be organized around the production of genius, but in allowing space for other values—although culture, of course, still retains pride of place—Nietzsche can be identified as a more moderate perfectionist, even if a strong version at that.

[40] For a similar account of Nietzsche's ideal future society, see Richardson, *Nietzsche's New Darwinism*, 206.

CHAPTER 5
REVALUATION

With *Thus Spoke Zarathustra*, Nietzsche has in his grasp his three fundamental philosophical notions: the eternal return, will to power, and overman. The "thought of eternal return," which Nietzsche considers to be the "basic idea of the work," the "highest possible formula of affirmation," came to him on a fateful day in August 1881. In Sils-Maria, "6,000 feet beyond people and time," on his daily walk around Silvaplana Lake, Nietzsche "stopped near Surlei by a huge, pyramidal boulder"—the rock of the eternal return—where the thought came to him (EH Z 1). Projecting himself back a couple of months from that occasion, he attributes the germs of the idea to a change in his musical taste, which he experienced with his "maestro and friend" Peter Gast in Recoaro, near Vicenza in Italy. Projecting himself this time forward, he writes that the closing section of the first book of *Zarathustra*, "On the Bestowing Virtue," was "completed at exactly the sacred hour when Wagner died in Venice" (EH Z 1).

Nietzsche considered *Thus Spoke Zarathustra* to be his most important work. It has a "special place" for him in his writings, and with it he claims to have given "humanity the greatest gift it has ever received" (EH P 4). It is not only the "most elevated book there is" but also the most "profound," so much so that he quotes copiously from it over the course of *Ecce Homo* and *Twilight of the Idols*.[1] It is the central work of Nietzsche's corpus, what he considers to be its apex, such that all three of his periods—early, middle, and late—relate to it in some manner, as I will now explore. This makes the work "singular" in the sense that it relates to all three periods, yet at the same time is separate from them.[2] On the one hand, it represents the final fruit of Nietzsche's path toward himself, undertaken in his middle period, and thus his final overcoming of the Wagnerianism that dominated his

---

[1] See EH P 4, Wise 8; Z 6–8, Destiny 2–5; TI Hammer. For perhaps Nietzsche's first quotation of *Zarathustra* in a published work, see BT P 7.

[2] See EH P 4; EH Z 6.

youth. On the other hand, Nietzsche conceives of his late, mature work, where he draws on his own philosophy, as a retrospective building block toward a full understanding of *Zarathustra*. They are the "no-saying, *no-doing*" part of his work that clear the way for the "yes-saying" part (EH BGE 1), which had already found its fullest expression in *Zarathustra* and "highest affirmation" in the doctrine of the eternal return.

If for Nietzsche *Zarathustra* is central to his writings, it also, from his retrospective and prospective projections of it, signals something new from what came before it. First, from the retrospective viewpoint of "taste," it represents a move away from the aphoristic style he had been developing since *Human, All Too Human*, including *Daybreak* and *The Gay Science*. Of this latter book he writes to Lou Andreas-Salomé, "With this book that series of writings beginning with *Human, All Too Human* comes to a close: in their totality, 'a new image and ideal of the freethinker' has been erected."[3] Nietzsche considers the period stretching from *Human, All Too Human* to *Zarathustra* to be his "freethinking" one, attempting to free himself from Wagner's grip.[4] It is thus conventionally labeled his middle period, sandwiched between his earlier Wagnerian-inspired work and his latter mature thought after *Zarathustra*. Instead of the aphoristic style that marked his middle period, Nietzsche chose to tell the story of Zarathustra as a "tragedy" (GS 342). Indeed, the singularity of *Zarathustra* is highlighted by its prose. Nietzsche will return, in his later work, to the aphoristic style (BGE, TI, and EH), along with developing the longer essay format (GM and AC), which is more reminiscent of *The Birth of Tragedy*. But nowhere would the novel style of *Zarathustra* be reproduced. Second, prospectively, *Thus Spoke Zarathustra* represents the final consummation of Nietzsche's break with Wagner.

I argued in chapter 2 that there existed an original political disagreement between Nietzsche and Wagner over the role of slavery in the production of high (Greek) culture. This, however, was papered over in *The Birth of Tragedy*, from which the offending passages were removed before publication. While disagreeing with the sociopolitical element of Wagner's total revolution, Nietzsche fully acquiesced at the time to Wagner's program of (Ger-

---

[3] Quoted in Mazzino Montinari, "Zarathustra before *Thus Spoke Zarathustra*," in *Reading Nietzsche*, ed. Mazzino Montinari, trans. Greg Whitlock (Champaign: University of Illinois Press, 2003), 77. On the back cover of the first edition of *The Gay Science*, Nietzsche echoes this thought, writing that "this book marks the conclusion of a series of writings by FRIEDRICH NIETZSCHE whose common goal is to erect *a new image and ideal of the free spirit*." For the notion that "freethinking" is a stage, if a necessary one, see HH P.

[4] In his review of *Human, All Too Human* in *Ecce Homo*, Nietzsche claims it is a "monument to a crisis"—namely, his disillusionment with Wagner. He notes that "the tone, the sound, has completely changed"—a reference to his newfound aphoristic style. Already in his prefaces of 1886, Nietzsche had identified the book as the beginning of his "great liberation" (HH P 3), and represents one of his "overcomings" (HH2 P 1).

man) cultural renewal. This at first brought the two together. Yet over the course of the next ten years, Nietzsche became disillusioned with Wagner, especially with what he saw as the latter's increasing pan-Germanism, anti-Semitism, and Christianity.[5] Already Nietzsche, no longer recognizing himself in his surroundings, had felt compelled to leave the first *Festspiel* in the middle of it.[6] It was Wagner's *Parsifal* that brought an end to their alliance. Their "quiet war," as Montinari labels it ("both of us remained silent"), began in 1878, when simultaneously Wagner received a copy of *Human, All Too Human* and Nietzsche a copy of *Parsifal*, as if two "*swords* had crossed" (EH HH 5).[7] "Wagner had become pious."

Nietzsche had been drawn to Wagner not solely by the latter's indubitable charisma but also because the master's desire to renew German culture was one that he shared. This union reached its apex with *The Birth of Tragedy*, which concluded with a rousing defense of Wagner's project.[8] But two problems were brewing, and both came to concern the direction that Wagner's work was to take. The first, as we saw earlier, related to the role of slavery in the (re-)creation of the high culture of the Greeks. The second was the role that Christianity would play in the "Artwork of the Future." Retrospectively, Nietzsche would claim that there was in *The Birth* a "consistently cautious and hostile silence about Christianity" (BT P 5), or again that there is a "deep, hostile silence about Christianity throughout the book. . . . At one point Christian priests are alluded to as an 'insidious type of dwarf,' as 'subterranean'" (EH BT 1). We can debate whether this represents too much of a recuperation by Nietzsche of his earlier work, but it is undeniable that he had placed his thinking at the time under the auspices of Apollo and Dionysus, rather than Apollo and Jesus, as Wagner had done. Wagner's ear-

[5] See variously HH2 P 3: "Wagner . . . sank down helpless and shattered before the Christian cross"; BGE 256: "Wagner . . . *way to Rome*"; EH HH 2: "Wagner had been translated into German . . . anti-Semite"; EH HH 5: "Wagner had become pious": NCW Broke Away 1: "since coming to Germany, Wagner had acceded step by step to everything that I hate—even to anti-Semitism. . . . Wagner . . . sank down helpless and shattered before the Christian cross." A brief chronology of the pair's relationship might go something like this: 1868, Nietzsche meets Wagner; 1872, publication of *The Birth* and high point of relationship; 1875, instead of attending rehearsals in Bayreuth, Nietzsche starts working on *Richard Wagner in Bayreuth*; 1876, Nietzsche leaves first *Festspiel*; and 1878, publication of *Human, All Too Human* and *Parsifal*.

[6] EH HH 2: "Where was I? I did not recognize anything; I hardly recognized Wagner. . . . I sifted through my memories in vain. Tribschen—a distant island of blissfulness; not a shadow of similarity. . . . *What had happened?*"

[7] Mazzino Montinari, "Nietzsche and Wagner One Hundred Years Ago," in *Reading Nietzsche*, ed. Mazzino Montinari, trans. Greg Whitlock (Champaign: University of Illinois Press, 2003), 40.

[8] Wagner's response to the book was: "I have never read anything more beautiful than your book! It is simply glorious. . . . I have just said to Cosima that you stand second only to her" (quoted in ibid., 40).

lier revolutionary writings, in which Nietzsche was well versed, had shown the potential to develop into something non-Christian, particularly through their attack on the church.[9] Yet this was abandoned with *Parsifal*, which saw Wagner take the "road to the cross." Rejecting this, Nietzsche consequently had to find his own way.[10] Thus while Nietzsche participated in what he had interpreted to be Wagner's early mission, the direction it subsequently took was not to his liking. He decided to follow his own path, and it is from this that the quiet war begins: Nietzsche's intellectual break from Wagner instigated the war.[11]

After his youthful following of Wagner, Nietzsche would in the subsequent years—his middle period—use the critical tools of science and the Enlightenment on himself and his time.[12] Not only would he continue on his anti-Christian path that philosophically separated him from Wagner but he would also come politically to reject the Wagnerian pan-Germanism and anti-Semitism that had marked his earlier period.[13] Applying the scalpel to himself, Nietzsche would become the exact opposite of what Wagner had become—namely, a good European, an anti-anti-Semite, and eventually an anti-Christ.[14] What Nietzsche was looking for in this period was himself, his own philosophy.[15] He achieved this for the first time with *Thus Spoke Zarathustra*—with his philosophy of the eternal return, will to power, and overman—which in turn ushers in his mature period. Wagner died in 1883, just when Nietzsche had finished writing the first part of *Zarathustra*. The quiet war came to an end, not simply because of Wagner's death, but

[9] Montinari (ibid., 41) writes, "The fourth of the *Untimely Meditations, Richard Wagner in Bayreuth*, still remains, in both Nietzsche and Wagner scholarship and elsewhere, as a fairly overlooked fact, in that it is an extremely adroit mosaic of quotations from Wagner's writings, such as *Art and Revolution, Artwork of the Future, Opera and Drama, An Announcement to My Friends*, and others."

[10] In his mid-teens, Nietzsche seemed to have lost his faith. He claims that "as an atheist, I never said grace at Pforta" (quoted in Mazzino Montinari, "Nietzsche's Recollections from the Years 1875–79 concerning His Childhood," in *Reading Nietzsche*, ed. Mazzino Montinari, trans. Greg Whitlock [Champaign: University of Illinois Press, 2003], 33).

[11] As Montinari ("Nietzsche and Wagner One Hundred Years Ago," 40–41) explains, "The irresistible single-mindedness of Nietzsche's intellectual development clarifies the personal schism, not vice versa. . . . Nietzsche's schism with Wagner was an intellectual act, a philosophical act."

[12] EH HH 1: "I used it to liberate myself from the things that *did not belong* to my nature. . . . The term 'free spirit' does not want to be understood in any other way: a spirit *that has become free*, that has taken hold of itself again. . . . The name 'Voltaire' on one of my writings—that was true progress—*toward myself.*"

[13] For Nietzsche's anti-Semitic comments about the "financial recluses," see GST, 171.

[14] See, respectively, BGE 241; letter to Franz Overbeck, mid-September 1888; AC.

[15] EH HH 4: "That lowermost self . . . slowly woke up, shyly and full of doubts—but it finally *started talking again* . . . this 'return *to myself.*'"

more important, because Nietzsche had now come up with his own personal means of achieving the cultural renewal that both had initially aimed
for. In the process of doing so, Nietzsche's version of cultural renewal took
on a European, anti-Christian, and anti-anti-Semitic aspect that was in contrast with the Wagnerian original. Through finding himself and his own
philosophy, Nietzsche had completed the trajectory that had started the war
with Wagner in the first place.

In this sense I concur with the philosophical division of Nietzsche's work
into three main periods, as Nietzsche himself suggests over the course of his
review of his work in *Ecce Homo*, although I have also stressed throughout
this book the continuities in Nietzsche's political thinking.[16] Nietzsche's
early period, his "youth" (EH HH 4), comprises *The Birth of Tragedy* and
those writings that relate to it, specifically "Philosophy in the Tragic Age of
the Greeks," "On the Future of Our Educational Institutions," and the "Five
Prefaces to Five Unwritten Books," which include the important essays on
"The Greek State" and "Homer's Contest." These writings carry the influence of Wagner, in particular his project of cultural renewal in *The Birth*,
and contain the elements of pan-Germanism and anti-Semitism that Nietzsche would later reject. Yet his studies of the Greeks already carried the
seeds of his falling out with Wagner, especially his view of ancient slavery,
along with his growing hostility toward Christianity. The *Untimely Meditations* can be considered transitional works, starting with a pamphlet against
Strauss that Nietzsche penned at Wagner's behest, to a discussion of Wagner
himself in the fourth and final *Untimely, Richard Wagner in Bayreuth*. As
Montinari remarks, Nietzsche's presentation of Wagner serves as a type of
mirror for Wagner in Bayreuth, as if to say "you were that, you wished to be
that, are you still that today?"[17] It was Nietzsche's challenge to Wagner to
remain loyal to the project that Nietzsche had understood Wagner to be
pursuing when they first met—a project that Nietzsche had originally
agreed with, but felt had taken a wrong turn.

In the euphoria of their early exchanges in Tribschen, perhaps a degree of
misunderstanding had crept in. This seems confirmed when the "vision of
the future" that Nietzsche paints at the end of the final *Untimely* is actually

---

[16] Ruth Abbey (*Nietzsche's Middle Period* [Oxford: Oxford University Press, 2000], xii) writes
that "it is possible to employ this schema while acknowledging that the boundaries between
Nietzsche's phases are not rigid, that some of the thoughts elaborated in one period were ad-
umbrated in the previous one, that there are differences within any single phase and that
some concerns pervade his oeuvre." For a discussion of themes that straddle the periods, see
Melissa Lane, "Honesty as Best Policy: Nietzsche on *Redlichkeit* and the Contrast between
Stoic and Epicurean Strategies of the Self," in *Histories of Postmodernism*, ed. Mark Bevir, Jill
Hargis, and Sara Rushing (London: Routledge, 2007), 25–51.

[17] Montinari, "Nietzsche and Wagner One Hundred Years Ago," 41.

his own vision, not Wagner's. Nietzsche did not fully realize that this was the case at the time, mixing in his own aspirations with those of Wagner. But looking back over the work in *Ecce Homo*, Nietzsche sees clearly that "the essay 'Wagner in Bayreuth' is a vision of my future" (EH UM 3). He adds, "The 'idea of Bayreuth' had transformed itself into something that will be no great mystery to anyone who knows my *Zarathustra*; it had transformed itself into that *great noon* when the most select people will devote themselves to the greatest task of all" (EH BT 4).

With *Zarathustra*'s philosophy, Nietzsche achieves his own version of the cultural revolution that he had originally planned with Wagner. But instead of the renewal of German culture, Nietzsche now aimed for a European, if not worldwide, cultural and philosophical revaluation of all values. Wagner's project was originally one of total revolution, where a cultural revolution was necessarily accompanied by social and political transformation. Wagner become less concerned with this latter aim, claiming that he focused his entire energy on the artistic side of the equation. Yet Wagner in reality went much further than simply leaving aside the revolutionary sociopolitical aspect of his total revolution. He accommodated himself to the new German political configuration to such a degree that he composed a *Kaisermarsch* in honor of the new Reich (WB 10). This seems to have left Nietzsche rather perplexed—we know his feelings about the new Reich.[18] He tried to reconcile himself with this by declaring that it was Wagner's "sublime trust" in the German spirit that allowed him to follow such "political aims."

If we consider *Richard Wagner in Bayreuth* to be a mirror held up by Nietzsche to Wagner to ask him to remain faithful to his original plans, then Nietzsche explicitly reminds him of the two-pronged nature of his project when he writes, "It is quite impossible to produce the highest and purest effect of which the art of the theater is capable without at the same time effecting innovations everywhere, in morality and politics, in education and society" (WB 4)—in short, a total revolution. In the same work, Nietzsche would later characterize Wagner as a "social revolutionary": "the possibility of a total upheaval of all things rose before his eyes, and he no longer shrank from his possibility" (WB 8). If in his later years Wagner did shrink from the possibility of a total revolution, accommodating himself to the political powers of the day so as to have his *Festspielhaus* built, Nietzsche did not. His "Revaluation of All Values" would contain an inseparable and still-revolutionary political dimension: his great politics.

---

[18] See, in particular, DS 1 and 2, where he criticizes the confused link between a German military victory and spiritual victory, insofar as while the French had lost the war, they certainly retained their cultural superiority.

NIETZSCHE'S *NACHLASS* AND HIS LAST WORKS

Like most of Nietzsche's books published during his lifetime, *Thus Spoke Zarathustra* did not sell well. Nietzsche was concerned it would not be understood.[19] He was right, it wasn't, and we still struggle with it today—which influenced his decision to publish part 4 privately, and even contemplated having parts 1 to 3 removed from the public altogether.[20] Yet when he was first writing it, Nietzsche conceived of *Zarathustra* as being his *"whole philosophy,"* his *"deepest seriousness"* that is the beginning of his *"disclosure,"* although he also admits that the work has a "legendary air" and uses "strange words."[21] On completion of the first three parts, he considered it to be the "entrance hall" to his philosophy, in the sense that for the first time, it presents his three philosophical notions together: the will to power, eternal return, and overman.[22] But this presentation was perhaps a little obscure, and Nietzsche decided to spend the subsequent part of his work explaining these concepts in a more literal manner. This was to be the no-saying, no-doing half of his project (EH BGE 1). All the works published after *Zarathustra* refer back to it in a certain manner, which is the yes-saying part of his task, again confirming its singularity.

Beyond Good and Evil, for instance, is described as being the *"deliberate* turning away from the sort of instincts that make a *Zarathustra* possible," in the sense that *Zarathustra* represents the "need to see into the *distance*," even as *Beyond Good and Evil* is "forced to focus on things that are closest to it, the age, our *surroundings*" (EH BGE 1). Thus if the yes-saying instincts of *Zarathustra* make it look far into the future, the no-doing ones concentrate on Nietzsche's present time. *Beyond Good and Evil* performs a *"critique of modernity"* so as to make way (retrospectively) for a new affirmative philosophy. In this it harks back to *Zarathustra*, with Nietzsche presenting himself in conclusion to the work as the "last disciple and initiate of the god Dionysus" (BGE 295), reminiscent of Zarathustra as the disciple of Dionysus. In *The Genealogy*, for its part, Zarathustra makes a direct appearance as the

---

[19] See letters to Peter Gast, April 6, 1883, where he states that it "disgusts me to think of *Zarathustra* going into the world as a piece of literary entertainment; who will be serious enough for it!" See also letter to Peter Gast, September 2, 1884, where he writes that *Zarathustra* is "dark and hidden and ridiculous to everyone," and that Heinrich von Stein admitted to only understanding "twelve sentences and no more" of it.

[20] See letter to Carl von Gersdorff, February 12, 1885; letter to Franz Overbeck, March 31, 1885.

[21] Letter to Carl von Gersdorff, June 28, 1883.

[22] See letter to Malwida von Meysenburg, end of March and early May 1884; letter to Franz Overbeck, April 7, 1884.

"younger, stronger" version of Nietzsche (GM II 25). Indeed, while *The Genealogy* applies itself to the no-doing task, this is because "there was no *counter-ideal*"—as Nietzsche makes explicit in his review of it in *Ecce Homo*—"*until Zarathustra*" (EH GM), until a yes-saying alternative. Finally, Zarathustra is omnipresent in *Twilight*, *Ecce Homo*, and *The Antichrist*, from Nietzsche announcing himself to be the "teacher of the eternal return" in the conclusion to *Twilight* (TI ancients 5), to copiously quoting from *Zarathustra* throughout both *Twilight* and *Ecce Homo*, to finally declaring that *The Antichrist* belongs to those "who will understand my *Zarathustra*" (AC P).[23]

If *Zarathustra* is the entrance hall to Nietzsche's philosophy, this seems to call for the construction of a "main building," a point that Nietzsche seemed patently aware of. He writes to Malwida von Meysenburg in early May 1884 that "now that I have built this entrance hall to my philosophy, I will have to start again and not grow tired until the main building also stands finished before me." Hence begins Nietzsche's project to write a Hauptwerk. To Franz Overbeck, on April 7, 1884, he explains that he means to "set about revising my metaphysical and epistemological views. I must now proceed step by step through a series of disciplines, for I have decided to spend the next five years on an elaboration of my 'philosophy,' the entrance hall of which I have built with my Zarathustra."[24] It would appear, then, that while Nietzsche had first presented his philosophical ideas in *Zarathustra*, he now felt the need to work them out in a more systematic fashion. This new work would be a mirror to *Zarathustra*, in the sense that it would present in a more conventional manner the ideas that had been put so lyrically there. Both works—*Thus Spoke Zarathustra* and the projected Hauptwerk—were conceived as amounting to being Nietzsche's magnum opus(es): they are two versions of the same thing, just stylistically different. Accordingly, Nietzsche will write in the close of his "Skirmishes" in *Twilight of the Idols* that "I have given humanity the most profound book in its possession, my *Zarathustra*; soon I will give it its most independent" (TI Skirmishes 51).[25]

Nietzsche started working on the Hauptwerk immediately after finishing part 3 of *Zarathustra* in summer 1884. One of the projected titles that stands out is "The Philosophy of Eternal Return: An Attempt at a Revaluation of All Values" (KSA 11 26 [259]), although Nietzsche also referred to it as "Noon and Eternity."[26] What is important to note here is the emphasis on

[23] See TI Hammer; EH P 4, Wise 8, books 1, 3, 4; BT 4; GS; Z; BGE 2; GM, Destiny 2, 3, 4, 5, 8.

[24] See also the letter to Peter Gast, September 2, 1884: "The next six years will be for working out a scheme that I have sketched for my 'philosophy.'"

[25] Nietzsche had already described himself to be the "*most independent man in Europe*" while talking about *Zarathustra* in a letter to Franz Overbeck on May 2, 1884, underlining the links between *Zarathustra* and the projected Hauptwerk.

[26] See Mazzino Montinari, "Nietzsche's Unpublished Writings from 1885 to 1888; or, Tex-

the eternal return, and its links to the notion of a revaluation of all values. After Nietzsche privately published part 4 of *Zarathustra*, these titles gradually faded until the infamous "The Will to Power" appeared in August 1885 (KSA 11 39 [1]). At first this title for Nietzsche's new planned magnum opus was concurrent with other titles, including *Beyond Good and Evil*.[27] But after the publication of *The Genealogy of Morality* in 1887, Nietzsche devoted his entire attention to "The Will to Power." Indeed, much in the same way that Nietzsche continually referred back to *Thus Spoke Zarathustra* as the affirmative part of his project in his work after it, he also referred to his forthcoming Hauptwerk in the same works. This underscores the fact that the works serve as mirrors to one another. So Nietzsche announced on the back cover of *Beyond Good and Evil* (1886) his "Works under preparation: The Will to Power: An Attempt at a Revaluation of All Values. In Four Books," and at the close of *The Genealogy* indicates that he is working on the theme of "On the History of European Nihilism," for which he refers his readers to a work he is writing: *"The Will to Power: Attempt at a Revaluation of All Values"* (GM III 27).

Even once the subtitle of "The Will to Power"—the "Revaluation of All Values"—is transformed into its full title, as I will soon explore, Nietzsche continues to make references to it in his last works. In *The Case of Wagner*, Nietzsche explains that he will "have an opportunity (in a chapter of my major work titled 'On the Physiology of Art') to go into detail about how this complete transformation of art into acting is an expression of physiological degeneration" (CW 7).[28] He dates *Twilight* "Turin, September 30, 1888, the day that the first book of the *Revaluation of all Values* was finished" (TI P), repeating this claim on the contents page of *Ecce Homo*. There, in his review of *Beyond Good and Evil*, he identifies his no-saying, no-doing part of his project directly with that of "the revaluation of values, the great war— summoning a day of decision" (EH BGE 1), and will continue to draw out this link between the two over the course of his review of all the subsequent works.[29] Thus, if the post-*Zarathustra* works represent Nietzsche's no-saying,

tual Criticism and the Will to Power," in *Reading Nietzsche*, ed. Mazzino Montinari, trans. Greg Whitlock (Champaign: University of Illinois Press, 2003), 80–102; Thomas Brobjer, "Nietzsche's *Magnum Opus*," *History of European Ideas* 32 (2006): 278–94.

[27] See KSA 12 2 [73]. Brobjer ("Nietzsche's *Magnum Opus*," 279) highlights how Nietzsche avoided using material intended for the Hauptwerk in *Jenseits von Gut und Böse* and *Zur Genealogie der Moral*, especially his analysis of nihilism. See, in particular, the "Lenzer Heide" text (KSA 12 5 [71] and 5 [75]).

[28] Nietzsche considers *The Case of Wagner* and *Nietzsche contra Wagner* as "breaks" (CW P) from his more important work, the "Revaluation of All Values," and thus for the purposes of this chapter, I will focus on *Twilight of the Idols*, *Ecce Homo*, and *The Antichrist* as being related to the "Revaluation."

[29] See EH GM: "There was no *counter-ideal—until Zarathustra*. I have been understood. A psychologist's three crucial preparatory works for a revaluation of all values"; EH TI: "I

no-doing part that clears the way for understanding the affirmative philosophy of *Zarathustra*, the "Revaluation of All Values" signifies that accomplishment of this destructive part, which ultimately arcs back round to merge with *Zarathustra*, as the introduction and main part of his main work, respectively. Within the cycle of transformations that Zarathustra had spoken in his first speech of *Zarathustra*, the "Revaluation of All Values" is the lion, who fights the dragon of "all values" so as to make possible a space within which children can play—namely, the affirmative philosophy first announced in *Zarathustra*.

Montinari has irrefutably demonstrated that *The Will to Power* editions—the 1901 edition and the reference 1906–11 edition translated into English by Kaufmann and R. J. Hollingdale—compiled by Gast and Nietzsche's sister Elizabeth Förster-Nietzsche, are frauds.[30] This was for two main reasons: most important, Nietzsche abandoned "The Will to Power" as the title for his planned Hauptwerk in favor of what had until then been its subtitle, the "Revaluation of All Values"; and the 1,067 aphorisms that made up the fraudulent edition of 1906–11 had not even followed the sequence of 374 aphorisms that Nietzsche had painstakingly organized as one of his most serious attempts at completing "The Will to Power" before he abandoned it.[31] Montinari concludes:

With that, the history of "Will to Power" as one of Nietzsche's literary projects comes to an end. That Nietzsche considered *Antichrist* to be his "Revaluation of All Values," from at the latest November 20, 1888, onward, such that the main title, "Revaluation of All Values," became the subtitle, as he expressly wrote Paul Deussen (November 26, 1888: "My 'Revaluation of All Values,' with the main title, *Antichrist*, is finished"), that he altered the subtitle again at the end of December: all this, together with the history of his autobiography, *Ecce Homo*, *Dionysian Dithyrambs*, and the short composition *The Case of Wagner*, along with his political proclamations against the Germany of young Kaiser Wil-

grasped the tremendous task of the *Revaluation* . . . great victory on September 30; the conclusion of the *Revaluation*"; EH CW: "The shattering lightning bolt of the *Revaluation*, a book that will rack the earth with convulsions."

[30] Montinari, "Nietzsche's Unpublished Writings," 91–101. See also Bernd Magnus, "Nietzsche's Philosophy in 1888: The Will to Power and the Übermensch," *Journal of the History of Philosophy* 24, no. 1 (1986): 79–98; Richard Roos, "Les derniers écrits de Nietzsche et leur publication," in *Lectures de Nietzsche*, ed. Jean-François Balaudé and Patrick Wotling (Paris: Le Livre de Poche, 2000), 33–70. While Kaufmann had rejected "The Will to Power" because of its association with Baeumler and the Nazi regime, he nonetheless decided to publish a translation of it, ostensibly so that the late notes could be made accessible to "those who cannot read these notes in the original German" (Friedrich Nietzsche, *The Will to Power*, ed. Walter Kaufmann, trans. Walter Kaufmann and R. J. Hollingdale [New York: Random House, 1968], xx).

[31] See KSA 13 12 [1–2]; Montinari, "Nietzsche's Unpublished Writings," 91–93.

helm II, belongs to the ostensibly confused conclusion to Nietzsche's lifework, which spelled the end of his intellect. *The Turin catastrophe came when Nietzsche was literally entirely finished with everything.*[32]

The status of Nietzsche's late works, and in particular his late notes, is subject to debate, not to mention controversy. For one, Baeumler based his "Hitler Prophecy," as Thomas Mann put it, on the spurious edition of *The Will to Power.* Perhaps in reaction to this, an older interpretation claimed that Nietzsche was already mad, or at least showing clear signs of madness, when he wrote his late works, especially *The Antichrist*, and consequently we would do best to ignore them.[33] This view is generally not reproduced in the contemporary literature; a study of Nietzsche's last letters show that he was lucidly correcting the proofs of *Ecce Homo* until early December 1888, "weighing each word on a gold scale," long after he had finished *Twilight* and *The Antichrist* at the end of September.[34] On the other hand, Heidegger declared that "what Nietzsche himself published during his creative life was always foreground. That is also true of his first treatise, *The Birth of Tragedy from the Spirit of Music* (1872). His philosophy proper was left behind as post-humous, unpublished work." This meant that *Twilight of the Idols*, *Ecce Homo*, and *The Antichrist* should only be considered "minor works."[35] Montinari's research was intended to confute Heidegger's view that to find Nietzsche's "real" philosophy one must first look into the unpublished notes. Instead, according to Montinari, Nietzsche not only abandoned "The Will to Power" on which Heidegger had based his interpretation but also was "finished with everything" when he collapsed in 1889, which is to say that he had presented his philosophy in his last works: *Twilight, Ecce Homo*, and *The Antichrist*.

On the basis of Montinari's philological work, Yannick Souladié, again rejecting Heidegger, has recently argued that Nietzsche's final philosophy should be understood as a "philosophy of *The Antichrist*."[36] And yet the debate continues, with Brobjer recently querying whether Nietzsche can truly be considered to be "finished with everything" when he experienced his mental collapse in 1889, particularly in view of his work on a Hauptwerk for

[32] Montinari, "Nietzsche's Unpublished Writings," 101.

[33] Eugen Fink (*Nietzsche's Philosophy* [London: Continuum, 2003], 121–29), for instance, describes *The Antichrist* as the work of a madman.

[34] Letter to Peter Gast, December 9, 1888. See Brobjer, "Nietzsche's *Magnum Opus*," 283; Yannick Souladié, "Nietzsche à la letter," in *Dernières lettres (hiver 1887–hiver 1889): De la volonté de puissance à l'antichrist*, by Friedrich Nietzsche (Paris: Editions Manucius, 2011), 14–15. Souladié dates Nietzsche's breakdown to January 3, 1889. This indeed seems to be when Nietzsche writes his "mad letters."

[35] Martin Heidegger, *Nietzsche* (San Francisco: HarperCollins, 1991), 1:8–9.

[36] See Yannick Souladié, "Présentation: *L'Inversion contra La Volonté de Puissance*," in *Nietzsche—L'inversion des valeurs* (Hildesheim: Olms, 2007), 3–25.

the final five years of his active life. As Brobjer writes, "It seems psychologically unlikely that Nietzsche was finished with everything when he collapsed 44 years old."[37] In what follows I will offer my own interpretation of how we should understand what Nietzsche was attempting to achieve in his last productive years, which takes something from each of these diverging accounts without entirely agreeing with any one of them. What I will maintain is that while Nietzsche was philosophically finished with everything when he published his final works, this nevertheless signaled the start of a necessary and complementary political phase of his endeavors.[38] As such, if Montinari is correct in declaring that Nietzsche had finished with everything on his collapse, what he had finished with was the philosophical dimension of his project, not the revaluation project as a whole. In fact, in his (correct) desire to philologically demonstrate Nietzsche's abandonment of "The Will to Power," Montinari's conclusion that Nietzsche's lifework ends in "confusion" appears a little premature. In throwing out the "Revaluation of All Values" with "The Will to Power," Montinari has inadvertently thrown out the baby with the bathwater.[39]

In early 1888, Nietzsche organizes 374 of his notes into four books, with each of these in turn subdivided into three.[40] This organization represents the most complete form that Nietzsche's project for "The Will to Power" was to take. Indeed, *The Will to Power* in its forged version uses the titles of this organization, but the 1,067 aphorisms that comprise it are not, needless to say, faithful to Nietzsche's organization of the 374. To Gast on February 13, 1888, Nietzsche explained that this represented his "first draft" of his "Attempt at a Revaluation," and that its assemblage was "torture." "In ten years I will try to do better." Thirteen days later, he writes again to Gast, "Do not think that I have created another work of 'literature' here; this composition was *for me* . . . . [T]he idea of 'going public with it' is completely out of the question."[41] It is clear that this "The Will to Power" version was a first personal draft for Nietzsche, never the completed thing. He continued to work on it, but remained dissatisfied with his work. He writes to both his mother and Meta von Salis that "this summer appears to have simply 'fallen through' in terms of his *'one grand and very specific task.'*"[42] Yet

[37] Brobjer, "Nietzsche's *Magnum Opus*," 292.
[38] Souladié ("Nietzsche à la letter," 18; my translation) is aware of this, writing that "after *Ecce Homo*, Nietzsche indeed seemed to have the intention to launch himself into direct political action."
[39] Cf. Hugo Drogon, "Twilight and Transvaluation: Nietzsche's Hauptwerk and the *Götzen-Dämmerung*," *Nietzscheforschung* 16 (2009): 175–82.
[40] See KSA 13 12 [1–2]. We can surmise that the titles of the books, not given there, relate back to KSA 12 7 [64].
[41] Letter to Peter Gast, February 26, 1888.
[42] See letter to Meta von Salis, August 22, 1888; letter to Franziska Nietzsche, August 30, 1888.

just a few days later, on September 7, 1888, Nietzsche would write again to Meta von Salis, explaining that "in the meantime I have been very produc-tive—to such a degree that I have reason to withdraw the sighs in my past letter about the summer that 'fell through.'"[43] Nietzsche felt that he had achieved "something *more*"—the "Revaluation of All Values," of which the first book is called *The Antichrist*.

What caused such a turnaround? In early September, Nietzsche had jot-ted down a list of twelve chapters on a loose sheet of paper that on the one side contained the title "Revaluation of All Values," and on the other titles such as *"Thoughts for the Day after Tomorrow*; Excerpts of My Philosophy," *"Wisdom for the Day after Tomorrow*: My Philosophy in Excerpts," and finally *"Magnum in Parvo*: A Philosophy in Excerpts" (KSA 13 19 [2–6]). The chap-ter titles are as follows: 1) "We Hyperboreans," 2) "The Problem of Socrates," 3) "Reason in Philosophy," 4) "How the True World Finally Became a Fable," 5) "Morality as Anti-Nature," 6) "The Four Great Errors," 7) "For Us—Against Us," 8) "The Concept of a Decadent Religion," 9) "Buddhism and Christianity," 10) "From My Aesthetics," 11) "Among Artists and Writers," and 12) "Arrows and Epigrams." Chapters 2, 3, 4, 5, 6, and 12 became the identically named chapters in *Twilight of the Idols*, while chapter 11 is the original title for "Skirmishes of an Untimely Man." Chapters 1, 7, 8, and 9 are sections of *The Antichrist*, with the titles still being visible, though stricken, in the printer's manuscript. "We Hyperboreans" becomes sections 1–7, "For Us—Against Us" turns into sections 8–14, "The Concept of a Dec-adent Religion" becomes sections 15–19, and "Buddhism and Christianity" ends up as sections 20–23.[44] By the end of the month (September 1888), Nietzsche had completed both *Twilight of the Idols* and *The Antichrist*.

Instead of the work "The Will to Power" where he would present his phi-losophy in a systematic manner, Nietzsche, reverting to type, decided to present them in "excerpt" form. In letters to Carl Fuchs, Gast, and Over-beck of September 1888, he describes *Twilight* as a "general overall introduc-tion" to his philosophy, or again as a "rigorous synthesis of my principal philosophical heresies."[45] Thus the "revisions" to his "epistemological" views that Nietzsche had planned in 1884 culminates in *Twilight of the Idols*. The fact that they are presented in an "abridged" rather than a more systematic form should not detract from their value, or indeed their completeness, given that Nietzsche set himself the task of saying "in ten sentences what

[43] Letter to Meta von Salis, September 7, 1888.
[44] See Montinari, "Nietzsche's Unpublished Writings," 98.
[45] Letter to Carl Fuchs, September 9, 1888; letter to Peter Gast, September 12, 1888; letter to Franz Overbeck, September 16, 1888. For *Twilight of the Idols* as a "rigorous synthesis," see, for instance, the fact that Nietzsche critiques the "philosopher's idiosyncrasies"—their "lack of historical sense"—in "Reason in Philosophy"—a theme he had already dealt with in both HH 2 and BGE 224.

other people say in a book" (TI Skirmishes 51). As Aaron Ridley remarks, "*Twilight* represents a pinnacle of aphoristic economy and wit, an example of Nietzsche's mature style at its very best."[46] All of Nietzsche's thoughts on epistemological questions are in *Twilight*, but expressed in his inimitable concise form as opposed to a thorough and scholarly one. So if one, like Heidegger, is looking for Nietzsche's "final philosophy," one should look no further than *Twilight* as a starting point, at least in terms of what concerns Nietzsche's epistemological views.[47]

Yet what Nietzsche himself terms the "metaphysical" elements of his philosophy—namely, the will to power, eternal return, and overmen—are not overly present in *Twilight*. This is because the second function of *Twilight* is to serve as an "initiation," an "appetizer," to the "Revaluation of All Values," which has as its focus these ideas.[48] As both books originated from the division of chapters from a common manuscript, we can see that they would revolve around, respectively, different elements: *Twilight* centers on the epistemological, and "Revaluation" the metaphysical. Nietzsche closes his "Skirmishes" in *Twilight*, the original conclusion to the work, with the line "I have given humanity the most profound book in its possession, my *Zarathustra*: soon I will give it its most independent" (TI Skirmishes 51)—the "Revaluation of All Values." In the following section, 'What I Owe to the Ancients," which signals the start of Nietzsche's "autobiography" *Ecce Homo*, Nietzsche signs off with the claim "I, the last disciple of the philosopher Dionysus—I, the teacher of the eternal return" (TI ancients 5), anticipating the final planned book of the "Revaluation," along with quoting from *Zarathustra*, its mirror work.

Nietzsche's rejection of a systematic work in favor of a presentation in excerpts of his epistemological views in *Twilight* brings us to the question of the systematicity of his overall thinking. Many have interpreted the apparent contradictions in Nietzsche's thought as leading to a "philosophy of contradiction," as the subtitle of a prominent study of Nietzsche suggests.[49] I have argued in the introduction to this chapter that Nietzsche went through three distinct phases, with the latter two in particular rejecting much of what the first one stood for. If we take Nietzsche's work as a bloc, certainly contradictions appear, as has been noted in the literature concern-

---

[46] Aaron Ridley, introduction to *Nietzsche: The Antichrist, Ecce Homo, Twilight of the Idols, and Other Writings*, trans. Judith Norman (Cambridge: Cambridge University Press, 2005), viii.

[47] See also Sarah Kofman, *Explosions I: De l'"Ecce Homo" de Nietzsche* (Paris: Editions Galilée, 1992); Sarah Kofman, *Explosions II: Les enfants de Nietzsche* (Paris: Editions Galilée, 1993).

[48] See letter to Peter Gast, September 12, 1888.

[49] Wolfgang Müller-Lauter, *Nietzsche: His Philosophy of Contradictions and the Contradictions of His Philosophy*, trans. David Parent (Champaign: University of Illinois Press, 1999). Note that Müller-Lauter himself goes beyond the antinomy that his subtitle suggests.

ing his views of truth.[50] But if we take into account his work's division, these then appear less as contradictions than as positions that Nietzsche would eventually "overcome."[51]

Nietzsche's comment in *Twilight* that he "distrusts all systematizers and avoid[s] them. The will to a system is a lack of integrity" (TI Arrows 26) is well known, and is taken to imply that Nietzsche rejects systematic thinking as a whole. Yet what we must remember here is the very German idea that a true philosopher has a "philosophy" that he must expound in an organized, elaborate, and systematic way in a "big book." It is first and foremost this notion that Nietzsche is rejecting when he rejects "systematizers": that for a philosophy to be systematic it must be exposed in a big book. While he rejected the need to present his philosophy in a systematic manner, this does not mean that he was not a systematic thinker, nor indeed that he did not have a philosophical system.[52] This becomes clear when we look at the notes from which this "arrow" was drawn, where he writes that "I distrust all systems and systematizers and avoid them; perhaps behind this book one can still find the system that I *avoided*" (KSA 12 9 [188]).[53] With *Twilight* and the "Revaluation," Nietzsche avoided writing a systematic big book, but behind these books we can still find his system.

Nietzsche's aphoristic style is central to him avoiding a form of systematic presentation of his ideas, yet this has led to the question of whether such an unsystematic style of exposition is synonymous with an unsystematic philosophy.[54] Nietzsche answers this question directly when he asks, in a short aphorism titled "Against the Shortsighted" in the second book of *Human, All Too Human*, "Do you think this work must be fragmentary because I give it to you (and have to give it to you) in fragments?" (AOM 128). He later explains that "to him who has thought a great deal, every new thought he hears or reads at once appears in the form of a link in a chain" (AOM 376), thereby underlining the unity of his thought. I think Karl Löwith got the tone about just right when he claimed that "Nietzsche's philosophy is neither a unified, closed system nor a variety of disintegrating aphorisms, but rather a system in aphorisms"[55]

---

[50] See Maudemarie Clark, *Nietzsche on Truth and Philosophy* (Cambridge: Cambridge University Press, 1991).

[51] See HH II P: "My writings speak *only* of my overcomings. . . . [T]hey always speak of something 'behind me.'"

[52] See John Richardson, *Nietzsche's System* (Oxford: Oxford University Press, 2002).

[53] See also KSA 12 10 [146]: "I am not dogmatic enough for a system—and not even my own system." Nietzsche's statement here suggests that he does have a system, but it is not dogmatic enough to present systematically.

[54] See the discussion in Abbey, *Nietzsche's Middle Period*, 155–58.

[55] Karl Löwith, *Nietzsche's Philosophy of the Eternal Recurrence of the Same* (Berkeley: University of California Press, 1997), 11.

Even though *Twilight* was conceived as an appetizer to the "Revaluation of All Values," and with *The Antichrist* already completed, Nietzsche decided he needed another, more personal introduction to the work.[56] He appeared haunted by the fear that the work would not be understood, and thus would go the same way of *Zarathustra*. In a letter to his editor C. G. Naumann written on November 6, 1888, Nietzsche writes, "I have become convinced that I need a new book, a work that serves as the highest *preparation* before I can present myself in about a year with the first book of the *Revaluation of All Values*. A real tension must be created—otherwise it will go the way of *Zarathustra*." This book is *Ecce Homo*, already anticipated in the final section of *Twilight*, "What I Owe to the Ancients." The work is supposed to serve as a "foretaste to *what is to come*": the "Revaluation."[57] There Nietzsche is intent on saying "who he is," and not being mistaken for who he is not, continually asking whether he has "been understood" (EH Destiny 7–9), in expectation that he will soon "have to confront humanity with the most difficult demand it has ever faced" (EH P 1).

THE *PASSAGE À L'ACTE*

From early September to mid-November 1888, Nietzsche consistently referred to *The Antichrist*, completed on September 30, as the "first book" of the "Revaluation of All Values."[58] In a letter to Overbeck on October 18, Nietzsche confirms that "there will be *four* books," and specifies that "they will be published one by one."[59] Yet one month later, on November 20 in a letter to Deussen, Nietzsche writes that "my *Revaluation of All Values*, with the main title *The Antichrist*, is finished."[60] *The Antichrist* has become the whole "Revaluation."

What happened to the other three books? Nietzsche continued to work on "The Immoralist," book 2, in both September and October, and also "The Free Spirit," book 3, although this is the only attention that this latter

[56] Letter to Peter Gast, October 30, 1888. Nietzsche writes that EH "speaks of me and my books with the greatest temerity."

[57] See letter to Peter Gast, November 13, 1888; draft letter to Georg Brandes, beginning of December 1888.

[58] See letters to Peter Gast, September 12, 1888, and October 30, 1888; letter to Paul Deussen, September 14, 1888; letter to Malwida von Meysenburg, October 4, 1888; letters to Franz Overbeck, October 18, 1888, and November 13, 1888.

[59] There are six plans for the "Revaluation of All Values" (see KSA 12 19 [8], 11 [416], 22 [14], 22 [24], 23 [8], 23 [13]), dating from September to October 1888. All have four books, with the most consistent arrangement being: book 1, "The Antichrist"; book 2, "The Immoralist"; book 3, "The Free Spirit"; and book 4, "Dionysus" (philosophy of the eternal return). There is some juggling between the orders of books 2 and 3.

[60] Letter to Paul Deussen, November 20, 1888.

book receives.[61] As we saw above, the draft letter to Brandes of early December describes the last section of *Ecce Homo*, "Why I Am a Destiny," as a "foretaste of what is *to come*." Nietzsche had recently reworked this section, adding the first two sections to the chapter.[62] While his tirade against Christianity—"*écrasez l'infâme*" (EH Destiny 8)—certainly anticipates *The Antichrist*, a closer reading suggests that it is extracted from material destined for "The Immoralist." Nietzsche presents himself there as "the first *immoralist*," critiques the "*good*" type of person, and attacks "*Christian* morality" and the "decadent priests" along with how they have come to power—themes all concordant with the detailed plans for "The Immoralist" (EH Destiny 2, 4, 7).[63]

If we are to fully understand what happens with the "Revaluation" project, we must understand its transformation from being solely a literary project to also becoming an "act." Nietzsche writes to Gast on October 30 that with *Ecce Homo*, he wishes to present himself "before committing the act so strangely solitary of the *Revaluation*," and this is echoed in the first section of "Why I Am a Destiny"—a later addition—where Nietzsche declares the "Revaluation of All Values" to be his "formula for an act of humanity's higher self-examination, an act that has become flesh and genius" in him (EH Destiny 1). Moreover, one of the first plans for the "Revaluation" has the "Revaluation of All Values" both as the main title and rewritten, underlined, at the end of the titles of the planned four books, as if writing it again constituted itself an act.[64] Nietzsche also concludes *The Antichrist*, now the full *literary* "Revaluation," with the exclamation "Revaluation of All Values!" (AC 62), so as to claim that the act had been accomplished with the start of a new, anti-Christian calendar.

Why does Nietzsche transform his "Revaluation" project into an act? I think we can answer this if we hark back to Wagner's—and Nietzsche's following of Wagner's—total revolution.[65] It is around this time that Nietzsche starts to realize that one can put "Nietzsche" in place of Wagner in the *Untimely Mediations* (EH BT 4; UM 3). Having presented his epistemological views in *Twilight*, and his metaphysical ones in *The Antichrist*, Nietzsche, having thereby completed his philosophy, would turn to the other part of his total revolution—politics. As he had said of Wagner, as quoted above: "It is quite impossible to produce the highest and purest effort of which the art

[61] See, respectively, KSA 13 19 [9], 22 [17]ff., 22 [25], 23 [3]ff; KSA 13 22 [24].

[62] For the first aphorism, the second being a quotation from *Zarathustra*, see KSA 13 25 [6]: 1.

[63] See KSA 13 23 [4–5].

[64] KSA 13 11 [416].

[65] See SE 6, where Nietzsche explains that one's first consecration to culture is to "attach one's heart to some great man," and that the second moment is to transform this "inward" into an "outward event."

of the theater is capable without at the same time effecting innovations everywhere, in morality and politics, in education and society" (WB 4). Having produced the highest and purest effort in philosophy, and indeed the German language with *Zarathustra*, Nietzsche would now move on to innovations everywhere, including morality, education, society, and politics.[66]

In *Wagner in Bayreuth*, Nietzsche had seen how Wagner "presents every dramatic event in a threefold rendering, through words, gestures, and music" (WB 8). *Thus Spoke Zarathustra*, as we saw above, was conceived as a *drama*, in the mode of Wagner's total work of art. As its mirror work, the "Revaluation of All Values," also in four books, can be viewed in the same manner: the "words" are *Twilight, Ecce Homo*, and the "literary act" that is *The Antichrist*; the "gestures" are the publication act of *The Antichrist*, which ignites Nietzsche's great politics and war of spirits; and finally, the music— how Nietzsche refers to *Zarathustra* (EH Z 1)—can be found in Nietzsche's "Hymn to Life" and the *Dionysian-Dithyrambs*.[67] With this Nietzsche has a total work of art, and a total revolution.

The need to express himself in other modes than prose, on top of the various styles of writing he experimented with over the course of his publications, was felt keenly, and early, by Nietzsche. Witness his inclusion of the "Songs of the Prince Vogelfrei" in his second edition of *The Gay Science*. Indeed, in his review of *The Birth of Tragedy* in 1886, Nietzsche had expressed frustration with how he had attempted to communicate his knowledge of Dionysus, concluding that it should have been "sung," and that he should have permitted himself "a *language of my very own*" (BT P 3, 6). In the note on "Toward the Teaching of Style" that he penned for Andreas-Salomé, Nietzsche left some insights into his way of thinking how one should express oneself, including notions such as "the richness of life reveals itself through a *richness of gestures*," "style ought to prove that one *believes* in an idea; not only thinks it but also *feels* it," and "the more abstract a truth that one wishes to teach, the more one must first *entice* the senses."[68] This gives us an insight into the manner in which Nietzsche thought one should con-

---

[66] See the draft letter to Jean Bourdeau, December 17, 1888. This thought was already expressed, at the time of writing *Zarathustra*, in a letter to Erwin Rohde, February 22, 1884.

[67] On Nietzsche's music and poetry, see Philip Grundlehner, *The Poetry of Friedrich Nietzsche* (Oxford: Oxford University Press, 1986); Curt Paul Janz, "The Form-Content Problem in Friedrich Nietzsche's Conception of Music," in *Nietzsche's New Seas: Explorations in Philosophy, Aesthetics, and Politics*, ed. Michael Gillespie and Tracy Strong, trans. Thomas Heilke (Chicago: University of Chicago Press, 1988), 97–116; Michael Gillespie, "Nietzsche's Musical Politics," in *Nietzsche's New Seas: Explorations in Philosophy, Aesthetics, and Politics*, ed. Michael Gillespie and Tracy Strong, trans. Thomas Heilke (Chicago: University of Chicago Press, 1988), 117–49.

[68] See Lou Andreas-Salomé, *Nietzsche*, trans. and ed. Siegfried Mandel (Champaign: University of Illinois Press, 2001), 77–78. On "Toward the Teaching of Style" and Nietzsche's

vince one's readers to join one's cause—how one goes about "fishing" for those who would give a hand with the necessary destruction (EH BGE 1). We can also note that the more traditional power of logic, along with its expression in a systematic big book, was far from his mind.

In one of his final notes, Nietzsche writes that the current political situation disgusts him too much for him to play only the role of a "spectator" (KSA 13 25 [6]: 2). As Strong has persuasively argued, Nietzsche, nearing the end of his life, expresses a desire to act; he wants to enter the political arena.[69] Why this desire? A first answer can be found in the discussion of Wagner's total revolution above: having successfully, in his own eyes, completed his total work of art, Nietzsche moves to the other part of his total revolution—politics. And this revolution takes a Nietzschean rather than Wagnerian form. If in *The Birth of Tragedy*, his first revaluation, Nietzsche had towed the Wagnerian line that a cultural renewal would see the rebirth of Greek culture—although there was already here a disagreement about the role of slavery in this renewal—Nietzsche's "Revaluation" proper inverses this relationship: it is a political revolution that will lead to the rebirth of classical culture. As Strong puts it, "At the beginning of his public life, he had argued in *The Birth of Tragedy* that an aesthetic moment was necessary for the reconstruction of European culture. . . . At the end of Nietzsche's life, however, politics has become the master trope."[70]

On top of following the structure of Wagner's total revolution, another way of understanding this move from art to politics is suggested, perhaps unwittingly, by Williams himself. In *Shame and Necessity*, he asks, "How do we respond to Greek tragedy? What are those 'structural substitutions,' as I called them, that are needed if it is to relate to our experiences?"[71] Williams's answer is politics. He explains that "Napoleon remarked to Goethe that what fate was in the ancient world, politics was in the modern, and in the same spirit Benjamin Constant said that the significance of the supernatural in ancient tragedy could be transferred to the modern theater only in political terms." In preparation for his "Revaluation," Nietzsche reread and made a number of notes on *The Birth*, indicating that the notion of tragedy was close to his mind.[72] Nietzsche was also—in a bizarre twist of

rhetorical uses more generally, see Tracy Strong, "In Defense of Rhetoric, or How Hard It Is to Take a Writer Seriously: The Case of Nietzsche," *Political Theory* 41, no. 4 (2013): 507–32.

[69] Tracy Strong, "Nietzsche's Political Aesthetics,'" in *Nietzsche's New Seas: Explorations in Philosophy, Aesthetics, and Politics*, ed. Michael Gillespie and Tracy Strong, trans. Thomas Heilke (Chicago: University of Chicago Press, 1988), 153–76.

[70] Ibid., 154.

[71] Bernard Williams, *Shame and Necessity* (Berkeley: University of California Press, 2008), 164.

[72] See KSA 13 14 [14–46], 16 [40], 17 [3]. Nietzsche titles the notes "Art in *The Birth of Tragedy*," some of which were to be incorporated into Nietzsche's review of *The Birth* in *Ecce Homo*.

fate—reading Constant's introduction to his own translation of Friedrich Schiller's *Wallenstein*, precisely the text that Williams cites where Constant argued for the move from the supernatural to the political. I do not mean to suggest here that it is in reading Constant's text that Nietzsche himself made a move to the political realm but rather that he came to the same conclusion as Constant's: if one wanted to re-create the conditions that made Greek tragedy possible, one could not start—this had been Wagner's mistake—with tragedy itself; one had to begin, as Nietzsche came to realize, with politics.

There is a strong echo in this move of what Nietzsche had learned from his study of the ancient Greeks: a healthy culture had to be restored before a healthy philosophy could come into existence again. To restore that culture, both politics and the instincts had to be reformed, and this is what Nietzsche will attempt to do with his revaluation. It is thus not surprising that Plato reappears in Nietzsche's writings of around this time. Not long before his declaration that he no longer wants to be a spectator to the politics of his day, Nietzsche had penned a preface to a "Tractatus Politicus," which he titled "On the Sovereignty of Virtues: How Virtue Comes to Power" (KSA 13 11 [54]). There he explains that virtue is brought to power by doing exactly the opposite of being virtuous—by lying, deceit, slander, and so on—which is precisely how for him the priests had come to power in the first place.[73] But men had never achieved true "perfection in politics," which Nietzsche associates with "Machiavellianism." Only Plato had come close to that ideal, and even he was not up to the task.

In referring to Plato within a tract on politics, Nietzsche thereby harks back to the twofold legislative mission that he had attributed to Plato in his early lectures on him: to legislate a new state and train the men to carry through his reform. Having achieved the philosophical basis for his new legislative project with the revaluation, Nietzsche would seek the men with whom he would carry out his reform. His project would take the following form: first men would be reeducated with healthy instincts through, among other things, a positively channeled will to power and the eternal return, away from the decadent moralism that Plato had unwittingly, because of Socrates, pursued; then these men would reform the political system so as to make way for a new set of laws that would reestablish a healthy culture on which a new healthy philosophy could take root. So while Nietzsche had retained a model from Wagner of how to structure a total revolution of both art and politics, he learns a model of political action from Plato.

In his philosophical biography of Nietzsche, Rüdiger Safranski writes that in his later period, Nietzsche starts to identify with the "ancient states-

---

[73] See also EH Destiny 7.

men" and "legislative philosophers" that he had studied in his youth.[74] Certainly Nietzsche's presentation of *The Antichrist* as an agitation edition in a draft letter to Brandes of December 9, 1888, seems to recall Nietzsche's theorization of Plato as an *"agitatorischen Politiker"* (PL P). Nietzsche thus appears to start taking up for himself the mantle of the philosophical lawgiver that he had likewise dubbed his new philosophers in *Beyond Good and Evil*: he desires to say, "This is how it *should* be!" (BGE 211). Already in Zarathustra's speech on the "Old and New Tables," which Nietzsche considers to be the "crucial section" of the book (EH Z 4), Zarathustra had tried his hand at legislating new values, commanding that one should "love your *children's land*" and *"become hard*!" (Z III Tables, 12, 29). This legislation, however, was more of the internal, ethical type, destined for the reeducation of the men to carry through the revaluation. Yet at the end of his productive life, Nietzsche starts to try his hand more directly at political legislation too, particularly with the infamous "Law against Christianity" that closes *The Antichrist*.

This "Law" was drawn from a number of "demands" that Nietzsche had formulated in his notes as the conclusion to *The Antichrist*, which he transformed into his *Law* in early December.[75] But these demands recall one of the chapters that Nietzsche had planned—and organized notes for—in the pivotal draft for "The Will to Power" in mid-February 1888, titled "Life Recipes for Us" (KSA 13 12 [2]). In fact, the move from "Life Recipes for Us" to a "Law against Christianity" tracks the move from an ethical to a more political conception of his role. This is important because there are strong continuities between "The Will to Power" versions that Nietzsche drafted and those of the "Revaluation of All Values." As Montinari indicates, "Viewed with respect to *contents*, the 'Revaluation of All Values' was in a sense the same as 'The Will to Power,' but precisely for this reason was its *literary* negation. Alternatively, *Twilight of the Idols* and *Antichrist* were created from the notes for 'The Will to Power'; the rest is—*Nachlass*, unpublished writings."[76] The plans for "The Will to Power" rather consistently seem to indicate chapters on nihilism, critique of values, the will to power as a new evaluative basis, and the philosophy of the eternal return—themes clearly taken up by the four books of the "Revaluation," with Christianity here being the European incarnation of nihilism.[77]

---

[74] Rüdiger Safranski, *Nietzsche: A Philosophical Biography*, trans. Shelley Frisch (London: Granta, 2003), 304–16.

[75] See KSA 13 22 [10]; draft letter to Georg Brandes, December 9, 1888, which contains the only explicit mention of the "Law." That it was found separately from *The Antichrist*—although perfectly well written, demonstrating that Nietzsche was still of sane mind when he penned it—appears to confirm that it was a later addition.

[76] Montinari, "Nietzsche's Unpublished Writings," 101.

[77] See KSA 12 2 [100], 7 [64]; KSA 13 12 [2], 19 [8], 22 [14, 24].

The theme of the philosopher as lawgiver is prominent in Nietzsche's conception—especially in its later conception—of book 4 of the "Revaluation": the last two plans have as titles for the final book "Dionysus: Legislator Type" and *"Dionysos Philosophos"* (KSA 13 23 [8, 13]). This seems to bring the *Law against Christianity* into the orbit of book 4 of "The Will to Power" cum "Revaluation of All Values." Moreover, sometime near the end of December, Nietzsche crossed out the "Revaluation of All Values" "subtitle" to *The Antichrist* that he had attributed to it on November 26, replacing it with the subtitle *A Curse on Christianity*.

Dionysus is the philosopher of the eternal return, and the projected book 4 of both "The Will to Power" and the "Revaluation of All Values" was systematically dedicated to the eternal return.[78] After having presented his epistemological views in *Twilight* and his metaphysical ones in *The Antichrist*, Nietzsche wanted to conclude his "Revaluation" with his crowning doctrine of the eternal return, thus linking it back again to *Zarathustra*. Yet apart from one or two reworkings of the notion in the notes in preparation for the Hauptwerk, the eternal return appears in them mainly as projected chapter titles, with the implication here being that the main work Nietzsche did on the eternal return was in preparation for *Zarathustra*.[79] Nietzsche appeared to have been satisfied with how he had presented the thought in *Zarathustra*, describing it as the "basic idea of the work" in his review of it in *Ecce Homo* (EH Z 1), quoting copiously from *Zarathustra* in his late works, along with closing *Ecce Homo* with the statement "I have not said anything I would not have said five years ago through the mouth of Zarathustra" (EH Destiny 8). There Nietzsche explains that the *"uncovering* of Christian morality is an event without equal, a real catastrophe . . . [that] splits the history of humanity into two parts." While *The Antichrist*, with its final transformation of the calendar, undeniably splits the history of humanity in two, Nietzsche is also referring to the doctrine of the eternal return, which splits humanity into ascending and descending forces, as I explored in the previous chapter.

In the first section of "Why I Am a Destiny"—one that was added later and that Nietzsche refers to as a "foretaste of what is *to come*" in the draft letter to Brandes of early December 1888—Nietzsche links the "Revaluation of All Values" with the notion of great politics. Yet great politics had already appeared as a subsection to book 4 in the pivotal draft of "The Will to Power" of early 1888.[80] Thus instead of having a final book that would reexplain the doctrine of the eternal return—a doctrine that Nietzsche felt

---

[78] See KSA 12 2 [100], 7 [64]; KSA 13 12 [2], 18 [17], 19 [8], 11 [416], 22 [14], 22 [24], 23 [8], 23 [13].

[79] See KSA 13 10 [3], 14 [188].

[80] See KSA 13 12 [2]. See also KSA 14 [169].

Zarathustra had sufficiently well presented in the first place—Nietzsche decided to focus on the political aspect of the thought as the conclusion to the "Revaluation." It is comprised of two parts. The first is a beginning of political legislation with the "Law against Christianity," which in the future, the new philosophers would have to turn into a positive legislation for the founding of a new society whose aim is to produce the overmen. But for this to happen, second, the war against the Christian party would have to be won. Nietzsche, following Plato, needs the men with whom he would win this war and found a new society. These men would form the party of life, which will fight a war of spirits against the party of Christianity, and it is for this party of life that Nietzsche writes a political strategy, a great politics, to which I now turn.

CONCLUSION

Contrary to Montinari, Nietzsche does not end his "life work" in confusion. He instead follows his "Revaluation" project to its natural end—one dictated by the logic of a total revolution: having presented his philosophy, he is moving into politics, he is getting ready to "rule the world."[81] What Nietzsche means by this is that once Christianity is no longer the only dominant form of morality, his philosophy will be able to direct certain segments of society. While Nietzsche's later, more megalomaniac statements undoubtedly show that he is starting to lose his grip on reality, I hope to have shown in this chapter at least the logic of Nietzsche's move into the political arena.[82] Nor are Nietzsche's final notes simply *Nachlass*, or just leftovers that distract from the main event, as Montinari would have it. Rather, they also contain important documents like the "Proclamation" of great politics and its associated letters, which I will examine in the next chapter. Indeed, as the "Proclamation" is lost to us, the notes are essential for reconstituting what Nietzsche intended for it, both in his final notebook and the relevant sections of his plans for "The Will to Power." What this also shows is that while Nietzsche prided himself in believing that the "ephemeral little

[81] Letter to Carl Fuchs, December 11, 1888; KSA 13 25 [19]: "During the next years, the world will be turned upside down; when the old God will have abdicated, it is I who will rule the world."

[82] There are signs that Nietzsche may have been aware of his impending doom. In his review of *Zarathustra*, he writes, "You pay a high price for being immortal: you have to die several times during your life. There is something I call the *rancune* of the great: once completed, everything great—a work, an act—immediately turns *against* the one who did it" (EH Z 5). To Gast he writes, "I now understand why I need not precipitate this tragic catastrophe of my existence that begins with *Ecce*" (December 16, 1888), and again remarks on December 30 that both *Ecce Homo* and "the man" are "over."

gossip of politics and national self-interest" was beneath him (AC P), when he does turn his attention to the contemporary political situation, he does so by redefining the "concept of politics" (EH Destiny 1), identifying what he believes to be the true core of politics—the breeding of a certain type of being—of which modern politics, under the sway of Christianity, has lost sight.[83]

Declaring that Nietzsche's final, systematic, philosophical project was "The Will to Power," Heidegger infamously constructed an interpretation of Nietzsche as the philosopher of the will to power. With this concept, Nietzsche, according to Heidegger, answered "*the* question of philosophy: "what is being?"[84] Nietzsche thus became, for Heidegger, the philosopher of the "end of metaphysics," although this was a project that Nietzsche failed to bring to a close, and a project that Heidegger would have us believe he was successful in completing. While Nietzsche's concept of the will to power is undeniably central to his thinking, it locates itself within a broader project of the "Revaluation of All Values." Therefore against Heidegger, I have argued that Nietzsche presented his final philosophy in his published works, notably *Twilight* and *The Antichrist*, and that following the logic of a total revolution, he moved, in the last element of the "Revaluation" project, to the political arena. Following Plato, he starts to legislate new values and writes a political strategy, a great politics, for his men—the party of life—to follow.

[83] For the links between breeding and Great Politics, see John Richardson, *Nietzsche's New Darwinism* (Oxford: Oxford University Press, 2004), 191.

[84] Heidegger, *Nietzsche*, 1:4.

CHAPTER 6

GREAT POLITICS

Nietzsche's productive life almost exactly spans Bismarck's era. He was a medical orderly in the Franco-Prussian War (1870–71), but fell ill and only served for two months. Serving as a medical orderly was quite a common experience for many of the more "spiritual" types of Nietzsche's generation. Most, however, were not as fortunate as he was to have actually survived, being decimated by various diseases contracted on the battlefield—illness already being a greater harvester of souls than war itself.[1] Nietzsche had previously volunteered as a cavalry officer in his local town, Naumburg, but after a self-described promising start, had a bad fall that prevented him from participating in the war effort in a combatant role. He published his first book, *The Birth of Tragedy*, in 1872, one year after German unification and the founding of the German Empire under Wilhelm I.[2] In his "Attempt at Self-Criticism" that would serve as preface to the reissuing of *The Birth* in 1886, he drew a clear parallel between the Franco-Prussian War and his own composition of the book:

> While the thunder of the Battle of Wörth rolled across Europe, the brooder and lover of riddles who fathered the book was sitting in some corner of the Alps, utterly preoccupied with his ponderings and riddles, and consequently very troubled and untroubled at one and the same time, writing down his thoughts about the *Greeks* .... A few weeks later he was himself beneath the walls of Metz and still obsessed with the question marks he had placed over the alleged "cheerfulness" of the Greeks; until finally, in that extremely tense month when peace was being discussed at Versailles, he too made peace with himself and, while recovering slowly from an illness that he had brought back from

---

[1] Peter Bergmann, *Nietzsche: "The Last Anti-political German"* (Bloomington: Indiana University Press, 1987).

[2] Friedrich *Wilhelm* Nietzsche was named after Wilhelm I's father, Friedrich Wilhelm IV, with whom he shared a birthday.

the field, reached a settled and definitive view in his own mind of the "Birth of Tragedy from the Spirit of *Music*" (BT P 1).[3]

Nietzsche departed his sane life in January 1889, although he was only to die eleven years later, in 1900. One year after Nietzsche's loss of his faculties, Bismarck would tender his resignation to the new emperor, Wilhelm II (March 1890), signaling the end of his political career. This moment was immortalized by the infamous cartoon cover of *Punch* magazine on March 29, 1890, drawn by John Tenniel and titled "Dropping the Pilot," which depicted Bismarck leaving the "ship of state" under the eyes of the new emperor.

Bismarck's politics—as it had done throughout most of Europe at that time—therefore defined the period of Nietzsche's intellectual, social, and political adult life. On the international stage this took the form of grosse Politik, Bismarck's power politics of making Germany a great power.[4] This *Machtpolitik* was backboned by the twin concepts of "blood and iron"— namely, war and advanced technology. With successive defeats of Denmark, Austria, and France, Bismarck achieved his goal of unifying Germany, with Prussia, as opposed to (Catholic) Austria, at its core. In doing so, Germany was able to take its seat among the great powers of Europe. From then on Bismarck's aim was to maintain Germany's position within the ever-shifting balance of power in Europe, going so far as to portray himself as the "honest broker" at the Congress of Berlin in 1878. Power politics' central thesis was the primacy of external relations to domestic politics, and Bismarck's other more explicitly domestic policies, in particular his Kulturkampf, played a role in his international politics.[5]

From at least *Human, All Too Human*, published in 1878, Nietzsche explicitly wrote and theorized about grosse Politik. At first this engagement was quite critical, linking it to the rise of democracy, mediocrity, and philistinism that he diagnosed as early as his first *Untimely Meditation, David Strauss, the Confessor and the Writer* (1873) as the legacy of Prussia's victory

[3] The 1886 reissuing changed the title to *The Birth of Tragedy, or: Hellenism and Pessimism*.

[4] See Tracy Strong, "'Wars the Like of Which One Has Never Seen': Reading Nietzsche and Politics," in *Friedrich Nietzsche*, ed. Tracy Strong (Farnham, UK: Ashgate, 2009). For Nietzsche's changing—from positive to negative at the end of his life—view of Bismarck, see Duncan Large, "The Aristocratic Radical and the White Revolutionary: Nietzsche's Bismarck," in *Das Schwierige 19. Jarhundert*, ed. Jurgen Barkhoff et al. (Tubingen: Max Niemeyer, 2000), 101–13. While Nietzsche may have kept a positive view of Bismarck *the person* for most of his adult life, until his final rejection of him in 1888, I argue in this chapter that at least from *David Strauss, the Confessor and the Writer* and *Human, All Too Human* onward, Nietzsche, after his initial enthusiasm for the Franco-Prussian War, became critical of Bismarck's politics.

[5] See Bergmann, *Nietzsche*, 162; Bruce Detwiler, *Nietzsche and the Politics of Aristocratic Radicalism* (Chicago: University of Chicago Press, 1990), 54. Bismarck's other (in)famous domestic politics was his antisocialist laws. See Frank Cameron and Don Dombowsky, eds., *Political Writings of Friedrich Nietzsche* (New York: Palgrave Macmillan, 2008).

over France. But with *Beyond Good and Evil* (1886), Nietzsche transformed grosse Politik into his own notion of what great politics should truly amount to. This he saw to be the unification of continental Europe led by a cultivated and interbred elite class of good Europeans, so that it may engage in the geopolitical struggle against the British Empire and Russia for mastery of the world.

Nietzsche's engagement with the notion of great politics is the best way, to my mind, of addressing the question of whether he "has a politics." As I contended in the introduction, Williams in *Shame and Necessity*, although he concludes that Nietzsche does not offer a politics, provides a framework within which to tackle this issue. Williams lays out four desiderata, which taken together, would amount to having a "coherent politics." These are: having "ethical and psychological insights"; an "intelligible account of modern society"; the ability to relate these insights to this account of society; and "a coherent set of opinions about the ways in which power should be exercised in modern societies, with what limitations and to what ends."[6]

The aim of this book has been to argue that Nietzsche does meet these criteria. In the chapters on the state and democracy in particular, I have brought to the fore that with regard to his ethical and psychological insights, Nietzsche posits slavery as a precondition for high culture, and underlines the role that the agon plays in perpetuating such culture. Furthermore, he appears to have a highly intelligible account of modern society, not simply his well-known grasp of the ethical and moral foundations of modernity, but also, in a more political vein, of the modern nation-state and democracy. In relating his notorious claim about the death of God to his theory of the decay of the modern state brought about through democracy, Nietzsche likewise demonstrates his ability to relate his ethical and psychological insights to his account of modern politics. Finally, in the chapter on democracy, I explored the vision of the future society that Nietzsche postulates, with its two spheres of existence and two separate moralities, each with their respective roles and responsibilities, and how power is to be shared between them.

The goal of this chapter is to build on these answers through analyzing Nietzsche's understanding of the international politics of his day. It will assert that along with his grasp of the modern state and democracy, Nietzsche reveals his insightful account of the power politics of his time, especially in how it is linked to the rise of mass politics. He is also able to relate his key twin concepts of slave and master morality to this understanding of international relations, criticizing what he labels the petty politics of his time from the perspective of slave morality, with its emphasis on fragmentation, medi-

---

[6] Bernard Williams, *Shame and Necessity* (Berkeley: University of California Press, 2008), 10–11.

ocrity, and philistinism, against which he will posit his own conception of a truly great politics on the basis of master morality. So while Nietzsche's engagement with the notion of great politics is constant throughout his work, and in contrast to his thinking about the state and democracy, which deepens within a given context over the course of his writings, a shift occurs between Nietzsche's earlier and later thoughts on the matter that tracks the development of his thinking about morality, in particular his separating out of it into its slave and master manifestations. This happens within a broader and continuous reflection on the topic, but allows Nietzsche to reorganize his thoughts on the matter from a different perspective, as I will examine over the course of this chapter.

Underlying Williams's four desiderata is the question, "What is to be done?" If Nietzsche can posit an ideal future society and provide a convincing account of the modern politics of his day, how does he propose that we move from his contemporary situation to this model future? What is his political strategy for getting from A to B? Does Nietzsche, in short, offer a politics understood as a political program? Through his call for the founding of a party of life, and the war of spirits it is brought to bear against its opposing Christian Reich and the party of Christianity, Nietzsche, I will argue, starts to formulate a concrete politics, a political strategy, and program to achieve his desired goal.

PETTY POLITICS

Human, All Too Human 481 is the first instance in Nietzsche's published work where he addresses himself explicitly to the issue of grosse Politik. The tone is set by the title of the aphorism: "Power Politics and What They Cost."[7] There, Nietzsche explains that the greatest cost incurred by those who prepare to engage in "power politics to secure a decisive voice among the mightiest states" are not to be found "where these are usually thought to lie." They are not to be found in the "interruption to trade and commerce, nor the maintenance of standing armies," on which Europe spends "between two and three billion annually." Instead, they are to be discovered in the "cost involved in the removal, year in, year out, of an extraordinary number of its efficient and industrious men from their proper professions and occupations so that they may become soldiers." Before power politics, these men had "other spheres of action open to them," but now "each able, industrious, intelligent, ambitious man of a people greedy for political glory is ruled by this greed and no longer belongs entirely to his own cause

---

[7] I translate *grosse Politik* as "power politics," or again "grand politics," when it refers to Bismarck's policies, reserving "great politics" for Nietzsche's own project.

as he once did." The "daily tribute" of politics taken from "every citizen's mental and emotional capital," this

> sum of all these sacrifices and losses of individual energy and labor is so enormous that almost necessarily, the political flowering of a people is followed by an intellectual impoverishment and exhaustion, a decreased ability to produce works that demand great concentration and single-mindedness.

"Is all of this worth it," Nietzsche asks to close the section, "if all the nobler, more tender, and spiritual plants" must be sacrificed to the "coarse and gaudy flower of the nation"?

For Nietzsche, the greatest cost of power politics is that those predestined for the "life of the soul," instead of accomplishing their destiny of furthering culture, will either be sacrificed for the good of the nation in one of its wars of expansion, or see their energy misdirected and wasted in perpetuating the apparatus, as one of its employees, of grand politics. No doubt harking back to Nietzsche's own experiences of the Franco-Prussian War, we can already discern the germ of this thought in his first *Untimely Meditation* on Strauss, where he had cautioned against believing that the recent military victory of Germany over France should also be understood as a cultural victory; quite the opposite, as a total investment in politics results in an equal loss in the domain of arts and culture. Germany was now perhaps a military power, but had accordingly ceased to be a cultural power. This claim is reiterated in the section "What the Germans Lack" in *Twilight of the Idols* (1889), one of Nietzsche's last works, underscoring the continuity of his thinking on the matter throughout his corpus. There Nietzsche explains that "if you invest all your energy in economics, world commerce, parliamentarianism, military engagements, power, and power politics," then "there won't be any left for the other direction"—that is, culture—concluding that "at the very moment Germany emerged as a great power, France won new importance as a *Kulturmacht*" (TI Germans 4).

Power politics is connected by Nietzsche to nationalism, racism, parliamentarianism, mediocrity, and philistinism—in a word, slave morality. Indeed, Nietzsche was quick to perceive the novelty of Bismarck's blood and iron *Machtpolitik* (BGE 254), and the new type of international relations it gave rise to. This was a politics that emanated from the arrival of the masses on the political stage, and their concomitant demand for great things that will satisfy their "*need for the feeling of power*," specifically war, as Nietzsche puts it in *Daybreak* (D 189). This last section is notable for being the first sketch of Nietzsche's theory of good and evil in relation to power, which he would affirm more fully in the opening paragraphs of *The Antichrist*, thereby stressing the link between Nietzsche's philosophy and politics. In *Beyond Good and Evil* 241 (1886), Nietzsche explains that grand politics can only come about in the "age of the masses," who "lie on their belly before every-thing that is massive," such that when a "statesman"—read Bismarck—erects for them "some monstrosity of empire and power," they call it "great." As witness the discussion between the two old patriots, the success of such a politics is success itself, that power is justified for power alone; the ends justify the means. In practicing grand politics, the statesmen revive the base passions and avidities of the people: nationalism—what Nietzsche will later call in *Ecce Homo* (1888) the "*névrose nationale* from which Europe is cur-rently suffering from" (EH CW 2)—narrowness of mind, racism, anti-Semitism, and anti-intellectualism.[8]

One of the main theses, as highlighted previously, of grand politics is the primacy of international relations over domestic politics. Nietzsche saw how colonization was being used as a way of trying to resolve the "social question" of the nineteenth century; the poor were being told "better to be master abroad than a slave at home" (D 206). He also perceived the interna-tional implications of Bismarck's Kulturkampf. One of Bismarck's biggest fears on the international stage was that France and Russia would form an alliance, thereby sandwiching Germany between two hostile powers—in particular France, which was animated by a spirit of *revanchisme* since its defeat in the Franco-Prussian War. From this angle Nietzsche interprets Bis-marck's Kulturkampf, his attack on German Catholics whom he was con-cerned would be more loyal to Rome that to the new Reich, as a means of driving a wedge between France and Russia. France was still a Catholic country, and thus felt aggrieved by such a policy, while Russia was known at the time to be oppressing Polish Catholics. In stoking the fires of this issue, Bismarck, Nietzsche understood, placed an obstacle in the way of a Franco-Russian alliance. As such, domestic politics served as a handmaiden to power politics.[9]

Bismarck's other concern on the international stage was the power strug-gle—what Arthur Conolly, a British intelligence officer of Irish extraction, coined "the great game," later popularized by Rudyard Kipling in his novel *Kim* (1901)—that was taking place between Britain and Russia over India (the "jewel in the crown") and Afghanistan. Whoever controlled that area, so it was thought, controlled the world. This conflict stretched back at least to the Crimean War of 1854–56 over the remains of the decaying Ottoman Empire, which the young Nietzsche had avidly followed with his friends, apparently siding with Russia.[10] If so, this would be consonant with Nietz-

---

[8] As the reference to the French—névrose nationale—reminds us, what might be lost in terms of culture for one culture might be won for another.

[9] William Altman, *Friedrich Wilhelm Nietzsche: The Philosopher of the Second Reich* (Lanham, MD: Lexington Books, 2013).

[10] The great game is usually dated from the Russo-Persian Treaty of 1813 to the Anglo-Russian Entente of 1907. See ibid.

sche's adult view of England, the only country he possibly had an entirely negative view of: he considered the utilitarianism of Jeremy Bentham and Mill—the "happiness of the greatest number"—as pure expressions of herd morality (BGE 228).[11]

It is within this international setting that Nietzsche's pronouncements on grand politics must be understood. Indeed, Nietzsche's first comments on the matter in *Human, All Too Human* intervene not long after the Russo-Turkish War of 1877–78, which arose as a consequence of the Crimean War: while the Ottoman Empire had to deal with the growing threat of Balkan nationalism, Russia, a natural ally to the Balkan cause due to its shared allegiance to the Eastern Orthodox Church, seized the opportunity to challenge Turkey in the Caucasus to recover territory it had lost during the Crimean War and reestablish itself in the Black Sea area. To mediate the conflict, Bismarck called the Congress of Berlin for June 13–July 13, 1878. This was the first time that Bismarck and Germany played the role of peacemaker, or "honest broker" as he liked to style himself, in a conflict between the great European powers, thus underlining the arrival of Germany itself as a great power on the international stage.

It is only with *Beyond Good and Evil*, and his theorizing of a positive vision of what great politics should amount to for him, that Nietzsche was to see the more immediate political ramifications of such a politics, content as he was in *Human, All Too Human* simply to measure its costs for culture. Armed with this reevaluation of grosse Politik, to which I now turn, Nietzsche was able to fully grasp the role that Bismarck had carved out for Germany in the European "balance of power." By placing itself between "two deadly hatreds," as Nietzsche puts it in *The Gay Science* 377, published in 1887 as part of an expanded edition of the work—chapter 5—to the original one published in 1882, Bismarck wanted to retain a "free hand" by serving as an intermediary between Britain and Russia. But the downside to such a politics is that for Germany to maintain its position, it must desire the "perpetuation of the petty state system in Europe." It must, therefore, foster nationalism, racism, and colonization—"India wars and complications in Asia"—along with "internal subversion, the shattering of empires into small states," and the "introduction of parliamentary imbecility," together with the "obligation for everyone to read the newspaper at breakfast" (BGE 208). Anticipating the move he would perform in *The Genealogy* concerning the notions of "good and bad" and "good and evil," Nietzsche recasts the grand politics of discord and herd morality as petty politics, to which he will oppose his own novel concept of great politics, for such a "disintegration politics" can only be an "interim politics" (BGE 256). "The time for petty politics is past; the next century will bring the struggle for the mastery of the world—the *compulsion* to great politics" (BGE 208).

[11] See also KSA 13 11 [127], 22 [1].

GREAT POLITICS

Aphorism 208 of *Beyond Good and Evil* marks the definitive shift in Nietzsche's published work of his thinking on great politics, from a critical stance as witnessed in *Human, All Too Human*, to elaborating his own positive conception of what great politics should be about. He explains that he desires for Europe to *"acquire one will* by means of a new caste that would rule Europe, a persistent, dreadful will of its own, that can set its aims thousands of years ahead." This new great politics will be in opposition to the petty politics that passed itself as "great" so far—"so that the long spun-out comedy of its petty statism and its dynastic as well as democratic splinter wills might finally be brought to a close" (BGE 208). So if grand politics up to that point, in particular how it was being practiced by Bismarck, involved maintaining Europe in a state of dissolution so as to retain Germany's "free hand" and its sense of grandeur, Nietzsche proposes instead the unification of Europe, led by a transnational and transracial European caste.

What Nietzsche is proposing, in short, is the reformulation of grosse Politik on the basis of a master—as opposed to slave—morality. This involves, first and foremost, the creation of a good European, to which his project of great politics is intimately linked: a new European humanity, transnational and transracial; recall Nietzsche's desire to marry Teutonic knights with Jewish financiers (BGE 251). Indeed, if Nietzsche is dejected by the international politics of his day, he also discerns an encouraging countermovement to such disintegration, which he identifies in the cultural, institutional, and economic European desire to *"become one"* (BGE 256), as I explored more fully in my chapter on democracy, and that he desires to see promoted. Instead of power being an end in itself, as it was with realpolitik, Nietzsche wants this new power to be channeled toward the creation, through the good Europeans, of a new European culture, which will have the "guidance and guardianship of universal world culture," as he puts it in *The Wanderer and His Shadow* 87.

By Europe, Nietzsche means *continental* Europe; he only has praise for Napoléon, who for him wanted to "consolidate Europe, and convert it into a political and *economic* unity for the sake of world government" (EH CW 2).[12] England, as we saw previously, had in effect, with its herd morality utilitarianism, excluded itself from world culture—Nietzsche thought Europe should come to "an understanding" with England, because it might need the material and human wealth of it colonies—while Russia was simply too much of a threat.[13] Whereas Nietzsche in his youth may have sup-

---

[12] See Don Dombowsky, *Nietzsche and Napoleon: The Dionysian Conspiracy* (Cardiff: University of Wales Press, 2014).

[13] KSA 12 37 [9].

ported Russia in the Crimean War, in his adult life—in a quite-common turnaround—he was very much aware, as were most of his compatriots, of the menace that Russia posed.[14] In the pivotal aphorism with which I opened this section, Nietzsche hopes that it is an increase in the threatening attitude of Russia that will finally tip the balance in favor of European unity: "I mean such an increase in the threatening attitude of Russia that Europe would make up its mind to become equally threatening" (BGE 208).

This sentence must be understood in the context of the Panjdeh Incident, which had taken place one year before the publication of *Beyond Good and Evil*, in 1885, where Russian troops, as part of the great game to control Central Asia, had seized an area of Afghanistan, almost triggering a full-scale conflict with Britain (diplomacy saved the day). What Nietzsche hoped for was an even more aggressive policy by Russia, so that Europe would feel sufficiently endangered to have to unify in face of a common threat. This explains why he lambasts Bismarck's policy of fostering "Indian wars and complications in Asia," along with "internal subversion," the introduction of "parliamentary imbecility," and the need for everyone to read the newspaper at breakfast, as a way of keeping it in check. If instead Russia were to exercise its accumulated will, then Europe would be forced to respond in kind and develop its own unified will.

Nietzsche's geopolitical vision is of a continental European power that will be on a level playing field with—and perhaps even come to dominate—Britain and Russia. But unlike the grand politics of the past, which had no further end than itself, this power will be put in the service of a good European cultural caste that will employ itself in the creation of a new trans-European culture, which itself is specially called on to lead world culture. This political power is necessary because if continental Europe were to come under the influence of Britain, than utilitarianism as herd morality would rule, and although Nietzsche does seem more sympathetic to the possibilities of Russian culture—we can note his later praise of Fyodor Dostoyevsky—Nietzsche here is not solely expressing an existential threat that he might have shared with the German people but also a concern about the disappearance of a specifically European culture, which in his eyes, successfully combines northern and Mediterranean influences, captured especially in Georges Bizet's music (BGE 254).[15] In his notes of the 1880s, Nietzsche does speculate about the possibility of Russia becoming the "master of Europe and Asia[;] . . . Europe as Hellas under the rule of

[14] In an article penned in 1944, Eric Voegelin ("Nietzsche, the Crisis, and the War," *Journal of Politics* 6, no. 2 [1944]: 177–212) underscores how real this menace was, and that German unification was only achieved because of Russian neutrality, having previously frustrated the attempt in 1849 to create a Prussian Union.

[15] Bizet is of course also used in this instance as a counterpoint to Wagner. But I think Nietzsche's enthusiasm for France and all things French is real and *recherché*.

Rome"—that is to say, European culture would continue to flourish under foreign rule, like Athenian culture under Roman rule.[16] But come 1886 and *Beyond Good and Evil*, Nietzsche seems much happier with the idea of a unified European power, which moreover builds on the different cultural, institutional, and economic trends that he claims to have discerned. Finally, this link between political and cultural power reemphasizes how, for Nietzsche, high culture cannot come about without a hierarchical political framework to underpin it.

Peter Bergmann has written that "Nietzsche embraced the concept of *grosse Politik* precisely at the moment when Germany was suddenly creating her colonial empire."[17] It is certainly the case that the years leading up to the publication of *Beyond Good and Evil* saw the intensification of the scramble for Africa, with Germany also starting to acquire colonies—most notably Cameroon in 1884—a policy that Bismarck had previously shunned. The Berlin Conference of 1884–85, presided over by Bismarck, formalized this partition of Africa. While the struggle to control the world no doubt played a part in how Nietzsche framed his own conception of great politics, as I discussed above, I do not think that the shift in Nietzsche's view of great politics between *Human, All Too Human* and *Beyond Good and Evil* is best located there. Rather, the context that seems the most significant in tracking Nietzsche's change of heart is the start of his project for a revaluation of all values, to which great politics, as we saw in the previous chapter, was intrinsically linked.

Indeed, Nietzsche's first statement about his own concept of great politics occurs in a letter to Overbeck in April 1884, where he writes "what *I* call great politics: (Nietzsche's emphasis).[18] It is also around this time that the term *Umwerthung* begins to appear in his notebooks.[19] It is thus only with this revalued notion of great politics in hand that Nietzsche holds a new (master morality) perspective from which to judge the international politics of his day. With this new conception, Nietzsche is able to recast the contemporary power politics of his time as petty politics—a term that only first appears in *Beyond Good and Evil* 208 of 1886, reappearing again in *Gay Science* 377 of 1887, and finally in *Ecce Homo*, "The Case of Wagner" 2, of 1888—that is, it is concurrent with his new theory of great politics. In this setting, petty and great politics represent the respective twin slave and master morality conceptions of grosse Politik, and must be understood together. So if the "struggle of the mastery of the world" (BGE 208) undeniably

---

[16] KSA 11 25 [112]. See Voegelin, "Nietzsche, the Crisis, and the War," 66.

[17] Bergmann, *Nietzsche*, 163.

[18] Letter to Franz Overbeck, April 30, 1884, KSB 6: 498. For this reference, I thank Vincent Garton, "The Transformation of Nietzsche's grosse Politik in the Epoch of Bismarck" (unpublished manuscript).

[19] See KSA 11 26 [259, 284].

played a part in mentally framing Nietzsche's own project of great politics, this was a consequence—and not the cause—of Nietzsche's revaluation of the term in the first place.

In a note of around this period (1885–86), Nietzsche, summarizing much of what has been said above, repeats that democratic Europe will give rise to a new interracial aristocracy destined to become the "masters of the earth" (KSA 12 2 [57]). He concludes with the line "Enough, the time is coming when we will relearn politics."[20] In has become commonplace in the scholarly literature to depict Nietzsche's political thought as in some ways going beyond a conventional understanding of politics. So Nietzsche's political thinking is often described as being "suprapolitical," or "atopian" or "archipolitical," among other formulations, drawing on the philosophy of Alain Badiou or Paul Ricœur.[21] These interpretations often come within what might be termed a "continental" approach to Nietzsche. Even though commentaries from Heidegger to Gilles Deleuze and Michel Foucault have no doubt been fundamental in shaping our understanding of Nietzsche, in this particular instance the end result seems to be a *double peine* of contributing neither to our understanding of Nietzsche nor a deepening of the philosophical project that this secondary literature calls on in the first place. It is derivative, anachronistic, and also, for want of a better word, ideological, in the sense that it is solely interested in placing Nietzsche within the structure of its own thought, without paying any attention to the subtleties of Nietzsche's own.

We need not appeal to extraneous notions to be able to make sense of Nietzsche's political thought; we can do so from within the structures that Nietzsche provides us with—analyzing contemporary politics from the perspective of either master or morality. The key, then, for Nietzsche is for us to be able to break away from a purely slave morality conception of politics that claims to be—much like herd morality—the *only* possible way of understanding politics. What Nietzsche wants us to do is *relearn* how to think about politics from the perspective of a reformulated master morality. He wants us to reopen the question of what we want humankind to be, as he puts it so starkly in *The Antichrist*—"what type of man should be bred" (AC

---

[20] The German is "die Zeit kommt, wo man über Politik umlernen wird"—thus "relearn" for "umlernen" instead of "unlearn," as other translations have it.

[21] See Paul van Tongeren, "Nietzsche as 'Über-Politischer Denken,'" in *Nietzsche, Power, and Politics: Rethinking Nietzsche's Legacy for Political Thought*, ed. Herman Siemens and Vasti Roodt (Berlin: De Gruyter, 2008), 69–83; Alex McIntyre, *The Sovereignty of Joy: Nietzsche's Vision of Grand Politics* (Toronto: University of Toronto Press, 2012); Vanessa Lemm, "Nietzsche's Great Politics of the Event," in *Nietzsche and Political Thought*, ed. Keith Ansell-Pearson (London: Bloomsbury, 2013), 179–95; Bruno Bosteels, "Nietzsche, Badiou, and Grand Politics: An Antiphilosophical Reading," in *Nietzsche and Political Thought*, ed. Keith Ansell-Pearson (London: Bloomsbury, 2013), 199–239.

3)—once we have decided that due to the death of God, the Christian answer is not the only one we must subscribe to, and to think about how politics should be rearranged to be able to make other answers come to fruition.

Some of that politics, as Williams correctly saw, might seem a little archaic, at least in the sense that it calls on a return to a more ancient understanding of political philosophy as political legislation, and here I find myself in agreement with Conway's claim that "taking advantage of the palpable degeneration of modern political institutions, [Nietzsche] dares to raise a calamitous, and previously unapproachable, question of political legislation: *what ought humankind to become.*"[22] But if we refuse a Christian answer to that question, which has been the dominant answer over the course of the last two millennia, then it is natural that at least in one instance we return to the original question we were trying to answer—Who do we want to be?—and to which we no longer find the answer convincing. Of course, in many ways this was precisely what Williams was advocating when he said that we have more in common with the Greeks than we usually believe, and we must come to recognize this not simply as a historical truth—we have returned to a situation more similar to the Greek world after the death of God—but more important a political truth.[23] In any case, that type of political question should not be so foreign to us that we need to come up with other categories, faute de mieux, which would allow for a discussion of them; we can do so within the categories we already have— categories that seem to have a strong posterity in twentieth-century thinking about politics.[24] And certainly this is only one aspect of what Nietzsche's politics looks like. The other—the unification of Europe on the basis of a master morality—should seem perfectly comprehensible to us, particularly in its content and, I hope, philosophical underpinning once we have grasped Nietzsche's view of morality.

This sheds light on the infamous antipolitical theme that appears in Nietzsche's work, and how we need not understand it, as Bergmann has convincingly argued, as *un*political in the manner that Thomas Mann pre-

---

[22] Daniel Conway, *Nietzsche and the Political* (London: Routledge, 1997), 3.

[23] Williams, *Shame and Necessity*, 11. We can note that Williams was sensitive to the fact that for Nietzsche, not only could we not return directly to a pre-Christian era, but also that Christianity had brought certain positive benefits with it, not least the type of reflection that Nietzsche himself engages in (see ibid., 9).

[24] I can't help but hear an echo of Nietzsche's question of "what type of man should be bred" in Weber's 1895—the same year that *The Antichrist* was first published—inaugural lecture "The Nation State and Economic Policy," when he writes that "the question which stirs us as we think beyond the grave of our own generation is not the *well-being* human beings will enjoy [that of the last man?] in the future but what kind of people they will *be*" (quoted in Peter Lassman and Ronald Speirs, eds., *Weber: Political Writings* [Cambridge: Cambridge University Press, 1994], 15).

sents it in his *Reflections of a Nonpolitical Man*.[25] In fact, the aphorism in which that phrase appeared in *Ecce Homo* was ultimately culled from what was to be the final version of that text.[26] We should instead understand Nietzsche's antipolitics as a rejection of the petty politics of his time. As he observes in the preface to *The Antichrist*, one must be used to seeing the "miserable, ephemeral little gossip of politics and national self-interest *beneath* you," so as to see the real question of "what type of man should be *bred*, should be *willed* as having greater value, as being more deserving of life, as being more certain of a future" (AC P, 3).[27]

RELEARNING POLITICS

In a draft letter to Brandes of early December 1888, Nietzsche describes the last chapter of *Ecce Homo*, "Why I Am a Destiny," as a "foretaste of what is to come."[28] While his tirade against Christianity there—"*écrasez l'infâme*" (EH Destiny 8)—certainly anticipates *The Antichrist*, Nietzsche had recently reworked the section, adding what we now know as the first two paragraphs. It is specifically to these two passages that the "foretaste" refers. In the first aphorism—the second, we can note, is simply a quote from *Zarathustra*—Nietzsche declares that his name will be associated with "a crisis such as the earth has never seen," the "act" of the revaluation of all values, which has become "flesh and genius" in him. When this "terrible truth" will come into "conflict with the lies of the millennia," then "the concept of politics will have then merged entirely into a war of spirits (*Geisterkrieg*), [and] all power structures from the old society will have exploded—they are all based on lies; there will be wars such as the earth has never seen. Starting with me, the earth will know *great politics*" (EH Destiny 1). This section was pulled from Nietzsche's last notebook of December 1888 to January 1889, which he titled "Great Politics."[29] It is in these last notes, along with their corresponding letters and material in the published texts, that we find Nietzsche's final articulation of his notion of grosse Politik, and its linked idea of the war of spirits—what politics will be transformed into in this new vision. Indeed, even though so far Nietzsche has contented himself with critiquing his contemporary politics and positing an opposing ideal, it

[25] See Bergmann, *Nietzsche*.

[26] See Mazzino Montinari, "A New Section in Nietzsche's Ecce Homo," in *Reading Nietzsche*, ed. Mazzino Montinari, trans. Greg Whitlock (Champaign: University of Illinois Press, 2003), 103–40.

[27] See also EH BGE 1, where Nietzsche explains that *The Birth* is "politically indifferent— 'un-German,'" meaning that it is opposed to the German power politics of its time.

[28] KSB 8.

[29] KSA 13 25 [6].

is with his joint concepts of great politics and the war of spirits that we start to see the emergence of his political strategy's content.

In this notebook, Nietzsche shows a singular command of his previous writings on the topic, denouncing on numerous occasions the "12 billion" that the "armed peace" cost every year (KSA 25 [14, 19])—a critique he had leveled at Europe's political leaders as far back as *Human, All Too Human*— thereby giving the lie to those who want to portray Nietzsche's final writings as already those of a madman.[30] He also reiterates his critique of Bismarck's petty nationalist and egoistic grand politics of *Beyond Good and Evil*, labeling Bismarck the idiot "par excellence" who only fought wars in favor of the dynastic politics of the Hohenzollern, instead of aiming for "*great* missions, universal and historical goals of a supreme and refined intellect" (KSA 25 [6, 14]).[31] Building on *The Genealogy* and his concurrent statements in *The Antichrist*, Nietzsche adds the priests to his critique of petty politics, explaining that the "dynastic" and "priestly" institutions are the "true mortal enemies of life." The first is an enemy of life because it "repays itself with the blood of the stronger, the more accomplished" by sacrificing them in its wars of aggrandizement—much like what Nietzsche had written in "Power Politics and What They Cost" in *Human, All Too Human*— while the latter tries to destroy these same men by making their instincts degenerate. "In this," Nietzsche concludes, "I find the emperor and the priests agree" (KSA 13 25 [15]).

To these Nietzsche "brings war," as he puts it in the opening of his notebook. He had planned a "Declaration of War" as the penultimate chapter of *Ecce Homo*—still visible on its content page—but this was to be superseded by a "Proclamation to the European Courts to Destroy the House of the Hohenzollerns," which he sent on January 1, 1889 to Jean Bourdeau, editor at the *Journal des débats*, to be published there. Although Bourdeau rejected this proclamation, and Nietzsche's mother tellingly burned his copy for fear of *lèse-majesté*—it did not sit well with her pro-Prussian and Bismarckian views—we can reconstruct it from the section titled "War to the Death against the House of the Hohenzollern" (KSA 25 [13]).[32]

Nietzsche's war is not "between peoples"; he does not find "words to express the disgust that the politics of the European dynasties inspire in [him], which make a principle, almost a duty, out of the exacerbation of the ego-

---

[30] On this point, see Aaron Ridley, introduction to *Nietzsche: The Antichrist, Ecce Homo, Twilight of the Idols, and Other Writings*, trans. Judith Norman (Cambridge: Cambridge University Press, 2005), vii–xxxiv.

[31] Large ("The Aristocratic Radical and the White Revolutionary," 113) dates Nietzsche's final break with Bismarck as 1888.

[32] Bourdeau's response on January 4 was: "I received your Turin manuscript, which bears witness to your anti-Prussian feelings. . . . [I]t does not appear to me to be publishable material" (KSB 8).

ism and antagonism of peoples." Nor is it between "classes," as there are no longer superior classes, in the sense that those who are on top today, having been molded for "two millennia" by (Christian) "physiological absurdities," are "physiologically condemned," such that they profess the *"opposite principle* of a superior species of men." Those types of war would simply reproduce what he decries as petty politics. Instead, Nietzsche's war is one that "cuts right through the absurd arbitrariness that are peoples, class, race professions, education, [and] culture" (KSA 25 [13]). It is a war between "ascending and declining, between will to live and the *desire for revenge* on life"—a war, in short, between the active and reactive forces, between a slave and master morality (KSA 13 25 [1]).

For this war, Nietzsche sets out what *his* principles of great politics should be, and it is here that we begin to see Nietzsche's new thoughts on the subject of great politics:

> *First principle*: Great politics wants physiology to be the queen of all other questions; it wants to create a power strong enough to *breed* a superior mankind as a whole, with greatest severity, against all that is degenerate and parasitic to life—against all that perverts, contaminates, denigrates, [and] ruins ... and see in the destruction of life the symbol of a superior type of soul.
>
> *Second principle*: War to the death against vice: all types of antinature are vices. The Christian priest is the most vicious type of man because he teaches antinature.
>
> *Second principle*: Create a party of life, strong enough for *great politics*; *great politics* makes physiology the queen of all other questions—it wants to *breed* mankind as a whole; it measures the order of race, peoples, [and] individuals, according to their future, according to the guaranty of life that their future contains—it puts to an end without pity all that is degenerate and parasitic.[33]
>
> *Third principle*: The rest follows from this (KSA 13 25 [1]).[34]

Nietzsche's great politics wants to breed a new, superior type of man through a correct use of physiology, and wants to fight against the Christian priest and all that is degenerate through the creation of a party of life, itself strong enough to pursue a great politics of breeding a new type of being.

For his party of life, Nietzsche calls for the foundation of associations, so as to provide him with "a few million partisans," with "immortal"—in the sense that they can continue his work once he is gone—and "numerous"

---

[33] It is Nietzsche who writes two "second principles."

[34] Note the similarities between this last line and the seventh, and final, proposition from the "Law against Christianity," underlining the links between the two.

hands to help him follow through on the "Revaluation of All Values," which he wants translated into French, once the "right moment" arrives. Like in *Beyond Good and Evil*, he identifies the Jewish bankers and military officers as his most likely candidates for the party of life. This is because "these two groups represent together the *will to power*," as "with military instincts in the body, one cannot be a Christian—in that case one would be a false Christian, and moreover a false soldier," and the Jewish bankers are "the only international power that by their origin and instinct, tie people together," as opposed to the névrose nationale—note the similarity to *The Case of Wagner*—Europe is currently prey to (KSA 13 25 [11]). At the beginning of December 1888, Nietzsche drafts a letter to Brandes, calling it the "first truly universal historical document: great politics par excellence."[35] Nietzsche adds that the Jews have an "instinctive hostility" to Christianity and socialism, and that his "international movement" needs their "great capital," such that when this "new power" of Jewish bankers and military officers is formed, it will become, in "the blink of an eye," the "foremost world power."[36] Nietzsche concludes his document by declaring that "if we are successful, we will have in our hands the government of the earth—and universal peace."[37] The "absurd barrier between races, nations, and classes" will have been overcome, with only a "hierarchy between men, [with] an infinitely long hierarchical ladder" remaining.

If Nietzsche uses the word "party," we should be careful not to confuse it with the political parties of the nineteenth century, which he clearly repudiated on the grounds of class, race, and nationalism. Nietzsche's party, whose membership is based on whether one represents ascending, in contrast to descending, life, is international in scope and aims for the mastery of the whole world, at least through its control of Europe.[38] We might thus better understand it as an "international movement," as Nietzsche presents it to Gast in a letter of December 9, 1888, in which he brings together seemingly disparate elements (financial Jews and military officers) to guide them toward a common goal of fighting the "Christian Party" in order to breed a new type of man.[39]

---

[35] The "material" for Nietzsche's Great Politics thus amounts to the notes in view of book 4 of "The Will to Power": the "Proclamation" of Great Politics, reconstituted from Nietzsche's last notebook, titled "Great Politics"; the "Law against Christianity" (it is only in the document of Great Politics to Brandes that the "Law" is referred to); the (draft) letters of Great Politics, in particular the document to Brandes; and the various references in Nietzsche's last books.

[36] See also the letter to Peter Gast, December 9, 1888 (KSB 8).

[37] Draft letter to Georg Brandes, early December 1888.

[38] See KSA 11 37 [9]: "In order . . . that Europe may engage in the battle for the mastery of the world with good prospects of victory."

[39] As Ernst Nolte has already noted (see *Nietzsche und der Nietzscheanismus* [Berlin: Propyläen, 1990]), the best counterpart to Nietzsche's party of life might be Marx's Communist

Nietzsche does not confine himself to simply outlining the principles of his great politics but rather proceeds to give some concrete suggestions over the course of both his published and unpublished notes about how to create a party of life strong enough to breed humanity as a whole. Physiology being the "queen of all questions," Nietzsche wants questions that he considers to be *immediately important*: nutrition, dress, cuisine, health, [and] procreation" to be handled with "rigor, seriousness, and sincerity" (KSA 13 25 [1]).[40] In *Ecce Homo*, Nietzsche had written about how to start "*reeducating*" oneself by focusing on what have previously been considered "petty concerns—nutrition, location, climate, recuperations, [and] the whole casuistry of selfishness" (EH Clever 10), thereby confirming the fundamental solidarity between the notes and published texts. In his early Basel lectures "On the Future of Our Educational Institutions," Nietzsche had also already discussed how to reform the education system, proposing that a true humanities education at the university be reserved for a small elite, with the rest being rerouted to a technical college where they would be taught the skills of their future, more manual trade. This claim is repeated in "What the Germans Lack" in *Twilight of the Idols*: " 'Higher education' and the *horde*—these are in contradiction from the outset. Any higher culture is only for the exceptions: you had to be privileged to have the right to such a high privilege. Nothing great or beautiful could ever be common property: *pulchrum est paucorum hominum*" (TI Germans 5).

Finally, Nietzsche offers some thoughts on the reorganization of marriage and procreation in view of creating his party of life in his later notes, although here we move into more controversial territory that sees Nietzsche, I think, fall victim to popular ideas about eugenics at the time, which have a longer posterity in European thought—both Left and Right—than we are usually keen to admit.[41] But I don't want to shy away from them. In his note "On the Future of Marriage," Nietzsche writes:

> a *hardening of taxes* on inheritance, etc., progressive hardening also of military service for bachelors from a certain age (decided by the community)

Party (see Karl Marx and Friedrich Engels, *The Communist Manifesto*, ed. Gareth Stedman Jones [London: Penguin, 2002]). While Nolte's comparison is instructive, I think he is mistaken to make them into exact and conscious opposites: that just because Marx's party leads to physical annihilation, as Nolte reads it, that Nietzsche's should too. As I will argue in the following section, Nietzsche's war is a nonphysical war that aims to maintain its opposition, not annihilate it entirely, with this latter desire being a manifestation of the slave morality that Nietzsche aspires to surpass.

[40] On physiology, see Nandita Biswas Mellamphy, *The Three Stigmata of Friedrich Nietzsche: Political Physiology in the Age of Nihilism* (Basingstoke, UK: Palgrave Macmillan, 2011).

[41] See Dan Stone, *Breeding Superman: Nietzsche, Race, and Eugenics in Edwardian and Interwar Britain* (Liverpool: Liverpool University Press, 2002).

>*advantages* of all kinds for fathers who bring many boys into the
>world: possibly a plural vote
>a *medical certificate* preceding every marriage and signed by the
>community authorities: where the engaged and doctors must
>answer a number of questions
>("family history")
>as an antidote to prostitution (or to ennoble it): provisional legal
>marriages (for years, months, days), with guarantees for the
>children
>all marriages under the responsibility of a certain number of men
>of confidence of the community: as a community affair (KSA
>13 16 [35])

On the opposite end, Nietzsche claims that having children in certain cases "would be a crime," indicating that not only should "chastity" be encouraged but also that society has a positive duty to intervene "without consideration for origin, social position, or spirit," and resort to the "strictest measures of constraint, withdrawal of liberty, and if need be, castration" (KSA 13 23 [1]).

While Nietzsche is not alone in defending plural voting—Mill, normally considered to be a much more liberal figure, is the more famous example—and although his views about medical examinations and somewhat-unorthodox stance on marriage might be, from a certain perspective, potentially commendable, it is hard not to characterize these statements as at minimum patriarchal.[42] To give it a more positive spin, one must return to what Zarathustra says about marriage and children, where he advances the notion that one should not aim to reproduce but rather "surproduce" in view of the coming of the overman (Z I On Child and Marriage). Nietzsche does criticize modern marriages in *Twilight*, but this is done so in a much less provocative way, with Nietzsche concluding that "marriage as an institution already affirms the greatest, most enduring form of organization" (TI Skirmishes 39). The fact that his more concrete suggestions remain in his notes indicates that these were ideas he was trying out, but did not represent his final views on the matter. Perhaps that's where they best belong.

THE WAR OF SPIRITS

Two concepts are key to understanding Nietzsche's war of spirits (*Geisterkrieg*): Bismarck's Kulturkampf and Christian "spiritual warfare," which I

[42] As Strong has remarked to me, "The first two clauses are standard today, the third was proposed by Margaret Mead, [and] the last is interestingly characteristic of some Jewish communities."

will now examine in turn. It is in opposing both these notions that we get a better sense of Nietzsche's own, and this also explains why Nietzsche uses a separate term—which I render as war of spirits—again to demark it from the other two.

In 1871, Bismarck started to pursue a number of policies that would come to be dubbed a Kulturkampf, a cultural struggle, against German Catholics. Having overseen the creation of the new Reich, with Protestant Prussia, as opposed to Catholic Austria, at its core, Bismarck was faced with the difficulty of having a strong Catholic minority within the newly founded empire that he suspected would pledge allegiance first and foremost to Rome, and not the Reich and over the next couple years, he would enact a number of bills aimed at reducing the power of the Catholic Church in society in general and education in particular.[43]

Nietzsche did not support this policy, writing to Rohde on February 28, 1875, that he did not want to be associated with this "odious Catholic business."[44] In a note from around that time, in preparation for his *Untimely Meditations*, Nietzsche sums up his views on the matter when he explains that "the struggle against the Catholic Church is an act of enlightenment, nothing else; and in the end it merely makes it disproportionately strong: which is wholly undesirable. Of course, in general it is correct. If only the state and the church would devour one another!" (KSA 7 32 [80]). Nietzsche presciently saw that the struggle against the Catholic Church would end up making it "disproportionally strong," the opposite of the desired effect: the result of Bismarck's policy was the ascent of the Catholic Center Party as one of the dominant forces in the Reichstag with which Bismarck would in the end have to make his peace.[45] By the end of the decade Bismarck had recognized his mistake, and after coming to an agreement with Pope Leo XIII, started to repeal the laws, although some were not repealed until as late as 1887. While Nietzsche believed that the struggle against the Catholic Church is "in general correct," this does not lead him to side with the German state, desiring instead that they devour one another.

But the more fundamental reason was that this struggle was in fact missing the main target. In the end, it was just a squabble within Christianity, a "skirmish at the outposts"; once reconciled with Rome, Bismarck, a devout Lutheran, would advocate the policy of "practical Christianity" as a foil within which to pass through social legislation to undermine the socialists,

---

[43] See Frank Cameron and Don Dombowsky, eds., *Political Writings of Friedrich Nietzsche* (New York: Palgrave Macmillan, 2008), 9–13; George Williamson, *The Longing for Myth in Germany: Religion and Aesthetic Culture from Romanticism to Nietzsche* (Chicago: University of Chicago Press, 2004), 234–84.

[44] KSB 1.

[45] The Center Party would later support Bismarck's social policies along with his more conservative turn.

who by then had become his main concern. On the ascension to the throne of Emperor William II, the court preacher and anti-Semite Adolph Stoecker, whom Nietzsche would label the "court preacher canaille," would advocate the development of a Christian Reich inspired by Martin Luther's *Of Early Government* (1523). Despite its more Protestant underpinnings, the Christian Reich would manage to reconcile the Catholics within its bosom. Nietzsche was thus confirmed in his first impression that fundamentally the Catholics, Protestants, and the state were all aiming for the same thing: a Christian state. The cultural struggle served as a smoke screen to the basic dividing point in European history: the struggle between master and slave morality. Ultimately, Bismarck's Kulturkampf was merely a struggle within the slave camp itself, whereas Nietzsche's war of spirits targeted Christianity as a whole.

In his *Epistle to the Ephesians* (6:12–17), Paul, in metaphorically supplying the Christian with the "armor of God," is thought to have inaugurated spiritual warfare (*geistlicher Kampf*). The passage reads as follows:

> For our struggle is not against flesh and blood but with the strong and the powerful—that is, with the lords of the world, who rule in this darkness, with the evil spirits under the heavens. Therefore put on the full armor of God, so that when the day of evil comes, you may be able to stand your ground, and after you have done everything, to stand. Stand firm then, with the belt of truth buckled around your waist, with the breastplate of righteousness in place, and with your feet fitted with the readiness that comes from the gospel of peace. In addition to all this, take up the shield of faith, with which you can extinguish all the flaming arrows of the evil one. Take the helmet of salvation and the sword of the Spirit, which is the word of God.[46]

The struggle is thus a spiritual war rather than a physical one, as the armor parts—the "belt of truth," the "breastplate of righteousness," the "shield of faith," and the "sword of the Spirit," which is "the word of God"—matching those of the Roman legionnaire, are to be used not against the "flesh and blood" but rather against the "evil spirits under the heavens" incarnated in the "strong and the powerful" and the "lords of the world" of the day.

In the first essay of *The Genealogy*, Nietzsche casts the struggle between slave and master morality as one between "Judea" and "Rome," with the former representing the "slave revolt in morality" that would lead to the first revaluation of good and bad into good and evil. The Pauline concep-

---

[46] Recent scholarship has questioned whether Paul wrote Ephesians, suggesting instead that it was penned by one of his disciples. Paul, however, very much does make comments in this direction; see Corinthians II 10 4–5: "The weapons we fight with are not the weapons of the world. On the contrary, they have divine power to demolish strongholds."

tion of spiritual warfare thus maps itself perfectly onto what Nietzsche identified as the slave revolt in morality: Paul, the quintessential Judeo-Christian priest, declares a spiritual war against the rulers and authorities of the day— namely, the Romans. Indeed, in the *Antichrist* Nietzsche is at pains to show that is it Paul who perverted Jesus's teaching of universal love into a slave revolt in morality against the masters. Nietzsche cites Paul's letter to the Corinthians (I:20), "God hath chosen the weak things of the world to confound the things that are mighty," as a "first-rate testimony to the psychology of every Chandala morality. . . . Paul was the greatest of all the apostles of revenge" (AC 45).[47] "What *he* needed was *power*," Nietzsche concludes. "With Paul, the priests wanted to return to power" (AC 42).[48]

The aim of Nietzsche's war of spirits is to reignite the struggle between slave and master morality, between Judea and Rome, in favor of the latter. Given that Christianity "inherited the Jewish revaluation" (GM I 7), the first act of Nietzsche's own revaluation, which inaugurates his war of spirits, is the publication of *The Antichrist*, which fittingly in terms of reversing spiritual warfare, is a deeply anti-Pauline tract. Yet he accepts that this battle will be a spiritual and intellectual one, as opposed to a physical one. This comes about because of the "internalization of the instincts" that Nietzsche accounted for over the course of *The Genealogy*. Once man, as we saw previously, is encased within the confines of the state and society, his natural urges can no longer be discharged outward and therefore are turned inward: "Every instinct that does not vent itself externally *turns inward*—that is what I call the *internalization* of man" (GM II 16). This internalization leads to the development of "bad conscience," which is what the priests seize on in their development of religion and ultimately in constructing a politics of ressentiment against the warrior class, as exemplified by Paul's spiritual warfare.[49]

But the internalization of the instincts has a silver lining in that it leads to the "spiritualization of hostility," which arises from the gradual realization of the "value of having enemies" (TI Morality 3). Even in the game of power politics this realization is becoming prominent: "Almost every party knows that its self-preservation depends on its opposition not losing too much strength." "A new creation in particular, like the new *Reich*," Nietzsche continues, alluding back to the role of Germany in petty politics, "needs enemies more that it needs friends. It only feels necessary when it

[47] The Chandala are the Indian slaves within the caste system as depicted by the Laws of Manu.

[48] For a different interpretation of Paul, see Alain Badiou, *Saint Paul: The Foundation of Universalism*, trans. Ray Brassier (Stanford, CA: Stanford University Press, 2003). I thank Keith Ansell-Pearson for this reference.

[49] See Mathias Risse, "The Second Treatise in *In the Genealogy of Morality*: Nietzsche on the Origin of Bad Conscience," *European Journal of Philosophy* 9, no. 1 (2001): 55–81.

faces opposition; it only *becomes* necessary when it faces opposition." So instead of desiring to entirely destroy one's enemy as slave morality wanted to, this new hostility desires to maintain one's enemy as a means of fortifying itself: "The church has always wanted to destroy its enemies. But we, on the other hand, we immoralists and anti-Christians, think that we benefit from the existence of the church" (TI Morality 3). As Nietzsche makes explicit in a late note,

> I have declared war against the anemic Christian ideal (together with what is related to it), not because I want to annihilate it but only to put an end to its *tyranny* and clear the way for other *ideals*, for *more robust* ideals. . . . The *continuance* of the Christian ideal belongs to the most desirable of desiderata: if only for the sake of the ideals that wish to take their stand beside it and perhaps above it—they must have opponents, and *strong ones* too, in order to grow *strong* themselves (KSA 12 10 [117]).

In short, Nietzsche revalues the spiritual warfare that the priests had inaugurated into a positive intellectual agon, where the continuation of strong Christian ideals is a precondition for the fortification and hopefully domination of those of the party of life.

Nietzsche's war of spirits will be an intellectual struggle fought by his party of life against the rulers and authorities of the day—the Christian Reich and its party of Christianity (KSA 13 11 [235]). It will be a battle over what type of man should be bred, with the aim that sufficient space—it need not be total, like the absolutist slave morality, which is what the spiritualization of hostility teaches—be carved out by the party of life to attempt to bring to light other types of existence than the Christian man. And this will be a spiritual battle; or it to be a physical one would be to fall back on to a petty politics that Nietzsche decries.

In his speech "On the Tarantulas," Zarathustra offers us an insight into how such a war of spirits is to be fought. He opposes the "preachers of equality" to those who wish for the coming of the overmen, and observes, "Inventors of images and ghosts shall they become in their hostility, and with their images and ghosts they shall yet fight with each other the supreme fight" (Z II Tarantulas). The implication is that each party comes up with theories and arguments (images and ghosts) with which to intellectually fight each other in order to have their values accepted. With Nietzsche's desire to publish millions of copies of the agitation publication *The Antichrist* across Europe, his writing of the "Proclamation" of great politics, and his numerous letters, we can get a sense of the form this war will take. Nietzsche again rules out the possibility of physical violence when he states a little earlier in Zarathustra's speech "On Priests" that "blood is the worst witness of truth; blood poisons even the purest teaching" (Z II Priests).

Nietzsche's war, after all, is to oppose the truth of his revaluation to the lie incarnated in the Christian Hohenzollern state (EH Destiny 1).

Nietzsche's Europe will come together through the various economic, political, and cultural factors driving it toward unity, as we have seen previously. So although inspired by Napoléon, due to the spiritualization of hostility it will not be a "union through empire" but rather a "union through association," brought together intellectually, culturally, and politically through the good Europeans and party of life. Indeed, one of the clearest indications that the wars Nietzsche plans are not physical wars of territorial appropriation but instead wars of intellectual domination comes in his demand in his "Proclamation" of great politics that his party of life should be trained as soldiers. But he explains that after such a military training, it would be "folly to then throw this youthful and powerful elite in front of the cannons" (KSA 13 25 [15]), which recalls his critique of power politics in *Human, All Too Human*. In his "Last Consideration," he affirms that "if we can dispose of wars, so much the better," repeating his belief that he can make better use of the twelve billion that the "armed peace" costs Europe every year (KSA 13 24 [19]).

When Nietzsche starts his descent into madness, the spiritual aspect sometimes spills over into a physical one, although this is mitigated by other claims. So in his final notes, Nietzsche demands that the "young criminal" William II be brought to him so that he may hang him (KSA 13 25 [14, 20]). It is his "criminal mind," however, that Nietzsche intends to burn. When Nietzsche declares that he can "dispense of war," he means to do so through a "correct opinion." While in his final "mad letters" Nietzsche states his intention to have the young emperor and all the anti-Semites shot, he had indicated in the letter to Bourdeau that accompanied the "Proclamation" that he "solemnly believes to be able to put some order to this European absurdity by an historic laughter, without shedding a drop of blood."[50]

It is undoubtedly the case that some of the measures Nietzsche toys with in terms of his breeding program might appear to us as strongly coercive, but it is remarkable that there is with Nietzsche a refusal of measures that would result *directly* in the shedding of blood. Though he states his desire to "annihilate everything parasitic," this must be understood as either the overcoming or dying out of such life-forms, as is made clear by the following note: "Future history: *this thought* [of the eternal return] will triumph more and more—and those who do not believe in it will finally, because of

[50] See letter to August Strindberg, December 31, 1888, KSB 8; letter to Franz Overbeck, January 4, 1889, KSB 8; letter to Jean Bourdeau, January 1, 1889, KSB 8. For Nietzsche, having all the anti-Semites shot was meant as a way of saying thanks to his friend Overbeck, himself a Jew.

their nature, *die out!*" (KSA 9 11 [338]). Nowhere does Nietzsche ever suggest that massacres should be committed.

CONCLUSION

In his review of *The Birth of Tragedy* in *Ecce Homo*, a book that he considers to be his first revaluation (TI Ancients 5), Nietzsche presents his vision for the future:

> Let us look forward a century and assume that I have succeeded in my attempt to assassinate two thousand years of antinature and desecration of humanity. The new party of life that takes on the greatest task of all, that of breeding humanity to higher levels (which includes the ruthless extermination of everything degenerate and parasitic), will make possible a *surplus of life* on earth that will necessarily regenerate the Dionysian state. I promise a *tragic* age: tragedy, the highest art of saying yes to life, will be reborn when humanity has moved beyond consciousness of the harshest though most necessary wars *without suffering from it*. (EH BT 4)

It is this vision of the future that Nietzsche develops most fully in his late notes, particularly in his last notebook, "Great Politics," thereby demonstrating the solidarity of purpose between his last texts and his final notes with his project for a "Revaluation of All Values." This future is one where the party of life fights a war against all that is degenerate and parasitic—Christianity and the Christian Reich—while attempting to breed a new type of (over-)man, thereby bringing into existence a new tragic, Dionysian age.[51] With his emphasis on consciousness and without suffering from it, we can see that what Nietzsche has in mind is fundamentally a war of spirits, an intellectual warfare to determine what type of man should be bred. We can also note that the notion of surplus—or slavery, as I identified in chapter 3—is central to this vision, and it is one that Nietzsche describes as being either tragic or Dionysian, thus strongly linking it back to the project that Nietzsche had set himself from the onset of his publishing career.

We can now also get a sense of the movement of Nietzsche's thought and role that his numerous figures play in building his vision.[52] So we move from the free spirits whose role it is to liberate themselves from the confines

[51] While van Tongeren has argued that Nietzsche's wars of spirits are "not wars between well-defined and determined parties," I think I have shown these to be quite determinate indeed.

[52] For the transitional element to Nietzsche's political thought, see Michel Haar, "The Institution and the Destitution of the Political according to Nietzsche," *New Nietzsche Studies* 2 (1997): 1–42.

of the herd morality of their epoch, to developing the mixed-race, transnational good Europeans, to finally participating in the party of life, whose role it is to fight a mind war against the Christian party so as to delineate a new sphere of existence, with its own, appropriate morality. The aim is to wrest a space from the absolutist claims of slave morality, and defend that as best possible, not to eradicate Christianity completely, which goes against the agonistic, spiritualization of hostility. Within this party a new type of ethics will be practiced as a way of "reeducating" oneself, as Nietzsche put it, focusing on the "whole casuistry of selfishness."[53] It is here that we might think the new philosophers or legislators come into play, as it is their role to devise a new table of values under which the cultured few will choose to live, with Nietzsche having already given the dual injunction of "loving your children's land" and "become hard" (Z III Tables 25). But once this intellectual struggle is successful, it will be their responsibility also to determine the rules within which their sphere of existence will coexist with the other sphere, especially in how that transfer of resources, so key to the development of the smaller sphere, will come about, as we saw in chapter 3. In many ways, these new philosophers represent a certain apex of Nietzsche's political organization, until they are replaced by a new nobility or again the overmen.[54]

In his foreword to his lectures "On the Future of Our Educational Institutions," which reads more like a manifesto, Nietzsche explains that while he will not offer either "tables or programs for schools," he does see "a time when serious men, in the service of a completely renewed and purified culture, and by common work, will become the legislators of our daily education—of education that leads to culture" (FEI F). He sees two aspects of the work that needs to be done: on the one hand, being capable of "covering all the roads from the depths of existence to the summits of the real problem of culture"; on the other hand, being able to descend to the "bottom of dry rules and the most elegant tables." Nietzsche declares that he will be satisfied if he succeeds in "climbing a substantial mountain to have a clearer horizon," therefore identifying at the time primarily with the former role. Yet with his detailing of the great politics of his party of life, Nietzsche in

[53] On this point, see Brian Domino, "The Casuistry of Little Things," *Journal of Nietzsche Studies* 23 (2002): 51–62. See also Leslie Paul Thiele, *Friedrich Nietzsche and the Politics of the Soul: A Study of Heroic Individualism* (Princeton, NJ: Princeton University Press, 1990).

[54] I have often pondered whether Herman Hesse's *The Glass Bead Game* (London: Vintage, 2000) painted, perhaps not fully consciously, a good picture of what this new world could look like: a small and poor cultural and intellectual elite living in a secluded "Castalia," but that performed the glass bead game—an abstract synthesis of the arts and science—to tie together and give meaning to existence as well as the world as a whole. Remember that Castalia has a diplomatic wing whose role it is to negotiate with the outside world to keep its funding. Of course Knecht leaves in the end, but there is one way of reading his ultimate drowning as a sacrifice so that the overman—Tito—can live.

his later life moves toward a much more substantive position on politics than is usually attributed to him. Of course there remain some unanswered questions—when aren't there?—and Nietzsche writes poignantly near the end of his intellectual life that "from this point I leave full freedom to another spirit than mine to continue" (KSA 12 10 [146]). Given that Nietzsche is calling for the development of new modes of life, this seems perfectly apposite, as he would not want to anticipate what forms these lives could take.

We can, however, speculate further about how, for instance, Nietzsche's party of life might operate, drawing from both Nietzsche's writings themselves and the context in which he is working. We saw in chapter 3 how Wagner's view of the artistic legislator could serve as an inspiration for Nietzsche's own thought: once the *Darsteller* has been invested with an idea, he raises himself to the position of poet, by convincing the other free members of the fellowship of his idea and thereby takes on its dictatorship until the project's completion. To ensure that the legislator would release his hold on the party once the project was completed, Nietzsche can draw on his understanding of Greek ostracism from "The Greek State," which he interprets as being a means within which to preserve a balanced agon, as I explored in chapter 4. Indeed, it is certainly the case that some form of agonistic struggle would be practiced within the party to ensure culture will be at its best, which Nietzsche believes can only come about through struggle. So there will be an external agon with the party of Christianity, and an internal one within the party itself. This vision seem compatible with Nietzsche's belief in the hierarchical nature of culture, and in an earlier note from *Assorted Opinions and Maxims*, Nietzsche explains that a self-selecting aristocracy of knowledge is the surest way of setting up a legislative body (AOM 318).

While I have drawn mainly from Nietzsche's own work so far, or at least those who had an important influence on him like Wagner, there are other areas to be explored to further give flesh to the bones of Nietzsche's ideas. In a scholarly article on Nietzsche's use of the Manu Code, Koenraad Elst looks at what he calls "the politics Nietzsche doesn't discuss."[55] He highlights how within Nietzsche's use of the Laws of Manu, he overlooks the "institutions that make caste society possible, e.g., the authority vested in the caste *pa´nchâyat* or intra-caste council governing caste matters and internal disputes; or in village *pa´nchâyat*, the inner-caste council in which each caste, even the lowest, had a veto right." Elst adds that "a consensus had to be reached between the castes [in the councils], which meant in practice

[55] Koenraad Elst, "Nietzsche and Hindu Political Philosophy," in *Nietzsche, Power, and Politics: Rethinking Nietzsche's Legacy for Political Thought*, ed. Herman Siemens and Vasti Roodt (Berlin: De Gruyter, 2008), 575–76.

that the harshest discriminations were somewhat mitigated." These suggestions offer some institutional direction to how Nietzsche's two spheres could operate, once his party of life were to be successful in its war of spirits to determine the future breeding of mankind.

To conclude, something must be said in terms of Nietzsche's relation to World War I, particularly with regard to the ambiguity of his phrase "wars the like we have never seen."[56] A few points are in order. First, Nietzsche, especially when we look at his reaction to the Franco-Prussian War and in general his decrying of petty politics, would not in the least have welcomed the First World War because it encapsulated precisely everything he had criticized as being the preserve of slave morality petty politics—nationalism, Christianity, philistinism, and so on—whereas what he was advocating were wars on the basis of a master morality. So if Nietzsche can be seen as the anticipator of World War I, it can only be in a negative sense: the war was exactly what Nietzsche feared would happen. Indeed, for some American commentators of the time, rather than being the forefather of the war, Nietzsche was the one who in fact pointed toward its resolution—through overcoming nationalism by "reuniting" peoples.[57] The only way, second, that Nietzsche might have welcomed the war is in an *instrumental* capacity: wars represent the "hibernation" time of culture, from which mankind emerges invigorated and willing to try new things (HH 444, 477). But ultimately these were not wars fought in man's name, which were meant to be intellectual wars to determine the future of mankind.

[56] See Altman, *Nietzsche*.
[57] See William Mackintire Salter, "Nietzsche and the War," in *Friedrich Nietzsche*, ed. Tracy Strong (Farnham, UK: Ashgate, 2009), 3–25.

CONCLUSION
NIETZSCHE NOW

A little over halfway through his "Can There Be a Nietzschean Politics?" Williams offers his answer to the question that formed the title of his piece. He explains that

> one effect of Nietzsche's work, as that of others, may be to make us question how far the criteria we think we have are actually expressed in anything that actually happens. What we have to do, rather, is to take up those elements of Nietzsche's thought that seem to make most sense to us in terms of such things as our ethical understanding, our understanding of history, and the relations of thought and action themselves, and try to let them animate the problems that seem to concern us most deeply politically.[1]

For Williams, Nietzsche forces us to rethink certain categories—ethics, truth, and history—that we have uncritically accepted in the past (What is the value of truth? as Nietzsche asks in *The Genealogy*), and the impact that his thinking can have today is to make us look afresh at our political problems from the perspective of these revalued—to use a Nietzschean term—categories. Rethinking those categories is precisely what Williams himself would go on to do with the concepts of truth and genealogy in his *Truth and Truthfulness*. But those categories are philosophical not political ones.

What I want to suggest is that the way in which Nietzsche makes us also rethink the political categories of, for instance, the state, modern democracy, and international politics, as I have explored over the course of this book, can be an even more stimulating way in which he can inform our reflection about our current political predicament. So while I completely agree with Williams that we cannot simply transfer Nietzsche's reflection

[1] Bernard Williams, "Can There Be a Nietzschean Politics" (unpublished manuscript), 10.

on politics to our present day—we cannot look for "some criterion of political or ethical desirability [in Nietzsche] that we can substitute for the kinds of criteria that we presently work with," which indeed would go against the very thesis of this book, which was that Nietzsche's political thought can only be properly understood in its nineteenth-century context—and that the best way of apprehending what a Nietzschean politics would look like for us today must be at a higher conceptual level, I do not agree that such a conceptual level need only be at the level of philosophy or history, although they are obviously of crucial importance too, but can also be at the level of political theory.[2]

Nietzsche reminds us that states are founded on an original act of violence, and that the relation between states and violence is one that is continuous throughout history. This is in sharp contrast to the social contract tradition, and I hope to have contributed to our understanding of Nietzsche's place within the canon of the history of political thought by positioning Nietzsche vis-à-vis that tradition along with the other concurrent theories of the "withering away of the state" of his time. What he seized on is the fact that culture cannot come about without a division of labor, and it has traditionally been the role of the state to enforce that division. But his critique of the modern Kulturstaat prompts us to remember that too great an encroachment by the state on the field of culture leads to its suffocation and wilting away. So a balance must be struck between state support—the Renaissance would never have achieved the cultural heights that Nietzsche lauds without patronage—and state intervention—a balance in constant need of being examined anew. Nietzsche helps us see those two spheres—that of politics and art—as deeply intertwined yet at the same time separate, and the relationship that the two spheres entertain with one—"at arm's length" was an old rallying slogan—is key to promoting a truly vibrant culture.

What that future state might look like is one that is worth debating, and Nietzsche certainly saw how it might start to appear much more regulatory, minimalist, globalized, and certainly in some cases postnational in a way that is recognizably our own. Indeed, Nietzsche's question of the role that democracy plays in the transformation of the modern state is one that merits further consideration. Democracy and culture have not always made the best bedfellows, and we would be wise to heed Nietzsche's warning about the need to defend the latter from the former. Moreover, the link he identifies between Christianity and democracy is not simply interesting from a historical point of view but also from a more contemporary perspective. If those links are verified, and we too live in the era of the death of God, how do we stand vis-à-vis democracy and equality? Does our loss of faith in God

[2] Ibid., 9.

preclude our belief in universal equality, which has historically been grounded in that faith? Does that loss of faith challenge our belief in the democratic order, or are we to follow the atheists in the marketplace who make fun of the madman with the torch announcing the death of God and continue to live our lives as if nothing has happened?

For those of us who live "now and around here," as Williams often put it—for those of us who have unlearned this faith—it is less Nietzsche's notion of the death of God that prompts a response from us but rather that of the shadows of God, in which while we recognize that God is indeed dead, we continue to live as if he were not—we continue to live according to some secularized Judeo-Christian worldview.[3] This raises the fundamental question that Nietzsche was getting at: If we no longer desire to be Christians, then who do we want to be? There is undeniably an element of self-fashioning in such a project, and it is no surprise that it would be attractive to many people in our contemporary, postreligious world. Nevertheless, and against some of literature on this topic, that self-fashioning cannot be understood to be happening in a vacuum, completely divorced from sociopolitical considerations; it cannot solely be a purely literary invention, in which everything becomes, to a degree, text, where any story can be told.[4] Moreover, that self-creation is linked to the need to give meaning to life, and Nietzsche surely hit on something when he said that it is only as an aesthetic phenomenon that life can be justified. Religion itself can easily be conceived as of itself having historically satisfied that need, so the question that remains for us is, What form is such an experience to take in the world of the death of God? Does Nietzsche's theory of the eternal return provide sufficient guidance for aesthetically fashioning one's life?

Of course many, if not most, still need this faith—something that Nietzsche was quite happy to entertain once it did not impinge on other's decisions to live differently. And while the type of religious extremism we experience today would have been novel for Nietzsche's time, he was one of the first to point out its dangers, particularly when that extremism was linked to a certain state—in his case, the Christian Reich. But in its more moderate formulation, we nonetheless come to the problem of combining what would seem to be two quite-distinct modes of existence, and possibly politics—a higher cultural one, and a lower democratic one—something Williams was interested in and that Nietzsche thought hard about.

Democracy, on Nietzsche's account, would lead to a new form of aristocracy, and if we certainly have the experience of democratic elites, they do

---

[3] See Geoffrey Hawthorn, introduction to *In the Beginning Was the Deed: Realism and Moralism in Political Argument*, by Bernard Williams (Princeton, NJ: Princeton University Press, 2005), xiii.

[4] See Alexander Nehamas, *Nietzsche: Life as Literature* (Cambridge, MA: Harvard University Press, 2002).

not come close to resembling what Nietzsche would have wanted. The same might be said of Europe: Nietzsche clearly would have welcomed its geopolitical unity, and indeed would have been happy to see his prediction about the economic and institutional factors driving that borne out. He would have been satisfied, furthermore, to see petty politics finally giving way to a great politics of European integration, although he would not have been blind to the grand positioning simmering beneath the surface. But more cuttingly, he would have asked, What purpose beyond itself does this unity serve? His was a Europe that had a special role in fostering a new European culture on the basis of good Europeans, and although the latter can sometimes be discerned, the former is patently lacking. Indeed, that such a culture is not being promoted has to do with the type of political elite that is leading Europe, and here the question of democratic elites and Europe combine.[5] So if we can sometimes discern the contours of the good Europeans, these have not been sufficiently brought to power in a way that the creation of a new European culture could come about.

There is with Nietzsche the belief that there will always be a certain ruling class. In his discussion of the "New and Old Conceptions of Government" in *Human, All Too Human*, he explains that

> to distinguish between government and people as though there were here two distinct spheres of power, a stronger and a higher and a weaker and lower, which treated and came to understanding with one another, is a piece of inherited political sensibility that even now corresponds exactly to the historical settlement of power situation in *most* states. (HH 450)

This is juxtaposed to the—risible, in Nietzsche's eyes—belief that "government is nothing but an organ of the people." But which belief dominates is of crucial importance to him, because every other social relationship maps itself onto the relationship between the government and the people. The true question of politics thus becomes with Nietzsche, What type of elite do we want to rule? And the answer to that question will determine much about how society is to be organized.

The key text that my study has relied on, particularly with regard to Nietzsche's theories of democracy and great politics, has been *Beyond Good and Evil*. Currently the main text used to teach Nietzsche is *The Genealogy of Morality*, which is evidently not without merit, but I wonder whether that is the best book to start with.[6] Part of the reason that *The Genealogy* is taught

[5] André Malraux is known to have said that if the European Union had to be constructed anew, then he would start with culture.

[6] I note that here have been a number of recent commentaries on BGE, including Laurence Lampert, *Nietzsche's Task: An Interpretation of Beyond Good and Evil* (New Haven, CT: Yale University Press, 2001), Christa Davis Acampora and Keith Ansell-Pearson, *Nietzsche's Beyond*

is historical. Nietzsche was often studied from the vantage point of the Frankfurt school, and the principle insight that was gleaned from him was the notion of the internalization of the instincts—a thought most prominently articulated in *The Genealogy*—which allowed those working in that tradition to move the issue of capitalist oppression from external to internal spheres: from economics to culture. Moreover, it is a practical text to use: it is quite unified, organized into three essays, and makes some of Nietzsche's most provocative claims. Yet if we are serious about studying Nietzsche as a political thinker in his own right, which we surely must be, then *Beyond Good and Evil* seems to me to be the more promising text to begin with, not simply because of the numerous political themes it deals with, but also because it does so from the perspective—pace *Human, All Too Human*, for instance—of Nietzsche having in his grasp all the hallmarks of his mature thought. This is not to downplay the significance of *The Genealogy*, but solely—if we are to start with one—to remind ourselves of the lexicographical priority of Nietzsche's work: *The Genealogy* was, after all, an "appendix" to *Beyond Good and Evil*.

A final thought concerns the relationship that philosophy entertains with politics, especially Nietzsche's idea that while philosophy might be helpful in identifying what is wrong with the world, it is not the right place to start to try to change it. We must first begin by reeducating ourselves before moving, as Nietzsche came to see, to politics. In many ways Williams reached a similar conclusion in what possibly remains his best work, *Ethics and the Limits of Philosophy* (1985), although perhaps without the politics: philosophy can help in trying to resolve questions of theory, but it is incapable, as the title suggests, of telling us how to live. As he put it in that wonderfully liberating phrase, "The only serious enterprise is living."[7]

Good and Evil: A Reader's Guide (London: Continuum, 2011); Maudemarie Clark and David Dudrick, *The Soul of Nietzsche's Beyond Good and Evil* (Cambridge: Cambridge University Press, 2012).

[7] Bernard Williams, *Ethics and the Limits of Philosophy* (Abingdon, UK: Routledge, 2011), 130.

BIBLIOGRAPHY

PRIMARY SOURCES
FRIEDRICH NIETZSCHE

IN GERMAN

Colli, Giorgio, and Mazzino Montinari, eds. *Sämtliche Briefe: Kritische Studienausgabe*. 8 vols. Berlin: De Gruyter, 2003.

Colli, Giorgio, and Mazzino Montinari, eds. *Sämtliche Werke: Kritische Studienausgabe*. 15 vols. Berlin: De Gruyter, 2009.

Colli, Giorgio, Mazzino Montinari, Volker Gerhardt, Norbert Miller, Wolfgang Müller-Lautre, and Karl Pestalozzi, eds. *Werke: Kritische Gesamtausgabe*. 40 vols. Berlin: De Gruyter, 1967–.

IN ENGLISH

Ansell-Pearson, Keith, ed. *On the Genealogy of Morality and Other Writings*. Translated by Carol Diethe. Cambridge: Cambridge University Press, 2006.

Bittner, Rüdiger, ed. *Writings from the Late Notebooks*. Translated by Kate Sturge. Cambridge: Cambridge University Press, 2003.

Breazeale, Daniel, ed. *Untimely Meditations*. Translated by R. J. Hollingdale. Cambridge: Cambridge University Press, 1997.

Cameron, Frank, and Don Dombowsky, eds. *Political Writings of Friedrich Nietzsche*. New York: Palgrave Macmillan, 2008.

Clark, Maudemarie, and Brian Leiter, eds. *Daybreak: Thoughts on the Prejudices of Morality*. Translated by R. J. Hollingdale. Cambridge: Cambridge University Press, 1997.

Cowan, Marianne, trans. *Philosophy in the Tragic Age of the Greeks*. Washington, DC: Regency Publishing, 1998.

Geuss, Raymond, and Alexander Nehamas, eds. *Writings from the Early Notebooks*. Translated by Ladislaus Löb. Cambridge: Cambridge University Press, 2009.

Geuss, Raymond, and Ronald Speirs, eds. *The Birth of Tragedy and Other Writings*. Translated by Ronald Speirs. Cambridge: Cambridge University Press, 1999.

Gray, Richard, trans. *Unpublished Writings from the Period of Unfashionable Observations*. Stanford, CA: Stanford University Press, 1995.

Hollingdale, R. J., trans. *Dithyrambs of Dionysus*. Vancouver: Anvil Press, 2004.

———. *Human, All Too Human: A Book for Free Spirits*. Cambridge: Cambridge University Press, 1996.

Horstmann, Rolf-Peter, and Judith Norman, eds. *Beyond Good and Evil: Prelude to a Philosophy of the Future*. Translated by Judith Norman. Cambridge: Cambridge University Press, 2001.

Middleton, Christopher, ed. *Selected Letters of Friedrich Nietzsche*. Translated by Christopher Middleton. Indianapolis, IN: Hackett, 1996.

Pippin, Robert, ed. *Thus Spoke Zarathustra: A Book for All and None*. Translated by Adrian Del Caro. Cambridge: Cambridge University Press, 2006.

Ridley, Aaron, and Judith Norman, eds. *The Anti-Christ, Ecce Homo, Twilight of the Idols, and Other Writings*. Translated by Judith Norman. Cambridge: Cambridge University Press, 2005.

Whitlock, Greg, ed. *The Pre-Platonic Philosophers*. Translated by Greg Whitlock. Champaign: University of Illinois Press, 2001.

Williams, Bernard, ed. *The Gay Science: With a Prelude in German Rhymes and an Appendix of Songs*. Translated by Josefine Nauckhoff and Adrian Del Caro. Cambridge: Cambridge University Press, 2001.

SECONDARY SOURCES

Abbey, Ruth. *Nietzsche's Middle Period*. Oxford: Oxford University Press, 2000.

Abbey, Ruth, and Fredrick Appel. "Domesticating Nietzsche: A Response to Mark Warren." *Political Theory* 27, no. 1 (February 1999): 121–25.

Acampora, Christa Davis. *Contesting Nietzsche*. Chicago: University of Chicago Press, 2013.

———. "Nietzsche contra Homer, Socrates, and Paul." *Journal of Nietzsche Studies* 24 (Fall 2002): 25–53.

Acampora, Christa Davis, and Keith Ansell-Pearson. *Nietzsche's Beyond Good and Evil: A Reader's Guide*. London: Continuum, 2011.

Allen, Danielle. *Why Plato Wrote*. Oxford: Wiley-Blackwell, 2010.

Altman, William. *Friedrich Wilhelm Nietzsche: The Philosopher of the Second Reich*. Lanham, MD: Lexington Books, 2013.

Anderson, Margaret. *Practicing Democracy: Elections and Political Culture in Imperial Germany*. Princeton, NJ: Princeton University Press, 2000.

Anderson, R. Lanier. "Nietzsche on Redemption and Transfiguration." In *The Re-Enchantment of the World: Secular Magic in a Rational Age*, edited by Joshua Landy and Michael Saler, 225–58. Stanford, CA: Stanford University Press, 2009.

———. "On the Nobility of Nietzsche's Priests." In *Nietzsche's On the Genealogy of Morality: A Critical Guide*, edited by Simo May, 24–56. Cambridge: Cambridge University Press, 2011.

Andreas-Salomé, Lou. *Nietzsche*. Translated and edited by Siegfried Mandel. Champaign: University of Illinois Press, 2001.

Ansell-Pearson, Keith. *An Introduction to Nietzsche as Political Thinker*. Cambridge: Cambridge University Press, 1994.

————. *Nietzsche contra Rousseau: A Study of Nietzsche's Moral and Political Thought.* Cambridge: Cambridge University Press, 1996.

Appel, Fredrick. *Nietzsche contra Democracy.* Ithaca, NY: Cornell University Press, 1999.

Aschheim, Steven. *The Nietzsche Legacy in Germany, 1890–1900.* Berkeley: University of California Press, 1994.

Badiou, Alain. *Saint Paul: The Foundation of Universalism.* Translated by Ray Brassier. Stanford, CA: Stanford University Press, 2003.

Bergmann, Peter. *Nietzsche: "The Last Antipolitical German."* Bloomington: Indiana University Press, 1987.

Berkowitz, Peter. *Nietzsche: The Ethics of an Immoralist.* Cambridge, MA: Harvard University Press, 1995.

Berry, Jessica. "Nietzsche and Democritus: The Origins of Ethical Eudaimonism." In *Nietzsche and Antiquity: His Reaction and Response to the Classical Tradition*, edited by Paul Bishop, 98–113. Rochester, NY: Camden House, 2004.

Bertram, Ernst. *Nietzsche: Attempt at a Mythology.* Champaign: University of Illinois Press, 2009.

Bosteels, Bruno. "Nietzsche, Badiou, and Grand Politics: An Antiphilosophical Reading." In *Nietzsche and Political Thought*, edited by Keith Ansell-Pearson, 199–239. London: Bloomsbury, 2013.

Brinton, Crane. *Nietzsche.* Cambridge, MA: Harvard University Press, 1948.

Brobjer, Thomas. "The Absence of Political Ideals in Nietzsche's Writings: The Case of the Laws of Manu and the Associated Caste Society." *Nietzsche-Studien* 27 (1998): 300–318.

————. "Critical Aspects of Nietzsche's Relation to Politics and Democracy." In *Nietzsche, Power, and Politics: Rethinking Nietzsche's Legacy for Political Thought*, edited by Herman Siemens and Vasti Roodt, 205–29. Berlin: De Gruyter, 2008.

————. "Nietzsche as Political Thinker: A Response to Don Dombowsky. *Nietzsche-Studien* 30 (2001): 394–96.

————. "Nietzsche's Knowledge of Marx and Marxism." *Nietzsche-Studien* 31 (2002): 298–313.

————. "Nietzsche's *Magnum Opus*." *History of European Ideas* 32 (2006): 278–94.

————. *Nietzsche's Philosophical Context: An Intellectual Biography.* Champaign: University of Illinois Press, 2008.

————. "Nietzsche's Wrestling with Plato and Platonism." In *Nietzsche and Antiquity: His Reaction and Response to the Classical Tradition*, edited by Paul Bishop, 241–59. Rochester, NY: Camden House, 2004.

Burckhardt, Jacob. "The State as a Work of Art." In *The Civilization of the Renaissance in Italy.* London: Penguin, 2004.

Burrow, J. W. *The Crisis of Reason: European Thought, 1848–1914.* New Haven, CT: Yale University Press, 2000.

Cameron, Frank, and Don Dombowsky, eds. *Political Writings of Friedrich Nietzsche.* New York: Palgrave Macmillan, 2008.

Cavell, Stanley. "Aversive Thinking: Emersonian Representations in Heidegger and Nietzsche." In *Conditions Handsome and Unhandsome*, 33–63. Chicago: University of Chicago Press, 1990.

Clark, Maudemarie. *Nietzsche on Truth and Philosophy*. Cambridge: Cambridge University Press, 1991.

Clark, Maudemarie, and David Dudrick. *The Soul of Nietzsche's Beyond Good and Evil*. Cambridge: Cambridge University Press, 2012.

Conant, James. "Nietzsche's Perfectionism: A Reading of *Schopenhauer as Educator*." In *Nietzsche's Postmoralism: Essays on Nietzsche's Prelude to Philosophy's Future*, edited by Richard Schacht, 181–257. Cambridge: Cambridge University Press, 2001.

Connolly, William. "Debate: Reworking the Democratic Imagination." *Journal of Political Philosophy* 5, no. 2 (1997): 194–202.

———. *Identity/Difference*. Ithaca, NY: Cornell University Press, 1991.

———. "Nietzsche, Democracy, Time." In *Nietzsche, Power, and Politics: Rethinking Nietzsche's Legacy for Political Thought*, edited by Herman Siemens and Vasti Roodt, 109–41. Berlin: De Gruyter, 2008.

Constantinidès, Yannis. "Les législateurs de l'avenir: L'affinité des projets politiques de Plato et de Nietzsche." *Nietzsche-Cahiers de L'Herne* 73 (2005): 128–43.

Conway, Daniel. "The Birth of the State." In *Nietzsche, Power, and Politics: Rethinking Nietzsche's Legacy for Political Thought*, edited by Herman Siemens and Vasti Roodt, 37–67. Berlin: De Gruyter, 2008.

———. *Nietzsche and the Political*. London: Routledge, 1997.

———. "Whither the 'Good Europeans'? Nietzsche's New World Order." *South Central Review* 26, no. 3 (2009): 40–60.

Crick, Bernard. *Democracy: A Very Short Introduction*. Oxford: Oxford University Press, 2002.

Dannhauser, Werner. *Nietzsche's View of Socrates*. Ithaca, NY: Cornell University Press, 1976.

Deleuze, Gilles. "Active and Reactive." In *The New Nietzsche: Contemporary Styles of Interpretation*, edited by David Allison, 80–106. Cambridge, MA: MIT Press, 1985.

———. *Nietzsche and Philosophy*. Translated by Hugh Tomlinson. London: Continuum, 2006.

Derrida, Jacques. *Spurs: Nietzsche's Styles / Eperons: Les Styles de Nietzsche*. Translated by Barbara Harlow. Chicago: University of Chicago Press, 1979.

Detwiler, Bruce. *Nietzsche and the Politics of Aristocratic Radicalism*. Chicago: University of Chicago Press, 1990.

Dombowsky, Don. "A Response to Th. H. Brobjer's 'The Absence of Political Ideals in Nietzsche's Writings.'" *Nietzsche-Studien* 30 (2001): 387–93.

———. *Nietzsche and Napoleon: The Dionysian Conspiracy*. Cardiff: University of Wales Press, 2014.

———. *Nietzsche's Machiavellian Politics*. Basingstoke, UK: Palgrave Macmillan, 2004.

Domino, Brian. "The Casuistry of Little Things." *Journal of Nietzsche Studies* 23 (2002): 51–62.

Drochon, Hugo. "Nietzsche and Politics." *Nietzsche-Studien* 39 (2010): 663–77.

———. "Nietzsche, Politics, and Gender." *Nietzsche-Studien* 39 (2010): 678–81.

———. "The Time Is Coming When We Will Relearn Politics." *Journal of Nietzsche Studies* 39 (Spring 2010): 66–85.

———. "Twilight and Transvaluation: Nietzsche's *Hauptwerk* and the *Götzen-Dämmerung.*" *Nietzscheforschung* 16 (2009): 175–82.

Elbe, Stefan. *Europe: A Nietzschean Perspective*. London: Routledge, 2003.

Elst, Koenraad. "Nietzsche and Hindu Political Philosophy." In *Nietzsche, Power, and Politics: Rethinking Nietzsche's Legacy for Political Thought*, edited by Herman Siemens and Vasti Roodt, 543–82. Berlin: De Gruyter, 2008.

Fink, Eugen. *Nietzsche's Philosophy*. London: Continuum, 2003.

Fossen, Thomas. "Nietzsche's Aristocratism Revisited." In *Nietzsche, Power, and Politics: Rethinking Nietzsche's Legacy for Political Thought*, edited by Herman Siemens and Vasti Roodt, 299–318. Berlin: De Gruyter, 2008.

Franco, Paul. *Nietzsche's Enlightenment: The Free-Spirit Trilogy of the Middle Period*. Chicago: University of Chicago Press, 2011.

Fukuyama, Francis. *The End of History and the Last Man*. London: Penguin, 1993.

Gauchet, Marcel. *The Disenchantment of the World: A Political History of Religion*. Princeton, NJ: Princeton University Press, 1997.

Geuss, Raymond. "Nietzsche and Morality." In *Morality, Culture, and History: Essays on German Philosophy*, 167–97. Cambridge: Cambridge University Press, 1999.

Gillespie, Michael Allen. "Nietzsche's Musical Politics." In *Nietzsche's New Seas: Explorations in Philosophy, Aesthetics, and Politics*, edited by Michael Gillespie and Tracy Strong, translated by Thomas Heilke, 117–49. Chicago: University of Chicago Press, 1988.

Grundlehner, Philip. *The Poetry of Friedrich Nietzsche*. New York: Oxford University Press, 1986.

Haar, Michel. "The Institution and the Destitution of the Political according to Nietzsche." *New Nietzsche Studies* 2 (1997): 1–42.

Halberstam, Michael. *Totalitarianism and the Modern Conception of Politics*. New Haven, CT: Yale University Press, 2000.

Hatab, Lawrence. "Breaking the Social Contract." In *Nietzsche, Power, and Politics: Rethinking Nietzsche's Legacy for Political Thought*, edited by Herman Siemens and Vasti Roodt, 169–88. Berlin: De Gruyter.

———. *A Nietzschean Defense of Democracy: An Experiment in Postmodern Politics*. Chicago: Open Court, 1995.

Hawthorn, Geoffrey. Introduction to *In the Beginning Was the Deed: Realism and Moralism in Political Argument*, by Bernard Williams, xi–xx. Princeton, NJ: Princeton University Press, 2005.

Heidegger, Martin. *Nietzsche*. Vols. 1–4. San Francisco: HarperCollins, 1991.

Hesse, Herman. *The Glass Bead Game*. London: Vintage, 2000.

Hobbes, Thomas. *Leviathan*. Edited by Richard Tuck. Cambridge: Cambridge University Press, 1996.

Honig, Bonnie. *Political Theory and the Displacement of Politics*. Ithaca, NY: Cornell University Press, 1993.

Hume, David. "Of the Original Contract." In *Political Essays*, edited by Knud Haakonssen, 186–201. Cambridge: Cambridge University Press, 1994.

Hussain, Nadeem. "Honest Illusion: Valuing for Nietzsche's Free Spirits." In *Nietzsche and Morality*, edited by Brian Leiter and Neil Sinhababu, 157–91. Oxford: Clarendon Press, 2007.

Janaway, Christopher. *Beyond Selflessness: Reading Nietzsche's Genealogy*. Oxford: Clarendon Press, 2009.

Janz, Curt Paul. "The Form-Content Problem in Friedrich Nietzsche's Conception of Music." In *Nietzsche's New Seas: Explorations in Philosophy, Aesthetics, and Politics*, edited by Michael Gillespie and Tracy Strong, translated by Thomas Heilke, 97–116. Chicago: University of Chicago Press, 1988.

Jaspers, Karl. *Nietzsche: An Introduction to the Understanding of His Philosophical Activity*. Baltimore: Johns Hopkins University Press, 1997.

Kahan, Alan. *Aristocratic Liberalism: The Social and Political Thought of Jacob Burckhardt, John Stuart Mill, and Alexis de Tocqueville*. New Brunswick, NJ: Transaction Publishers, 2001.

Kaufmann, Walter. *Nietzsche: Philosopher, Psychologist, Antichrist*. Princeton, NJ: Princeton University Press, 1974.

Kaufmann, Walter, ed. *The Will to Power*. Translated by Walter Kaufmann and R. J. Hollingdale. New York: Random House, 1968.

Klossowski, Pierre. *Nietzsche and the Vicious Circle*. London: Continuum, 2005.

Kofman, Sarah. *Explosions I: De l'"Ecce Homo" de Nietzsche*. Paris: Editions Galilée, 1992.

———. *Explosions II: Les enfants de Nietzsche*. Paris: Editions Galilée, 1993.

Lampert, Laurence. "Nietzsche and Plato." In *Nietzsche and Antiquity: His Reaction and Response to the Classical Tradition*, edited by Paul Bishop, 205–19. Rochester, NY: Camden House, 2004.

———. *Nietzsche's Task: An Interpretation of Beyond Good and Evil*. New Haven, CT: Yale University Press, 2004.

Lane, Melissa. "Founding as Legislating: The Figure of the Lawgiver in Plato's Republic." In *Dialogues on Plato's Politeia (Republic): Selected Papers from the Ninth Symposium Platonicum*, edited by Luc Brisson and Noboru Notomi, 104–14. Berlin: Akademia Verlag, 2012.

———. "Honesty as Best Policy: Nietzsche on *Redlichkeit* and the Contrast between Stoic and Epicurean Strategies of the Self." In *Histories of Postmodernism*, edited by Mark Bevir, Jill Hargis, and Sara Rushing, 25–51. London: Routledge, 2007.

Lane, Melissa, and Ruehl, Martin, eds. *A Poet's Reich: Politics and Culture in the George Circle*. London: Camden House, 2011.

Large, Duncan. "The Aristocratic Radical and the White Revolutionary: Nietzsche's Bismarck." In *Das Schwierige 19. Jarhundert*, edited by Jurgen Barkhoff et al., 101–13. Tubingen: Max Niemeyer, 2000.

———. "A Note on the Term 'Umwerthung.'" *Journal of Nietzsche Studies* 39 (2010): 5–11.

Lassman, Peter, and Ronald Speirs, eds. *Weber: Political Writings*. Cambridge: Cambridge University Press, 1994.

Leiter, Brian. *Nietzsche on Morality*. London: Routledge, 2003.

Lemm, Vanessa. "Is Nietzsche a Perfectionist? Rawls, Cavell, and the Politics of Culture in Nietzsche's 'Schopenhauer as Educator.'" *Journal of Nietzsche Studies* 34 (2007): 5–27.

———. "Nietzsche's Great Politics of the Event." In *Nietzsche and Political Thought*, edited by Keith Ansell-Pearson, 179–95. London: Bloomsbury, 2013.

Locke, John. *Two Treatises of Government*. Edited by Peter Laslett. Cambridge: Cambridge University Press, 1988.

Loeb, Paul. *The Death of Nietzsche's Zarathustra*. Cambridge: Cambridge University Press, 2010.

Löwith, Karl. *Nietzsche's Philosophy of the Eternal Recurrence of the Same*. Berkeley: University of California Press, 1997.

MacIntyre, Alasdair. *After Virtue: A Study in Moral Theory*. London: Duckworth, 2007.

Magnus, Bernd. "Nietzsche's Philosophy in 1888: The Will to Power and the Übermensch." *Journal of the History of Philosophy* 24, no. 1 (1986): 79–98.

Martin, Nicholas. "Breeding Greeks: Nietzsche, Gobineau, and Classical Theories of Race." In *Nietzsche and Antiquity: His Reaction and Response to the Classical Tradition*, 40–53. Rochester, NY: Camden House, 2004).

Marx, Karl, and Friedrich Engels. *The Communist Manifesto*. Edited by Gareth Stedman Jones. London: Penguin, 2002.

McIntyre, Alex. *The Sovereignty of Joy: Nietzsche's Vision of Grand Politics*. Toronto: University of Toronto Press, 2012.

Mellamphy, Nandita Biswas. *The Three Stigmata of Friedrich Nietzsche: Political Physiology in the Age of Nihilism*. Basingstoke, UK: Palgrave Macmillan, 2011.

Montesquieu, Charles de. *The Spirit of the Laws*. Edited by Anne Cohler, Basia Miller, and Harold Stone. Cambridge: Cambridge University Press, 1989.

Montinari, Mazzino. "A New Section in Nietzsche's *Ecce Homo*." In *Reading Nietzsche*, edited by Mazzino Montinari, translated by Greg Whitlock, 103–40. Champaign: University of Illinois Press, 2003.

———. "Nietzsche and Wagner One Hundred Years Ago." In *Reading Nietzsche*, edited by Mazzino Montinari, translated by Greg Whitlock, 36–49. Champaign: University of Illinois Press, 2003.

———. "Nietzsche's Recollections from the Years 1875–79 concerning His Childhood." In *Reading Nietzsche*, edited by Mazzino Montinari, translated by Greg Whitlock, 23–35. Champaign: University of Illinois Press, 2003.

———. "Nietzsche's Unpublished Writings from 1885 to 1888; or, Textual Criticism and the Will to Power." In *Reading Nietzsche*, edited by Mazzino Montinari, translated by Greg Whitlock, 80–102. Champaign: University of Illinois Press, 2003.

———. "Zarathustra before *Thus Spoke Zarathustra*." In *Reading Nietzsche*, edited by Mazzino Montinari, translated by Greg Whitlock, 69–79. Champaign: University of Illinois Press, 2003.

Moore, Gregory. *Nietzsche, Biology, and Metaphor*. Cambridge: Cambridge University Press, 2004.

Müller-Lauter, Wolfgang. *Nietzsche: His Philosophy of Contradictions and the Contradictions of His Philosophy*. Translated by David Parent. Champaign: University of Illinois Press, 1999.

Nehamas, Alexander. *Nietzsche: Life as Literature*. Cambridge, MA: Harvard University Press, 2002.

Nolte, Ernst. *Nietzsche und der Nietzscheanismus*. Berlin: Propyläen, 1990.

Nussbaum, Martha. "Is Nietzsche a Political Thinker?" *International Journal of Philosophical Studies* 5, no. 1 (1997): 1–13.

Ottmann, Henning. *Philosophie und Politik bei Nietzsche*. Berlin: De Gruyter, 1999.

Owen, David. "Nietzsche, Ethical Agency, and the Problem of Democracy." In *Nietzsche, Power, and Politics: Rethinking Nietzsche's Legacy for Political Thought*, edited by Herman Siemens and Vasti Roodt, 143–68. Berlin: De Gruyter, 2008.

———. *Nietzsche, Politics, and Modernity*. London: Sage, 1995.

———. "Nietzsche's Freedom: The Art of Agonic Perfectionism." In *Nietzsche and Political Thought*, edited by Keith Ansell-Pearson, 71–81. London: Bloomsbury, 2013.

Patton, Paul. "Nietzsche and Hobbes." In *International Studies in Philosophy* 33, no. 3 (2001): 99–116

———. "Nietzsche, Genealogy, and Justice." In *Nietzsche and Political Thought*, edited by Keith Ansell-Pearson. London: Bloomsbury, 2013.

Perreau-Saussine, Emile. *Catholicism and Democracy: An Essay in the History of Political Thought*. Princeton, NJ: Princeton University Press, 2012.

Plato. *The Republic*. Edited by G.R.F. Ferrari. Translated by Tom Griffith. Cambridge: Cambridge University Press, 2000.

Ratner-Rosenhagen, Jennifer. *American Nietzsche: A History of an Icon and His Ideas*. Chicago: University of Chicago Press, 2012.

Rawls, John. *A Theory of Justice*. Cambridge, MA: Harvard University Press, 1999.

Reginster, Bernard. *The Affirmation of Life: Nietzsche on Overcoming Nihilism*. Cambridge, MA: Harvard University Press, 2009.

Richardson, John. *Nietzsche's New Darwinism*. Oxford: Oxford University Press, 2004.

———. *Nietzsche's System*. Oxford: Oxford University Press, 2002.

Ridley, Aaron. Introduction to *Nietzsche: The Antichrist, Ecce Homo, Twilight of the Idols, and Other Writings*, translated by Judith Norman, vii–xxxiv. Cambridge: Cambridge University Press, 2005.

Risse, Mathias. "The Second Treatise in *In the Genealogy of Morality*: Nietzsche on the Origin of the Bad Conscience." *European Journal of Philosophy* 9, no. 1 (2001): 55–81.

Roos, Richard. "Les derniers écrits de Nietzsche et leur publication." In *Lectures de Nietzsche*, edited by Jean-François Balaudé and Patrick Wotling, 33–70. Paris: Le Livre de Poche, 2000.

———. "Nietzsche et Épicure: l'idylle héroïque." In *Lectures de Nietzsche*, edited by Jean-François Balaudé and Patrick Wotling, 283–350. Paris: Le Livre de Poche, 2000.

Rousseau, Jean-Jacques. *"The Discourses" and Other Early Political Writings*, edited by Victor Gourevitch. Cambridge: Cambridge University Press, 1997.

Ruehl, Martin. *"Politeia* 1871: Young Nietzsche on the Greek State." In *Nietzsche and Antiquity: His Reaction and Response to the Classical Tradition*, edited by Paul Bishop, 79–97. Rochester, NY: Camden House, 2004.

Safranski, Rüdiger. *Nietzsche: A Philosophical Biography*. Translated by Shelley Frisch. London: Granta, 2003.

Salter, William Mackintire. "Nietzsche and the War." In *Friedrich Nietzsche*, edited by Tracy Strong, 3–25. Farnham, UK: Ashgate, 2009.

Schotten, Heike. *Nietzsche's Revolution*: Décadence, *Politics, and Sexuality*. New York: Palgrave Macmillan, 2009.

Schrift, Alan. "Nietzsche's Contest: Nietzsche and the Culture Wars." In *Why Nietz-

sche Still? Reflections on Drama, Culture, and Politics, edited by Alan Schrift, 184–203. Berkeley: University of California Press.

———, ed. *Why Nietzsche Still? Reflections on Drama, Culture, and Politics*. Berkeley: University of California Press.

Shaw, Tamsin. *Nietzsche's Political Skepticism*. Princeton, NJ: Princeton University Press, 2010.

Siemens, Herman. "Nietzsche's Political Philosophy: A Review of Recent Literature." *Nietzsche-Studien* 30 (2001): 509–26.

———. "Reassessing Radical Democratic Theory in the Light of Nietzsche's Ontology of Conflict." In *Nietzsche and Political Thought*, edited by Keith Ansell-Pearson, 83–105. London: Bloomsbury, 2013.

———. *Nietzsche, Power, and Politics: Rethinking Nietzsche's Legacy for Political Thought*. Berlin: De Gruyter, 2008.

Simmel, George. *Nietzsche and Schopenhauer*. Translated by Helmut Loiskandl, Deena Weinstein, and Michael Weinstein. Champaign: University of Illinois Press, 1991.

Skinner, Quentin. "Meaning and Understanding in the History of Ideas. In *Visions of Politics, Volume I: Regarding Method*, 57–89. Cambridge: Cambridge University Press, 2002

———. "The State." In *Political Innovation and Conceptual Change*, edited by Terence Ball, James Farr, and Russell Hanson, 90–131. Cambridge: Cambridge University Press, 1989.

Smith, Verity, and Strong, Tracy. "Trapped in a Family Portrait? Gender and Family in Nietzsche's Refiguring of Authority." In *Dialogue, Politics and Gendre*, edited by Jude Browne, 146–72. Cambridge: Cambridge University Press, 2013.

Souladié, Yannick. "La Laideur de Socrates." *Nietzsche-Studien* 35 (2006): 29–46.

———. "Nietzsche à la lettre." In *Dernières lettres (hiver 1887–hiver 1889): De la volonté de puissance à l'antichrist*, by Friedrich Nietzsche. Paris: Editions Manucius, 2011.

———. "Présentation: *L'Inversion contra La Volonté de Puissance*." In *Nietzsche—L'inversion des valeurs*, 3–25. Hildesheim: Olms, 2007.

Stack, George. *Lange and Nietzsche*. Berlin: de Gruyter, 1983.

Stone, Dan. *Breeding Superman: Nietzsche, Race, and Eugenics in Edwardian and Interwar Britain*. Liverpool: Liverpool University Press, 2002.

Strong, Tracy. *Friedrich Nietzsche and the Politics of Transfiguration*. Champaign: University of Illinois Press, 2000.

———. "In Defense of Rhetoric, or How Hard It Is to Take a Writer Seriously: The Case of Nietzsche." *Political Theory* 41, no. 4 (2013): 507–32.

———. "Nietzsche and the Political: Tyranny, Tragedy, Cultural Revolution, and Democracy." *Journal of Nietzsche Studies* 35–36 (Spring–Fall 2008): 48–66.

———. "Nietzsche's Political Aesthetics." In *Nietzsche's New Seas: Explorations in Philosophy, Aesthetics, and Politics*, edited by Michael Gillespie and Tracy Strong, translated by Thomas Heilke 153–76. Chicago: University of Chicago Press, 1988.

———. *Politics without Vision: Thinking without a Banister in the Twentieth Century*. Chicago: University of Chicago Press, 2012.

————. "'Wars the Like of Which One Has Never Seen': Reading Nietzsche and Politics." In *Friedrich Nietzsche*, edited by Tracy Strong, xi–xxxiii. Farnham, UK: Ashgate, 2009.

Strong, Tracy. "The World as It Finds Us." In *Politics without Vision: Thinking without
a Banister in the Twentieth Century*, 370–96. Chicago: University of Chicago Press,
2012.

Swift, Paul. *Becoming Nietzsche: Early Reflections on Democritus, Schopenhauer, and
Kant.* Lanham, MD: Lexington, 2005.

Taylor, Charles. *A Secular Age.* Cambridge, MA: Harvard University Press, 2007.

Thiele, Leslie Paul. *Friedrich Nietzsche and the Politics of the Soul: A Study of Heroic
Individualism.* Princeton, NJ: Princeton University Press, 1990.

van Tongeren, Paul. *Die Moral von Nietzsches Moralkritik: Studie zu "Jenseits von Gut
und Böse."*Bonn: Bouvier, 1989.

————. "Nietzsche as 'Über-Politischer Denken.'" In *Nietzsche, Power, and Politics:
Rethinking Nietzsche's Legacy for Political Thought*, edited by Herman Siemens and
Vasti Roodt, 69–83. Berlin: De Gruyter, 2008.

Voegelin, Eric. "Nietzsche, the Crisis, and the War." *Journal of Politics* 6, no. 2 (1944):
177–212.

Wagner, Richard. "Art and Revolution" (1849). In *Richard Wagner's Prose Works*, translated by William Ashton Ellis, 1:23–65. London: Kegan Paul, 1895.

————. "The Artwork of the Future" (1849). In *Richard Wagner's Prose Works*, translated by William Ashton Ellis, 1:69–213. London: Kegan Paul, 1895.

————. "On State and Religion" (1864). In *Richard Wagner's Prose Works*, translated
by William Ashton Ellis, 4:5–34. London: Kegan Paul, 1895.

Warren, Mark. *Nietzsche and Political Thought.* Cambridge, MA: MIT Press, 1991.

Whitlock, Greg. *The Pre-Platonic Philosophers: Friedrich Nietzsche.* Champaign: University of Illinois Press, 2001.

Wilamowitz-Moellendorf, Ulrich von. *"Zukunftsphilologie."* In *Der Streit um Nietz-
sches "Geburt der Tragödie,"* edited by Karlfried Gründer, 27–55. Hildesheim: Georg
Olms Verlag, 1989. Translated and edited by Babette Babich, *"Future* Philology!"
New Nietzsche Studies 4 (2000): 1–32.

Williams, Bernard. "Can There Be a Nietzschean Politics? Unpublished manuscript,
1–16.

————. *Ethics and the Limits of Philosophy.* Abingdon, UK: Routledge, 2011.

————. Introduction to *The Gay Science."* In *The Sense of the Past: Essays in the History
of Philosophy*, edited by Miles Burnyeat, 311–24. Princeton, NJ: Princeton University Press, 2006.

————. "Nietzsche's Minimalist Moral Psychology." In *The Sense of the Past: Essays in
the History of Philosophy*, edited by Miles Burnyeat, 299–310. Princeton, NJ:
Princeton University Press, 2006.

————. *In the Beginning Was the Deed*, 1–17. Princeton, NJ: Princeton University
Press, 2007.

————. *Shame and Necessity.* Berkeley: University of California Press, 2008.

————. "There Are Many Kinds of Eyes." In *The Sense of the Past: Essays in the History
of Philosophy*, edited by Myles Burnyeat, 325–30. Princeton, NJ: Princeton University Press, 2006.

—. *Truth and Truthfulness: An Essay in Genealogy*. Princeton, NJ: Princeton University Press, 2002.

—. "Unbearable Suffering." In *The Sense of the Past: Essays in the History of Philosophy*, edited by Miles Burnyeat, 331–37. Princeton, NJ: Princeton University Press, 2006.

Williamson, George. *The Longing for Myth in Germany: Religion and Aesthetic Culture from Romanticism to Nietzsche*. Chicago: University of Chicago Press, 2004.

Zucker, Catherine. "Nietzsche's Rereading of Plato." *Political Theory* 13, no. 2 (1985): 213–38.

INDEX

Abbey, Ruth, 64n35, 71n1, 73n10, 133n16
Acampora, Christa Davis, 33n27, 183n6
Afghanistan, 19, 23, 158, 161
agon, 16, 22, 44–45, 72–73, 100–110, 126, 155, 167, 174, 177–78
Allen, Danielle, 45n55
Altman, William, 158n9, 179n56
Anderson, Margaret, 76, 102
Anderson, R. Lanier, 89n40, 105n3
Andreas-Salomé, Lou, 130, 146
Ansell-Pearson, Keith, 50, 98–99, 183n6
The Antichrist, 11, 18–19, 35, 40–51, 88–95, 114, 119–23, 136–74
antipolitical (unpolitical), Nietzsche as, 1, 19–20, 22, 50, 164
Appel, Frederick, 72, 73n10
Arendt, Hannah, 6, 72, 101
aristocracy, 14, 21, 31, 71–74, 79–79, 85–102, 124, 163, 178, 182
aristocratic radicalism, 6, 20
Aschheim, Steven, 21n32, 95n44, 101n53
Assorted Opinions and Maxims, 178

Badiou, Alain, 173n48
Baeumler, Alfred, 21–22, 139
Bakunin, Mikhail, 76
Beethoven, Ludwig von, 87
Bergmann, Peter, 72, 74n12, 153n1, 162, 164
Berkowitz, Peter, 34n30, 72
Bertram, Ernst, 22
Beyond Good and Evil, 2, 14, 19, 36, 41–46, 69, 79–99, 135–37, 149, 155–68, 183–84
The Birth of Tragedy, 2, 3, 6–12, 24–26, 30–43, 51–59, 92, 109–13, 130–33, 139, 146–47, 153–54, 176

Bismarck, Otto von, 2, 14, 20, 75, 77, 153–72
Bizet, Georges, 161
blond beasts of prey, 10, 15, 58–60, 84, 107, 120, 122
Bosteels, Bruno, 163n21
Brahmins, 90
Brandes, Georg, 6, 145–50, 165–68
breeding (eugenics), 14–15, 35, 43, 69, 79, 85–87, 123–24, 152, 167–69, 175–79
Brinton, Crane, 29n17, 74n13
Britain (British Empire, England), 2, 19–20, 155–61
Brobjer, Thomas, 37n38, 47n61, 61n31, 68n44, 75n15, 89, 139–40
Brown, Wendy, 1, 72
Burckhardt, Jacob, 57, 76
Burrow, J. W., 69n46, 84n31

Caesar, Julius, 87
caste society, 13, 17, 57, 83–115, 127, 160–1, 178
Cavell, Stanley, 117n20, 126
Chamberlain, Houston Stewart, 85
Christian Reich, 16–18, 156, 172–76, 182
Christianity, 15, 19, 25, 33–34, 42–47, 66, 69, 80, 89, 103–4, 119–23, 131–33, 145, 149–52, 165, 168, 171–81
Clark, Maudemarie, 143n50, 184n6
Conant, James, 117n20
Connolly, William, 1, 71–72
Constant, Benjamin, 17, 147–48
Constantinidès, Yannis, 41n46
Conway, Daniel, 50, 56n23, 68n43, 117n26, 164
Crick, Bernard, 101

Dannhauser, Werner, 29n17
David Strauss, the Confessor and the Writer, 26, 44, 133, 154, 157
Daybreak, 34, 71, 130, 157
death of God, 3–4, 10–15, 68, 155, 164, 181–82
Deleuze, Gilles, 105n1, 107n4, 111n8, 114n15, 163
democracy, 1–21, 62–104, 154–56, 160, 180–83
Derrida, Jacques, 105n1
Detwiler, Bruce, 21, 50, 72
Dionysus, 29, 131–35, 142, 146, 150
Dombowsky, Don, 50, 72, 89n38, 154n5, 160n12
Domino, Brian, 177n53
Dostoyevsky, Fyodor, 161

Ecce Homo, 9, 24, 31–45, 118–20, 129–46, 150, 158–69, 176
Elbe, Stefan, 68n43
Elst, Koenraad, 90n41, 178n55
England. *See* Britain
eternal return, 6, 16–17, 22–25, 39, 105–15, 126–50, 175, 182
eugenics. *See* breeding

Fink, Eugen, 139n33
Fossen, Thomas, 95n45
Foucault, Michel, 163
Fukuyama, Francis, 116n18
"The Future of Our Educational Institutions," 8, 45, 133, 169, 177
Franco-Prussian War, 2, 53, 153, 157–58, 179

Gauchet, Marcel, 103n57
The Gay Science, 10, 32, 64, 71, 80, 93, 111, 125, 130, 146, 159, 162
The Genealogy of Morality, 10–12, 50–52, 58–64, 80–96, 119–23, 135–37, 159, 166, 172–3, 180–84
Geuss, Raymond, 80n23
German Reich (Kaiserreich), 46, 64, 75, 77, 134, 156, 158, 171, 173
Germany, 1–2, 4, 11, 20, 46, 49, 53, 75–76, 84–85, 102–3, 120, 131–34, 138, 143, 146, 153–54, 157–162, 173
Gillespie, Michael, 146n67
Gobineau, Joseph-Arthur, comte de, 15, 75, 84–86
Goethe, Johann Wolfgang, 17, 35, 40, 87, 126–28, 147

good Europeans, 2, 11, 15, 86, 155, 160, 175–77, 183
great game, 19, 158–61
great politics (grosse Politik, grand politics, power politics, realpolitik, Machtpolitik), 2, 4, 8–22, 48, 66, 77, 98, 105, 111, 118, 134, 146, 150–77, 183
Greeks, 3, 6–7, 10–13, 17, 24–57, 93, 101–64
"The Greek State," 10–16, 37, 50–69, 88–93, 101–8, 133, 178
Grundlehner, Philip, 146n67

Hatab, Lawrence, 1, 56n23, 72–73
Hawthorn, Geoffrey, 182n3
Hegel, Georg Wilhelm Friedrich, 20, 41–42, 98
Heidegger, Martin, 22, 25, 126, 139, 142, 152, 163
Heine, Heinrich, 87
Heraclitus, 7, 26–31, 110–13
herd morality. *See* slave morality
Hesse, Herman, 177n54
Hobbes, Thomas, 49–59
"Homer's Contest," 16, 72, 100–106, 133
Honig, Bonnie, 1, 72
Human, All Too Human, 2, 5, 9, 11, 18–19, 51–52, 62–67, 71, 77, 81, 88, 93, 97, 130–31, 143, 154–56, 159–62, 166, 175, 183–84
Hume, David, 55n21, 59n28
Hussain, Nadeem, 106n3

India, 19, 84–89, 158–161

Janaway, Christopher, 39n39, 90n40
Janz, Curt Paul, 146n67
Jaspers, Karl, 22
Journal de Goncourt, 75
Journal des débats, 75, 166

Kahan, Alan, 73n9
Kaiserreich. *See* German Reich
Kant, Immanuel, 41–42, 114–15
Kaufmann, Walter, 1–2, 21–22, 26n4, 29n17, 49–50, 66, 114n15, 138
Klossowski, Pierre, 105n1
Kulturkampf, 2, 18, 154, 158, 170–72
Kulturstaat, 4, 10, 51, 61, 181

Lane, Melissa, 22n34, 41n48
Lampert, Laurence, 41n47, 47, 61n31, 183n6
Large, Duncan, 24n2, 154n4, 166n31

last man/men, 16, 98, 106, 113–24
Law against Christianity, 42, 149–51
Law of Manu, 88–91, 99, 178
Leiter, Brian, 1, 10, 49, 55, 60, 65–66
Lemm, Vanessa, 117n20, 163n21
Locke, John, 49, 55, 56n25, 59
Loeb, Paul, 111n10
Löwith, Karl, 143n55

Machtpolitik. *See* great politics
MacIntyre, Alasdair, 50, 125n34
Magnus, Bernd, 8, 138n30
Malraux, André, 183n5
Mann, Thomas, 21, 139, 164
Martin, Nicholas, 84n33, 85n34, 85n36, 108n5
Marx, Karl (Marxism), 21, 55, 68–69, 169n39
master morality, 2, 4, 9, 18, 80–85, 155–79
McIntyre, Alex, 163n21
Mellamphy, Nandita Biswas, 169n40
Mill, John Stuart, 73, 159, 170
misarchism, 15, 75, 80–81, 93, 101–3
Montesquieu, Charles de, 85n35
Montinari, Mazzino, 18, 130–33, 136–40, 149–51
Moore, Gregory, 83n30, 84n33, 84n37
Müller-Lauter, Wolfgang, 105n1

Nachlass (late notes), 2, 8, 19, 35, 139, 149–51, 176
Napoleon, 17, 87, 119, 147, 160, 175
Nazis (National-Socialism), 1–2, 21–22, 49
Nehamas, Alexander, 1, 50, 113, 124
Nolte, Ernst, 168n39
Nussbaum, Martha, 5, 55

Ostracism, 105, 108–9, 178
Ottmann, Henning, 41n46
overman (Übermensch, overmen), 6, 11–17, 25, 45, 50, 94–135, 142, 151, 170–77
Owen, David, 1, 71–72

Panjdeh Incident, 19, 161
party of Christianity, 16, 66–69, 151–56, 174–78
party of life, 4, 7, 11, 16–18, 43–44, 66, 69, 105, 118, 125, 151–56, 167–79
pathos of distance, 6, 13, 20, 95–99, 108, 115, 124–25
Patton, Paul, 71
Paul, 172–73

perfectionism, 16–17, 91, 106, 117–28
Perreau-Saussine, Emile, 103n57
petty politics, 2, 9, 18–20, 155–79, 183
"Philosophy in the Tragic Age of the Greeks," 7–8, 26–35, 110, 120, 133
Plato, 7–8, 25–55, 60–69, 80, 89–90, 102–3, 121–28, 148–52
postmodern readings of Nietzsche, 1–2, 14, 72, 79, 101
power politics. *See* great politics
"Pre-Platonic Philosophers," 7, 26–32, 42–48, 121

Ratner-Rosenhagen, Jennifer, 12n20
Rawls, John, 17, 55, 106, 126–28
realpolitik. *See* great politics
Reichstag, 14, 75, 77, 86, 171
Reginster, Bernard, 105n2
revaluation of all values, 12, 19, 24, 35, 44–48, 68, 80, 110, 119, 123, 134–37, 140, 148–49, 162–65, 172–76
"Revaluation of All Values" (book project), 18, 24–27, 30, 35, 39–48, 136–52, 168, 176
Revue des deux mondes, 44, 75
Richard Wagner in Bayreuth, 133–34
Richardson, John, 13n21, 15n22, 37n35, 69n46, 85n36, 91n43, 97n48, 99n50, 112n12, 123n30, 128n40, 152n83
Ridley, Aaron, 120n25, 142
Risse, Mathias, 173n49
Roos, Richard, 127n38, 138n30
Rousseau, Jean-Jacques, 49, 55–56, 59
Ruehl, Martin, 51–53
Russell, Bertrand, 21, 49
Russia, 2, 19–23, 155–61

Safranski, Rüdiger, 46n56, 149n74
Salter, William Mackintire, 179n57
Schlegel, Friedrich, 84
Schmitt, Carl, 72
Schopenhauer, Arthur, 39, 87
Schopenhauer as Educator, 51, 60–62, 65, 121, 125–26
Schotten, C. Heike, 116n19
Schrift, Alan, 1, 71–72
shadows of God, 103, 182
Shaw, Tamsin, 64–66
Siemens, Hermann, 100, 107, 108n5
Simmel, George, 39n39
Skinner, Quentin, 73n11

slave morality (herd morality), 2–4, 9, 15, 18, 41–42, 80–84, 93, 101–4, 155–63, 172–74, 177–79

slavery, 11–12, 20, 25, 37, 50–73, 83–101, 108, 127–33, 147, 155, 158, 176

Socrates, 7–8, 26–44, 61, 80, 121–82, 148

Souladié, Yannick, 139–40

Spencer, Herbert, 69

Stack, George, 37n35

state: ancient, 10, 59–68, 148; decay of, 4, 10–15, 50–52, 62–68, 98, 155; modern, 4–20, 55–69, 98, 125, 155, 181; postmodern, 51, 68–70

Stendhal, 87

Stone, Dan, 15n23, 169n41

Strong, Tracy, 17, 22, 42n50, 73n8, 91, 104n58, 147, 170n42

Swift, Paul, 27n9

Taylor, Charles, 103n57

Thus Spoke Zarathustra (Zarathustra), 5–6, 9–17, 39, 42, 69–70, 98–120, 129–51, 165, 170, 174

Tocqueville, Alexis de, 73–74

Tongeren, Paul van, 95n45, 163n21

Twilight of the Idols, 7, 11, 27–36, 44–64, 96, 106, 110–57, 169–70

Übermensch. *See* overman

Untimely Meditations, 6, 9, 18, 26–7, 44, 53, 60, 133, 145, 154, 157, 171

Villa, Dana, 1, 72

Voegelin, Eric, 161n14

Wagner, Richard, 6–17, 25–27, 35–68, 75, 84–93, 129–48, 162–68, 178

The Wanderer and His Shadow, 14, 71–86, 92, 102, 160

war of spirits, 16–18, 66–69, 98, 146, 151–56, 165–79

Warren, Mark, 1, 4, 72, 74n13

Weber, Max, 21n32, 68n42, 72, 164n24

Whitlock, Greg, 26n5

Wilamowitz-Moellendorf, Ulrich von, 26n4

Williamson, George, 171n43

will to power (philosophy), 6, 16–17, 22, 25, 35, 39, 105–10, 129–35, 142–52, 168

"Will to Power" (book project), 8, 17–21, 39, 91–94, 137–41, 149–52

Williams, Bernard, 1–23, 50, 66, 147–48, 155–56, 164, 180–84; "Can There Be a Nietzschean Politics," 5–6, 180; *Ethics and the Limits of Philosophy*, 184; *In the Beginning Was the Deed*, 182n3; "Nietzsche Minimalist Moral Psychology," 3n7, 122n29; *Shame and Necessity*, 3, 5–6, 17–18, 90n40, 147, 155; "There Are Many Kinds of Eyes," 4, 6; *Truth and Truthfulness*, 3, 180

World War I, 175

World War II, 1, 21, 49, 55

Zuckert, Catherine, 27n12, 61n31

Lightning Source UK Ltd.
Milton Keynes UK
UKHW01f1439050618
323755UK00002B/146/P